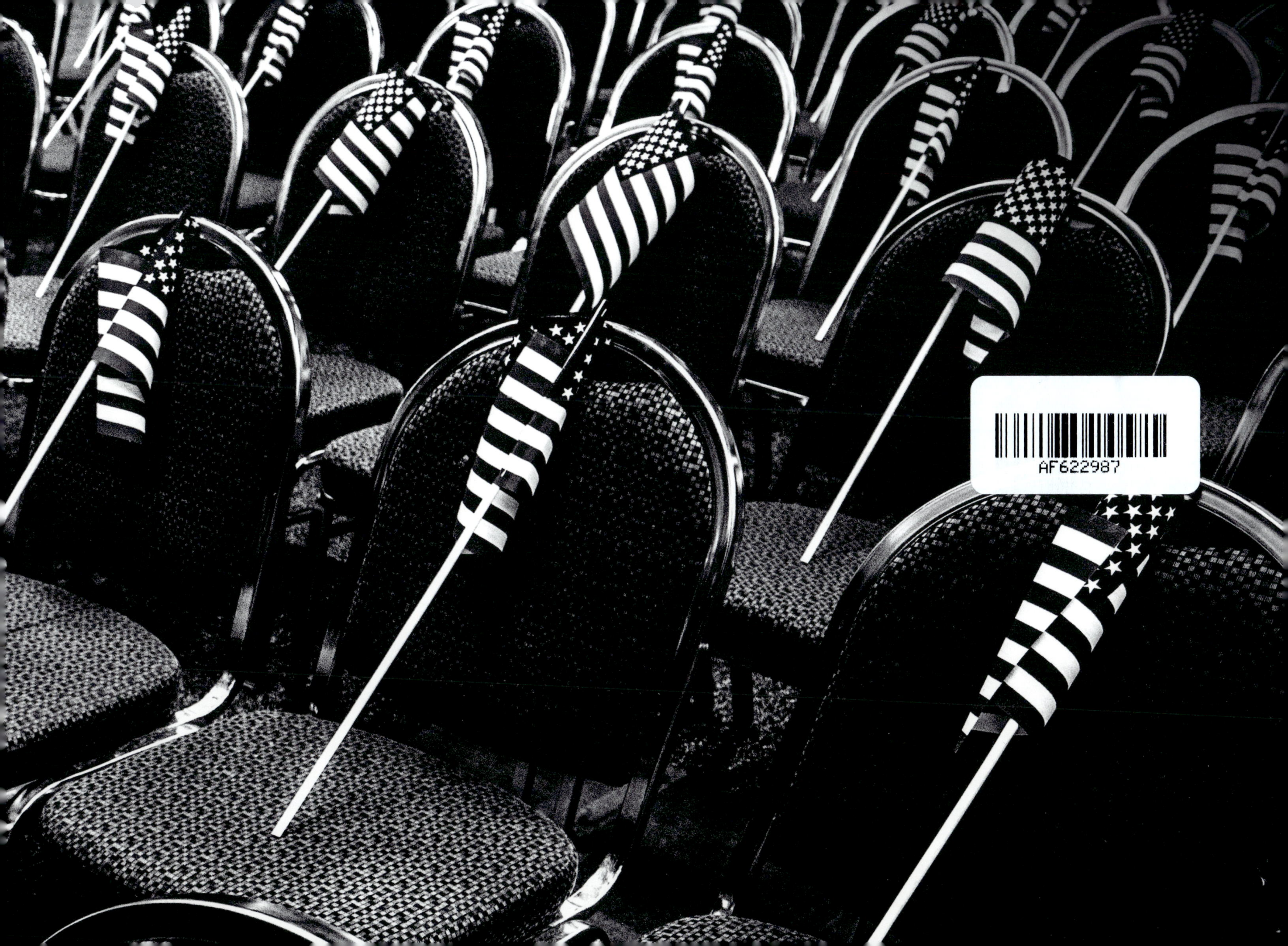

"There are no bad pictures; that's just how your face looks sometimes"—**ABRAHAM LINCOLN**

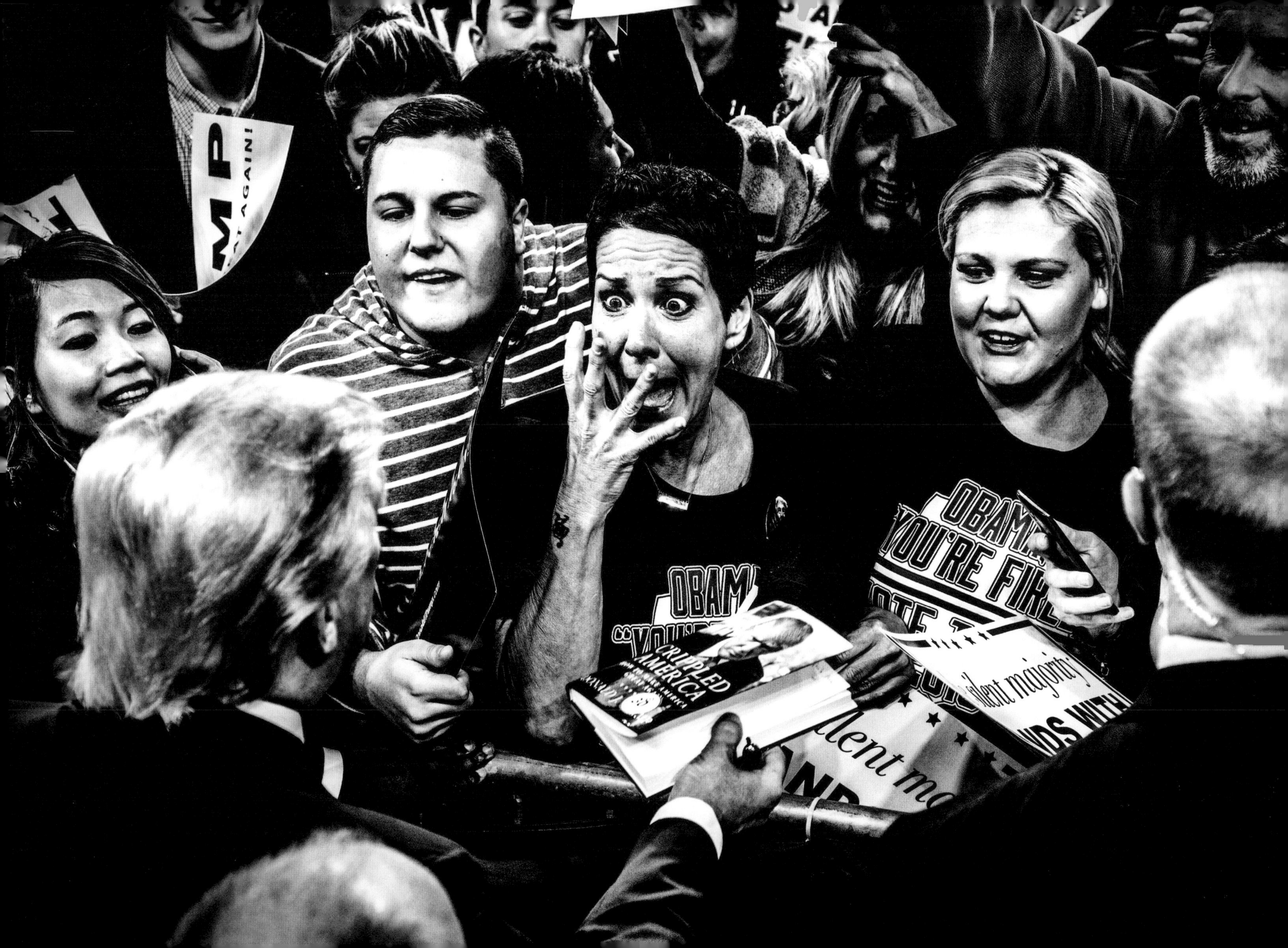
CRIPPLED AMERICA
silent majority
OBAMA

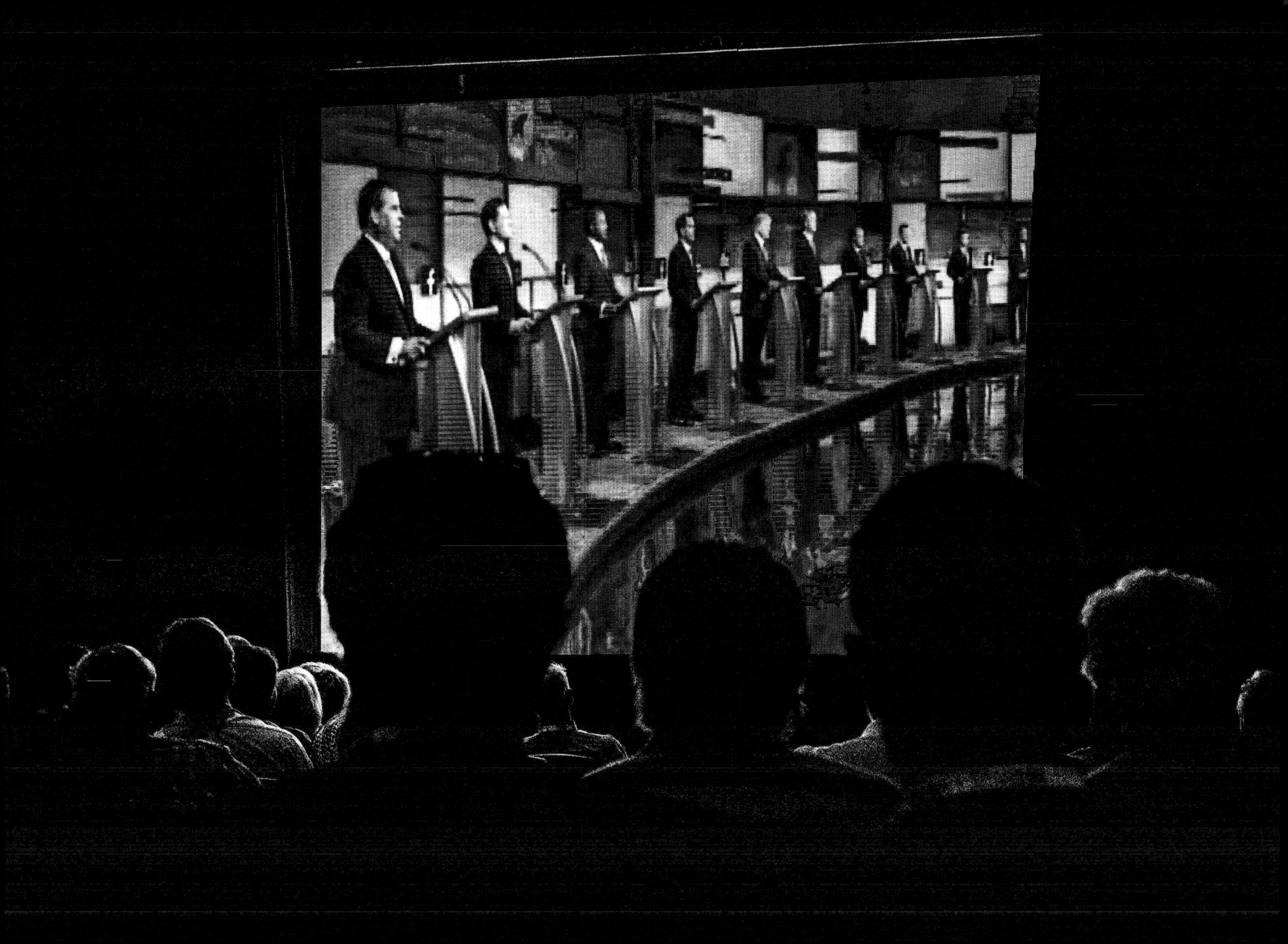

POLITICAL THEATRE

MARK PETERSON

ESSAY BY JOHN HEILEMANN

STEIDL

"Journalism is printing what someone else does not want printed: everything else is public relations." —**ATTRIBUTED TO GEORGE ORWELL**

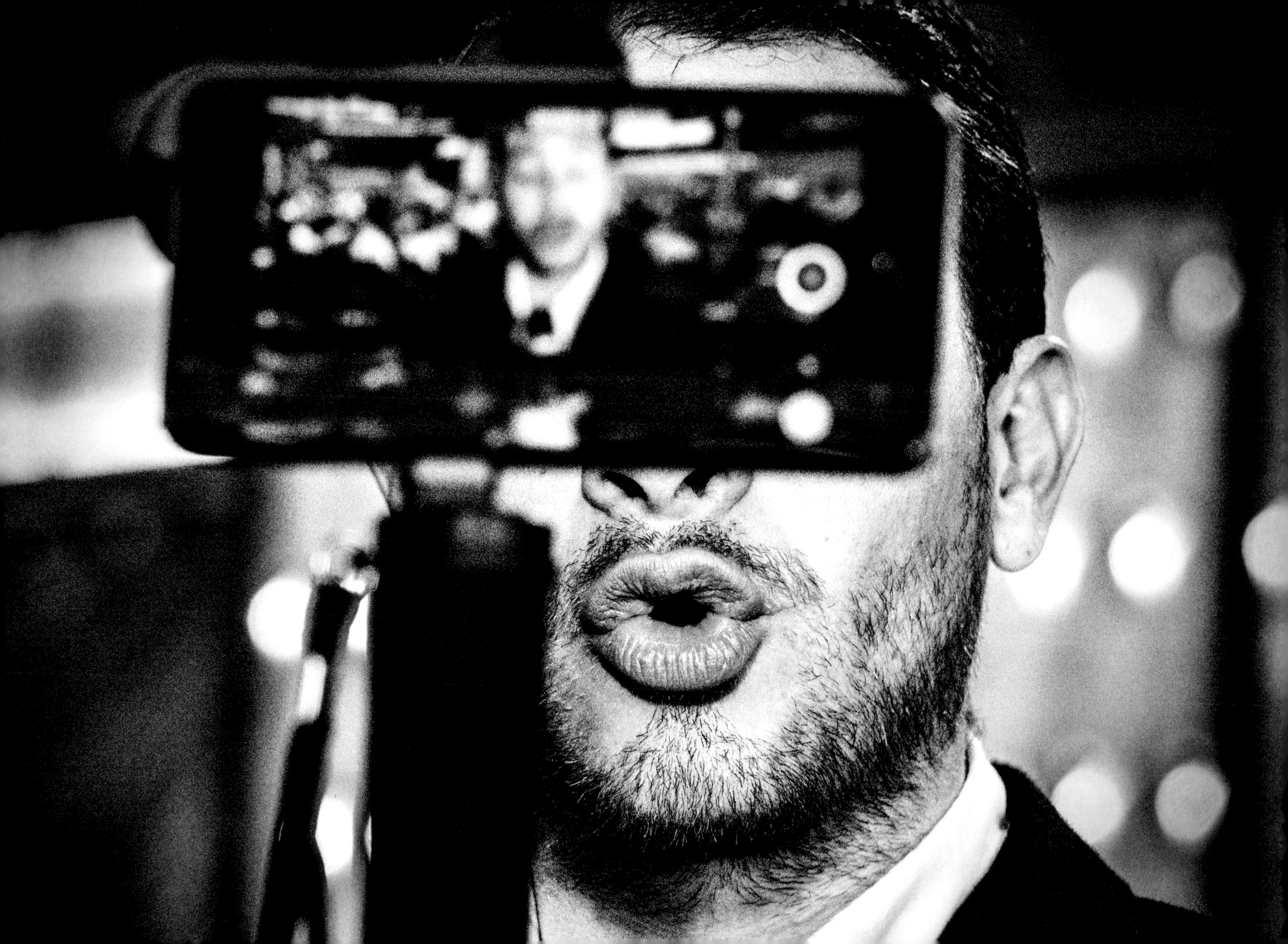

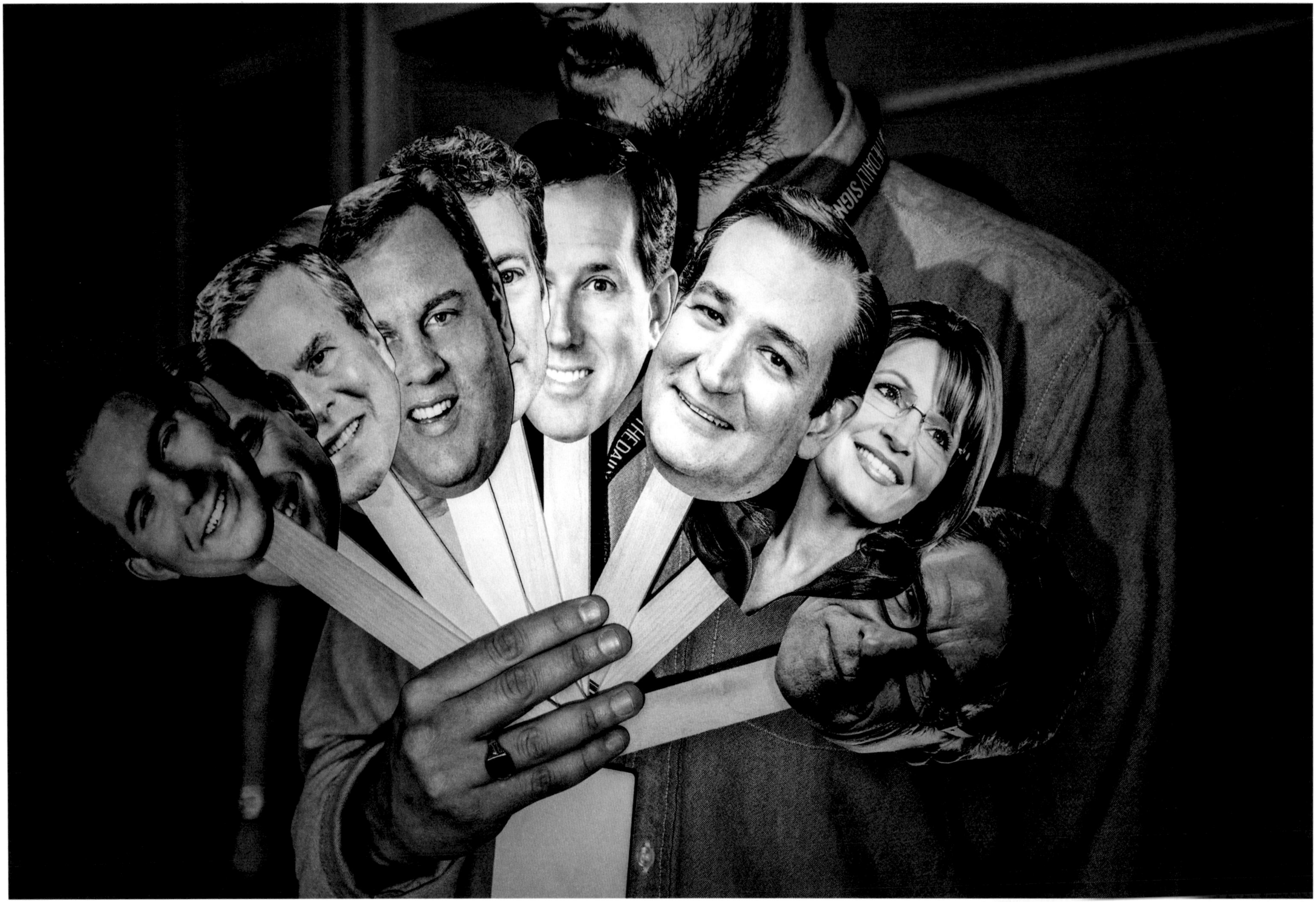

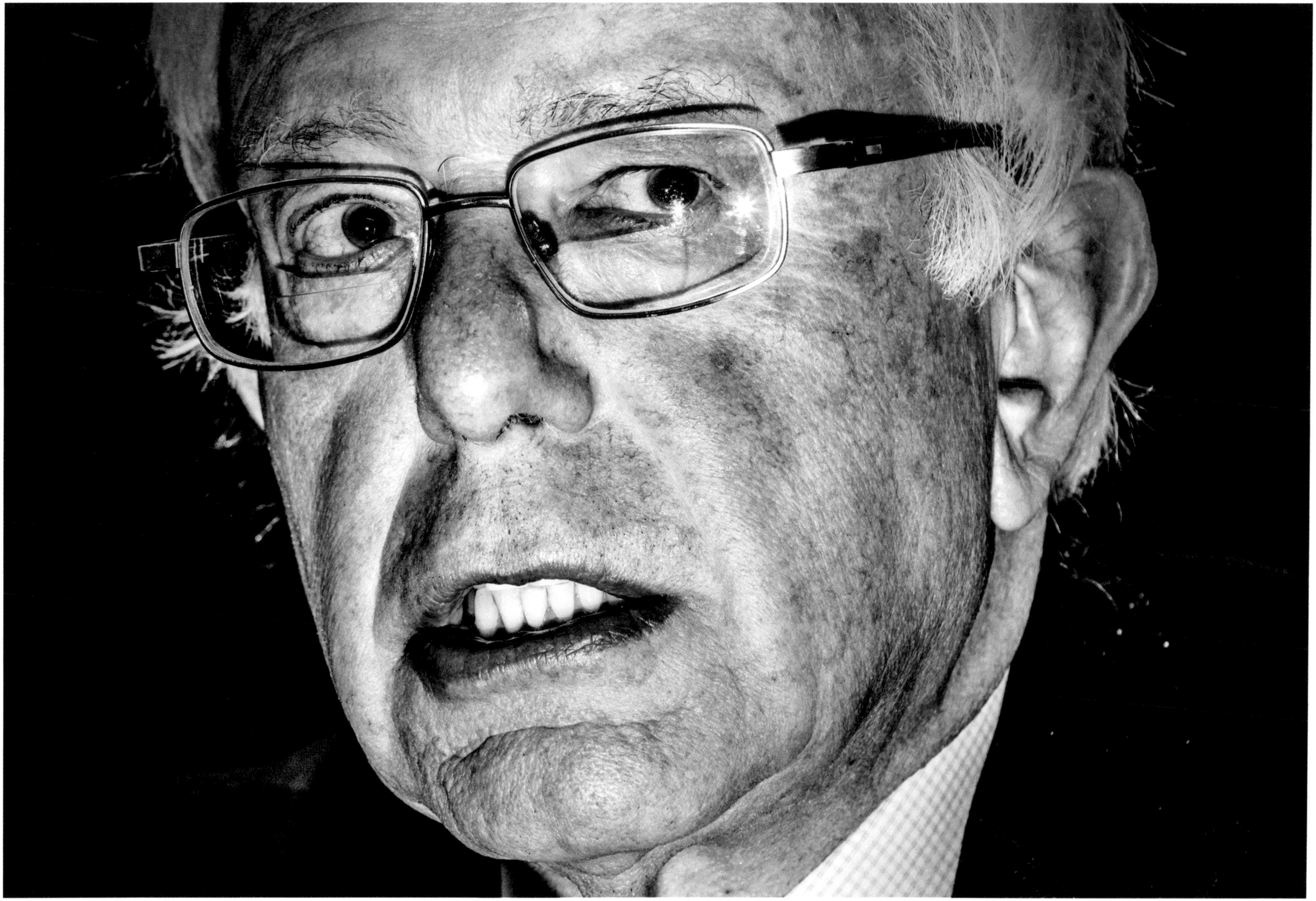

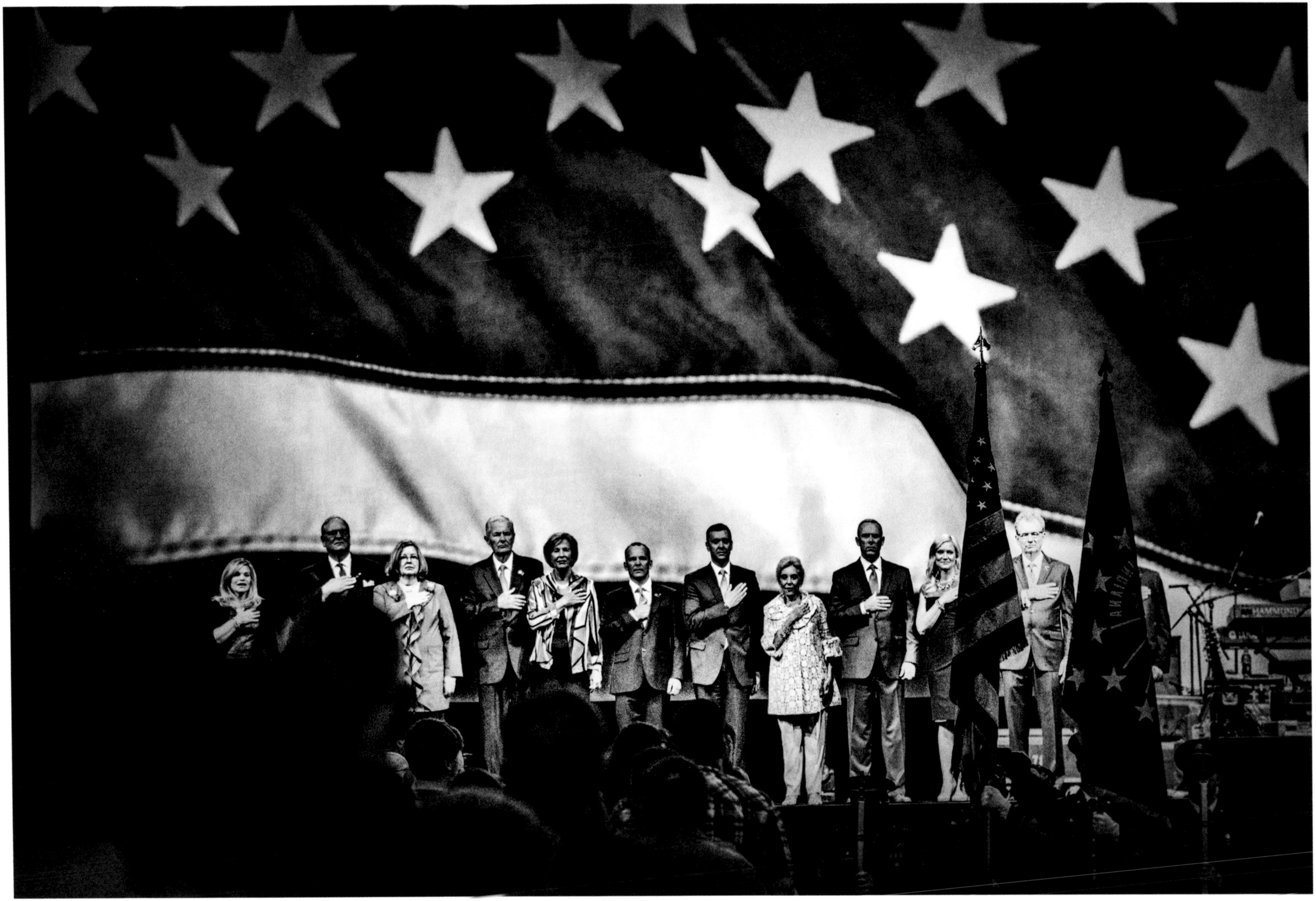
HAMMOND

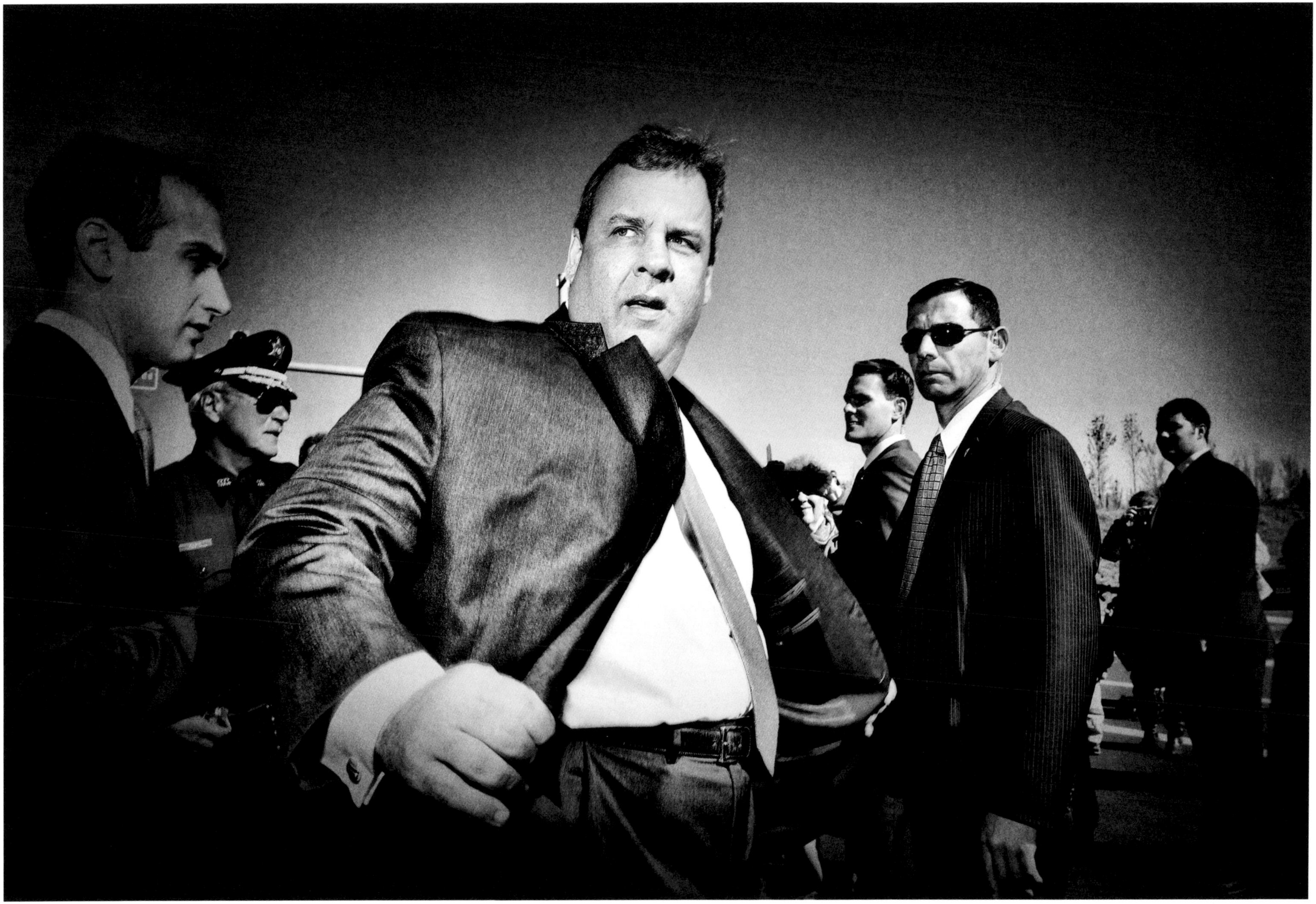

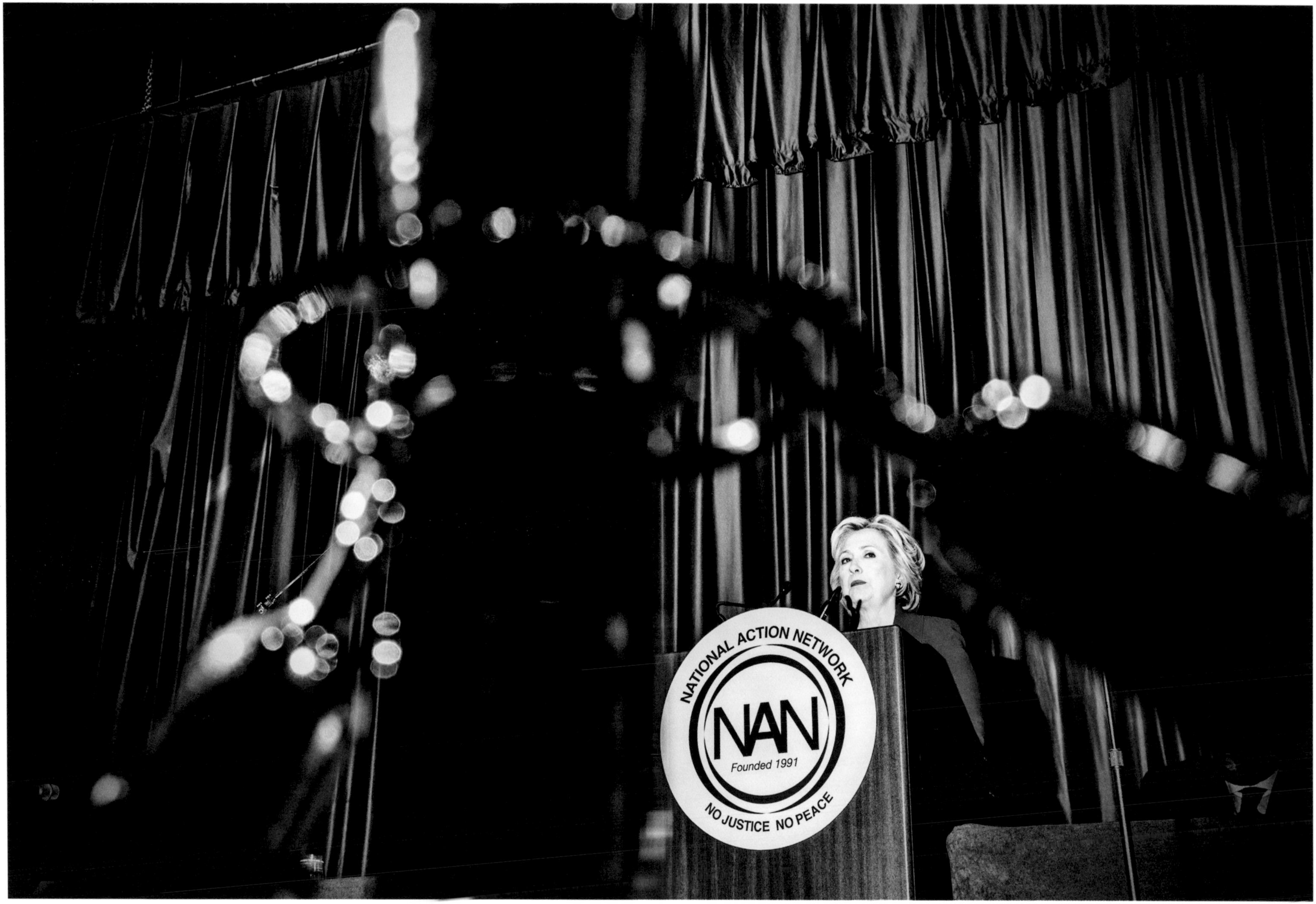
NATIONAL ACTION NETWORK
NAN
Founded 1991
NO JUSTICE NO PEACE

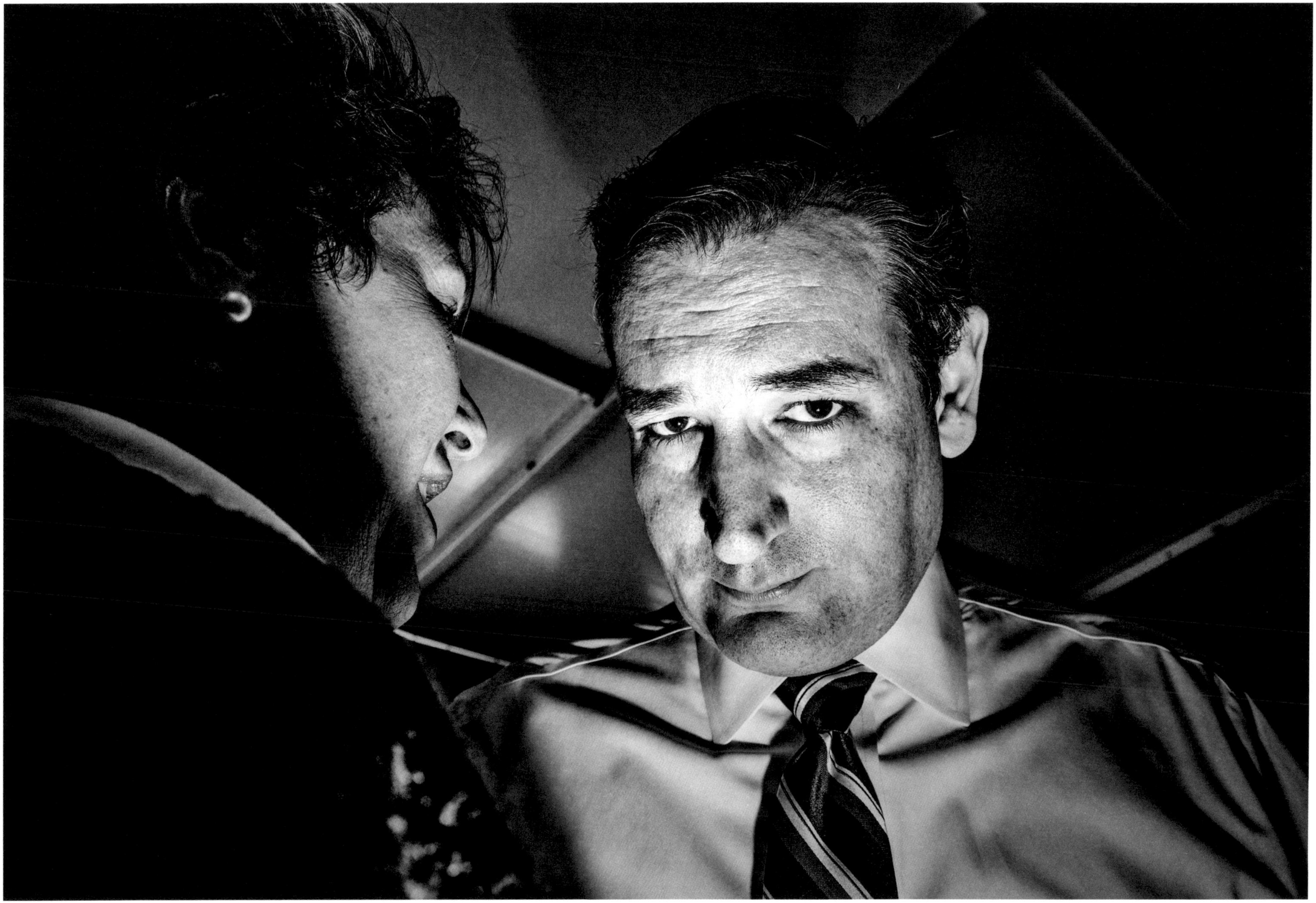

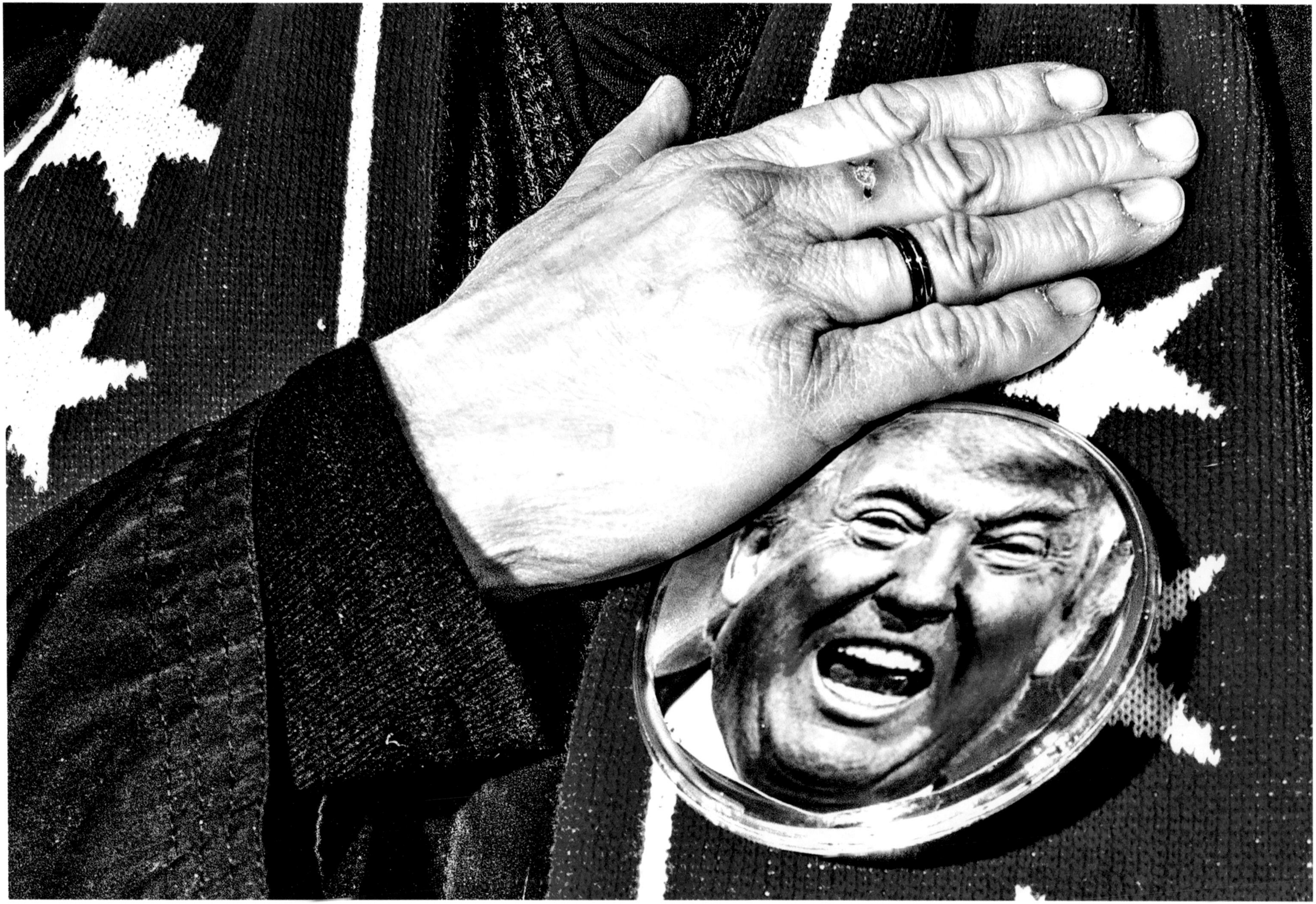

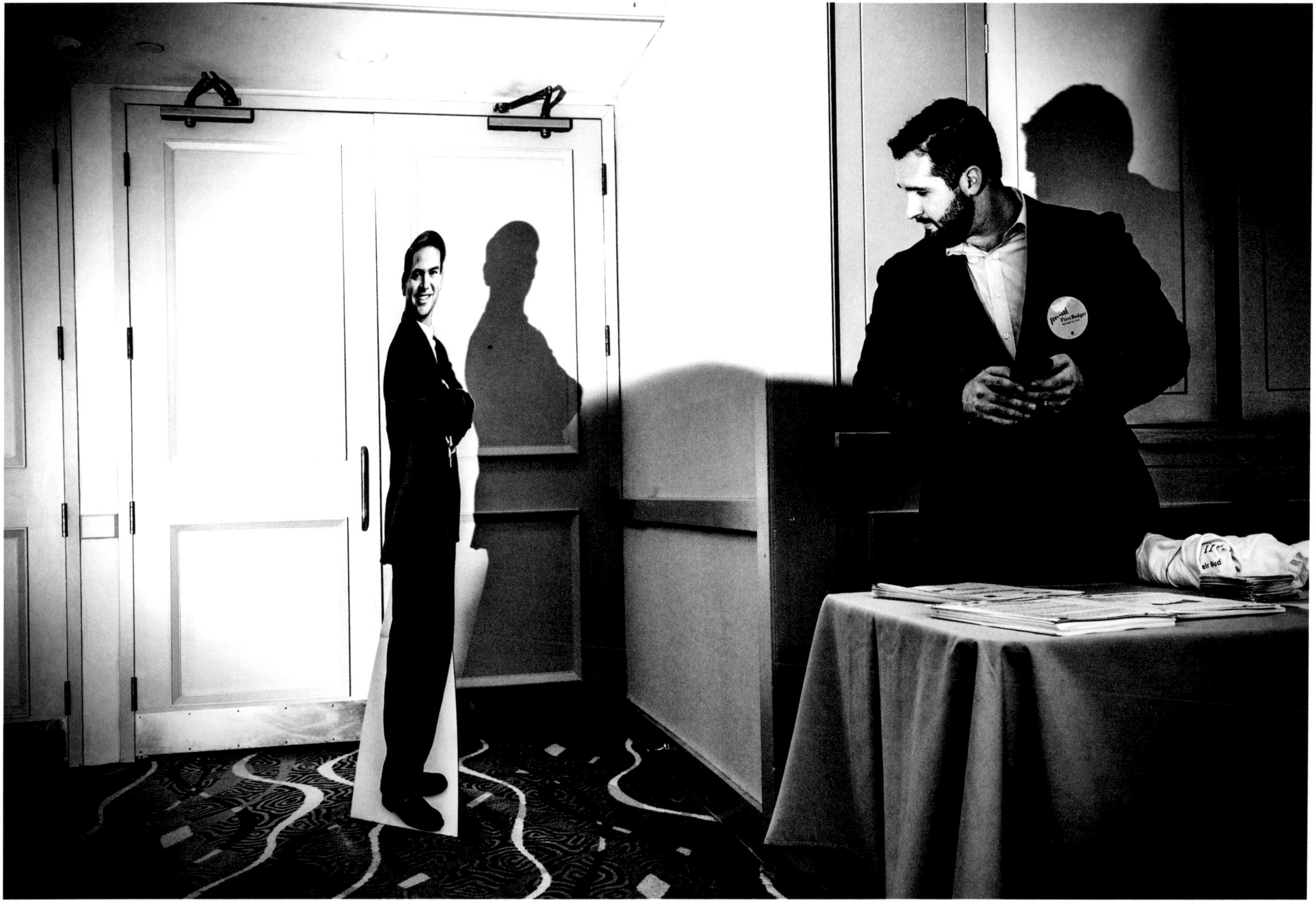

"You know what else they say about my people?

The polls, they say I have the most loyal people.

Did you ever see that?

Where I could stand in the middle of Fifth Avenue and shoot somebody and I wouldn't lose any voters, okay? It's like incredible."—**DONALD TRUMP**

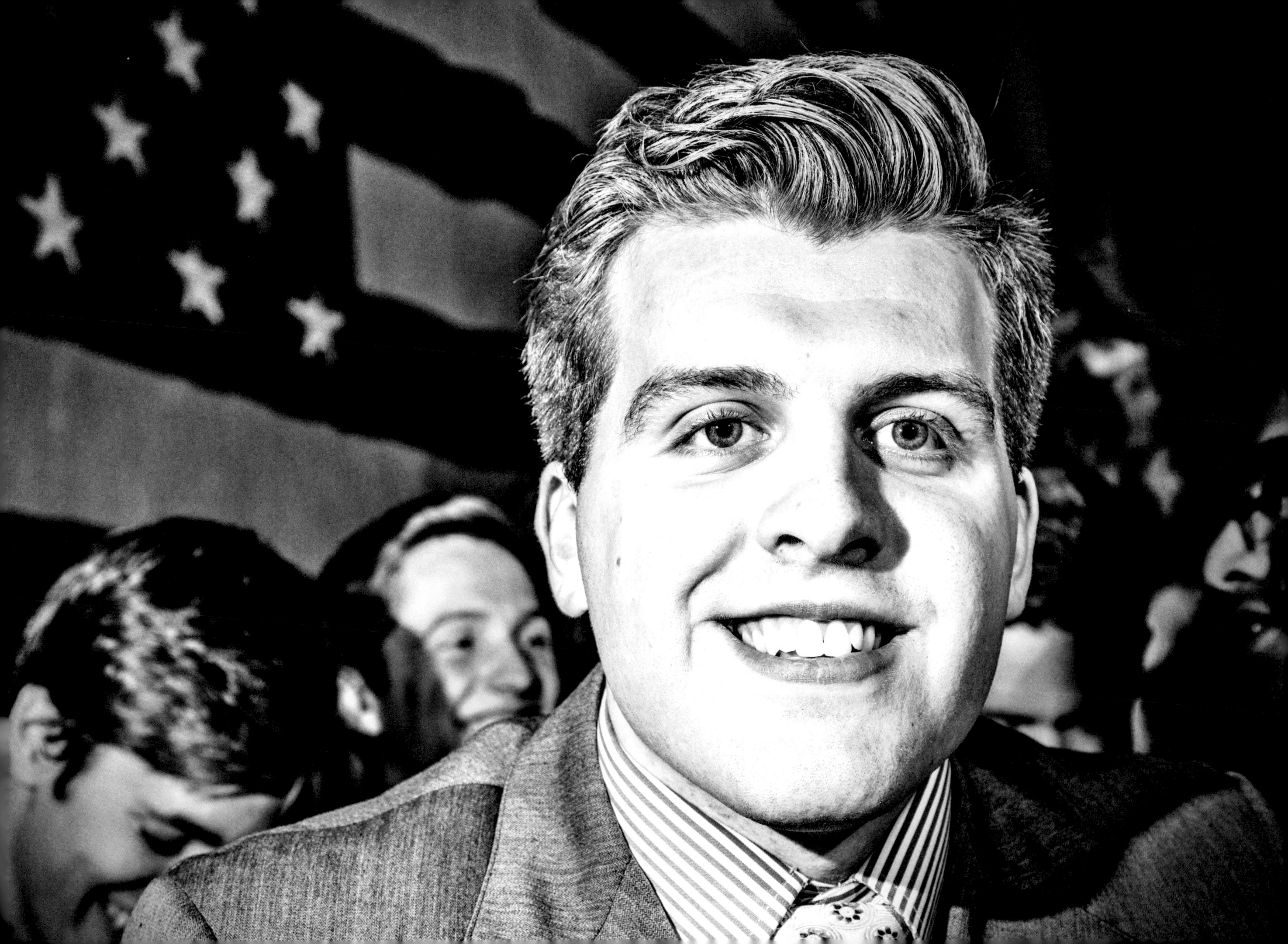

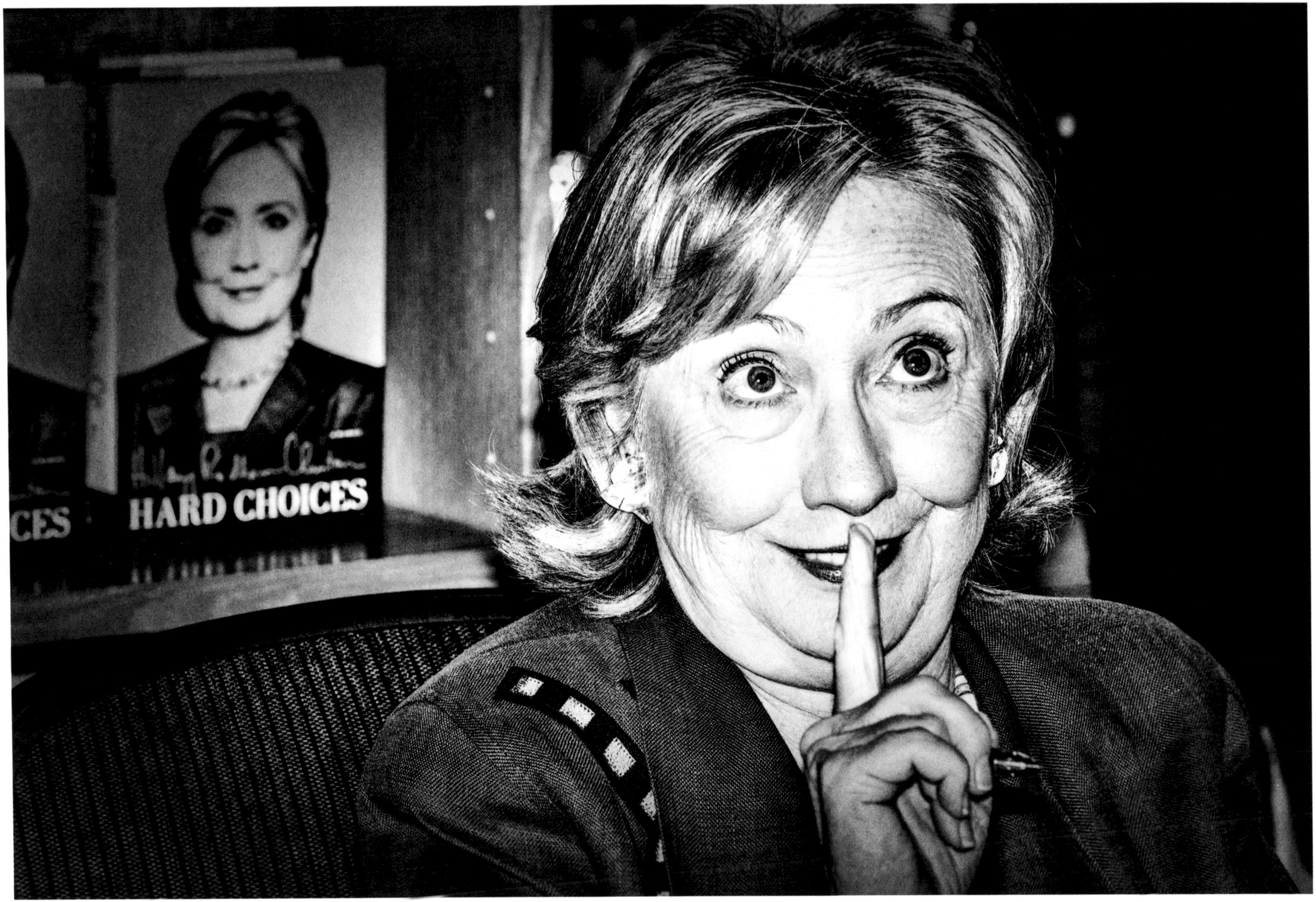
CES
HARD CHOICES

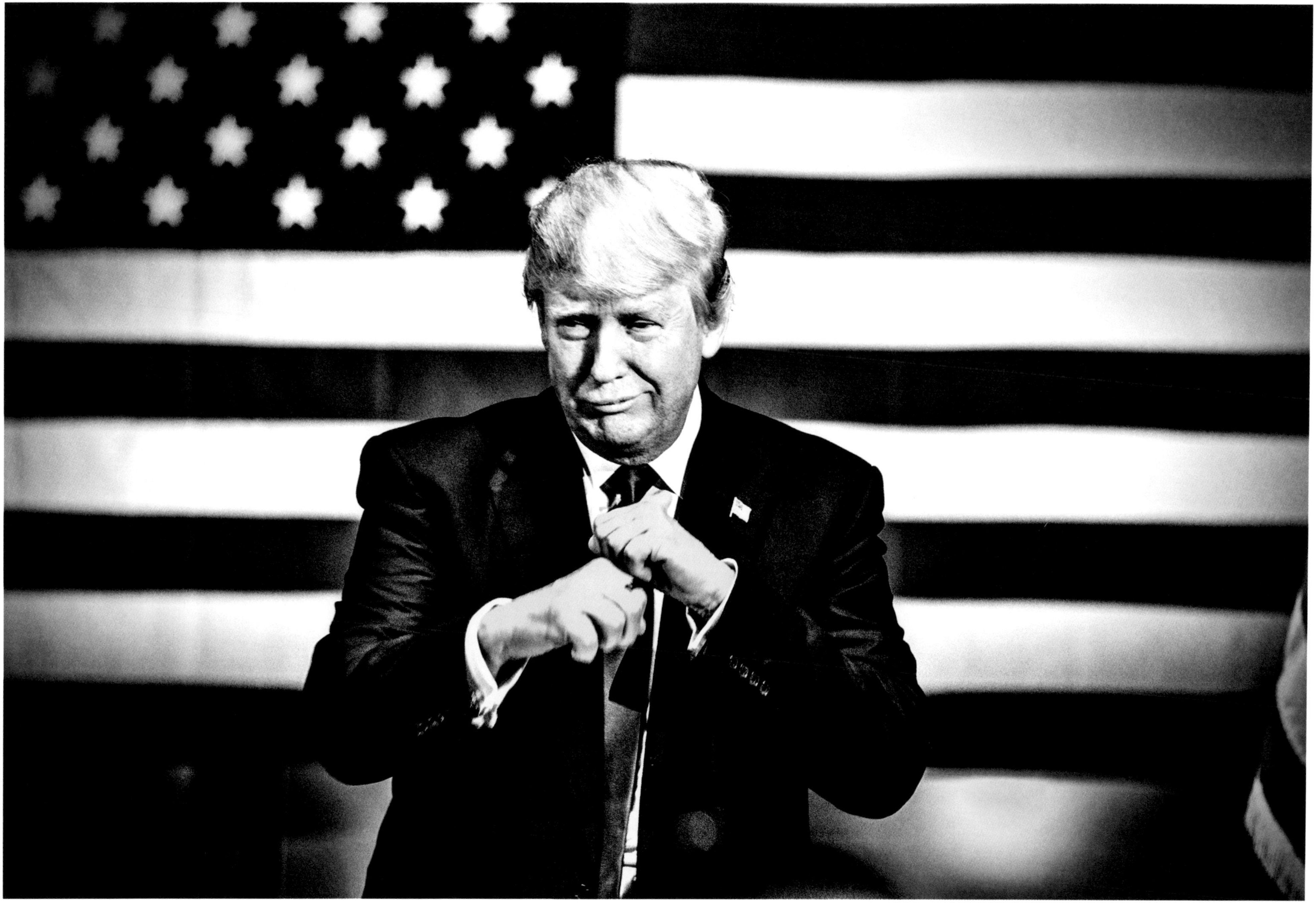

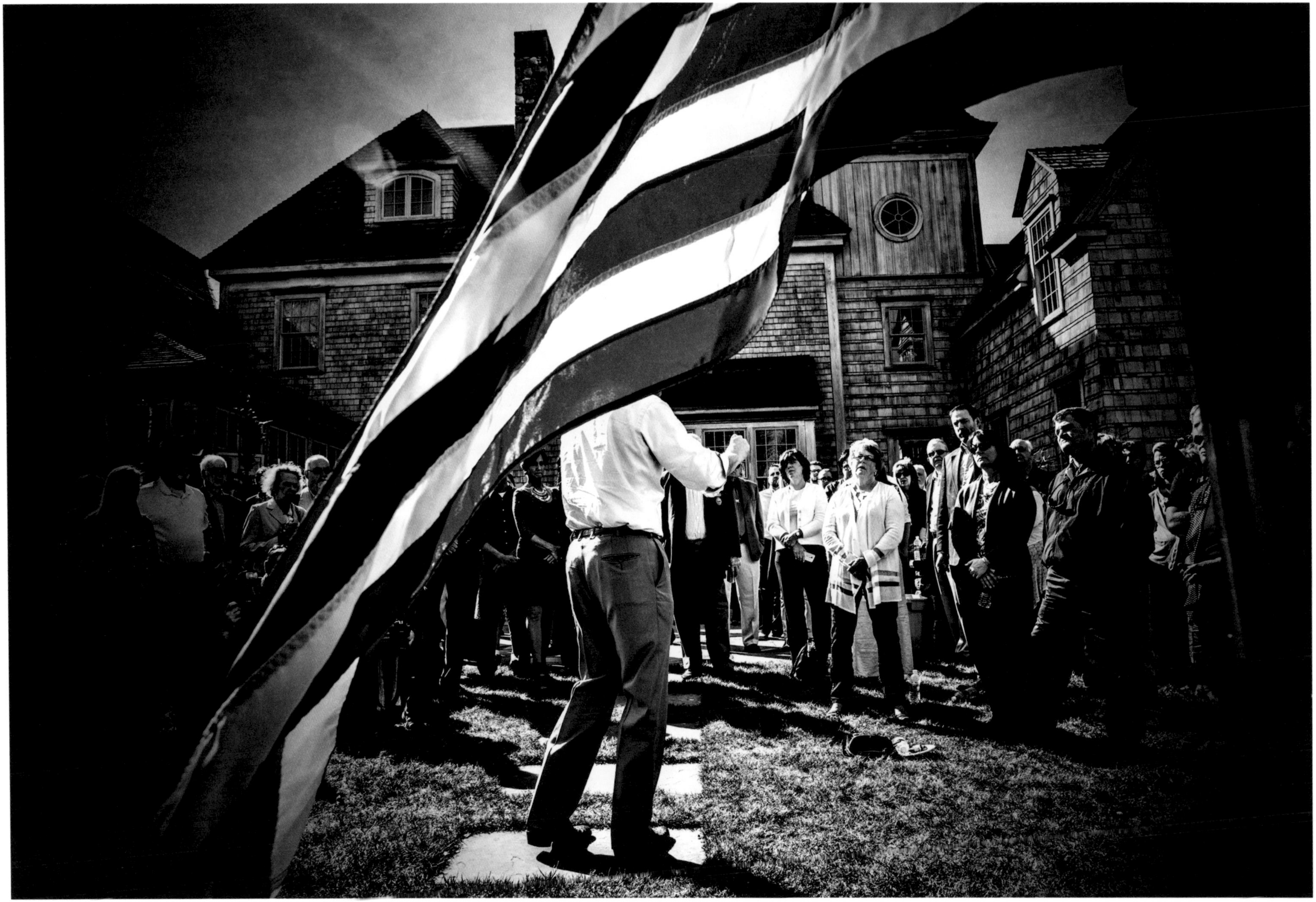

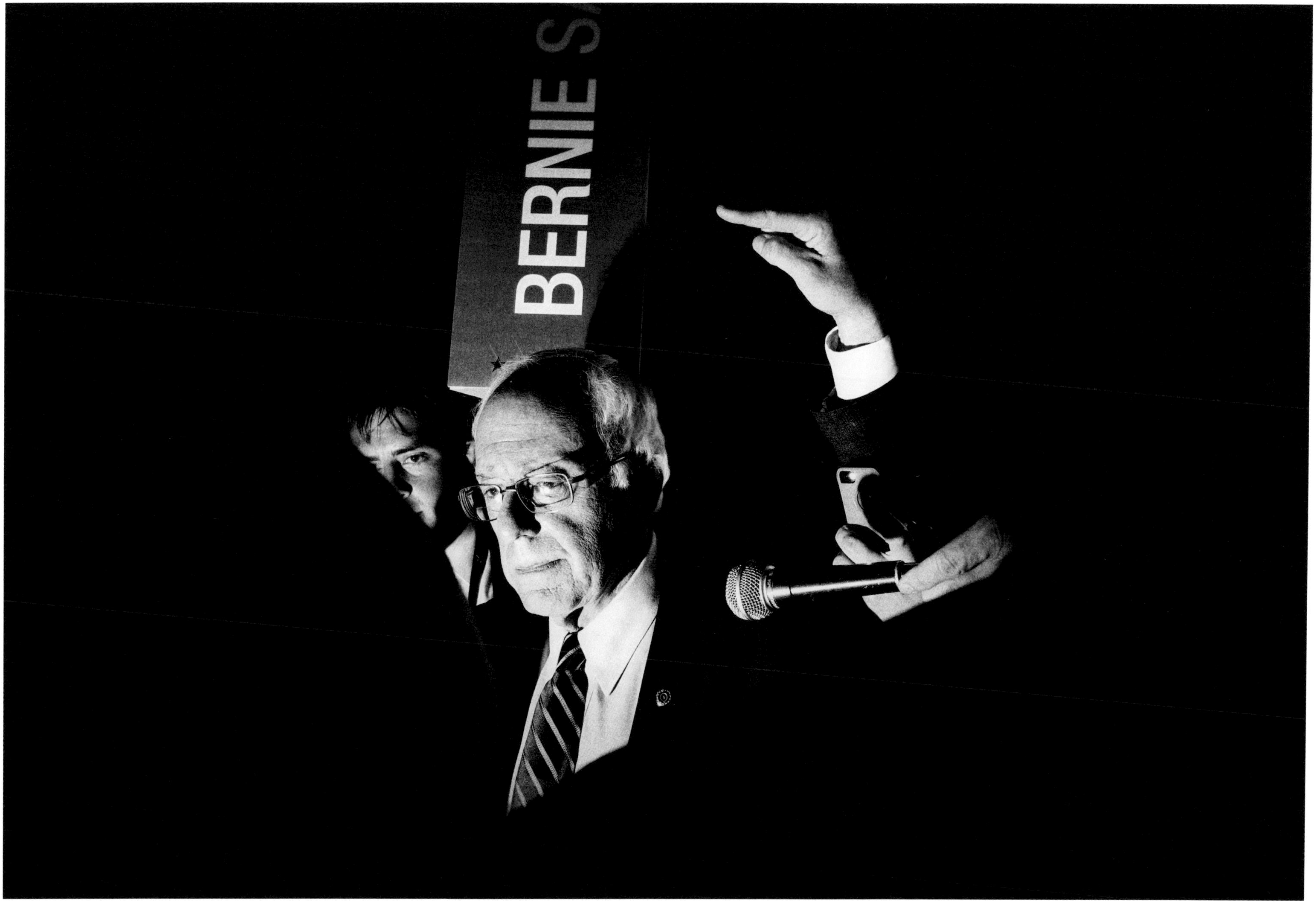
BERNIE

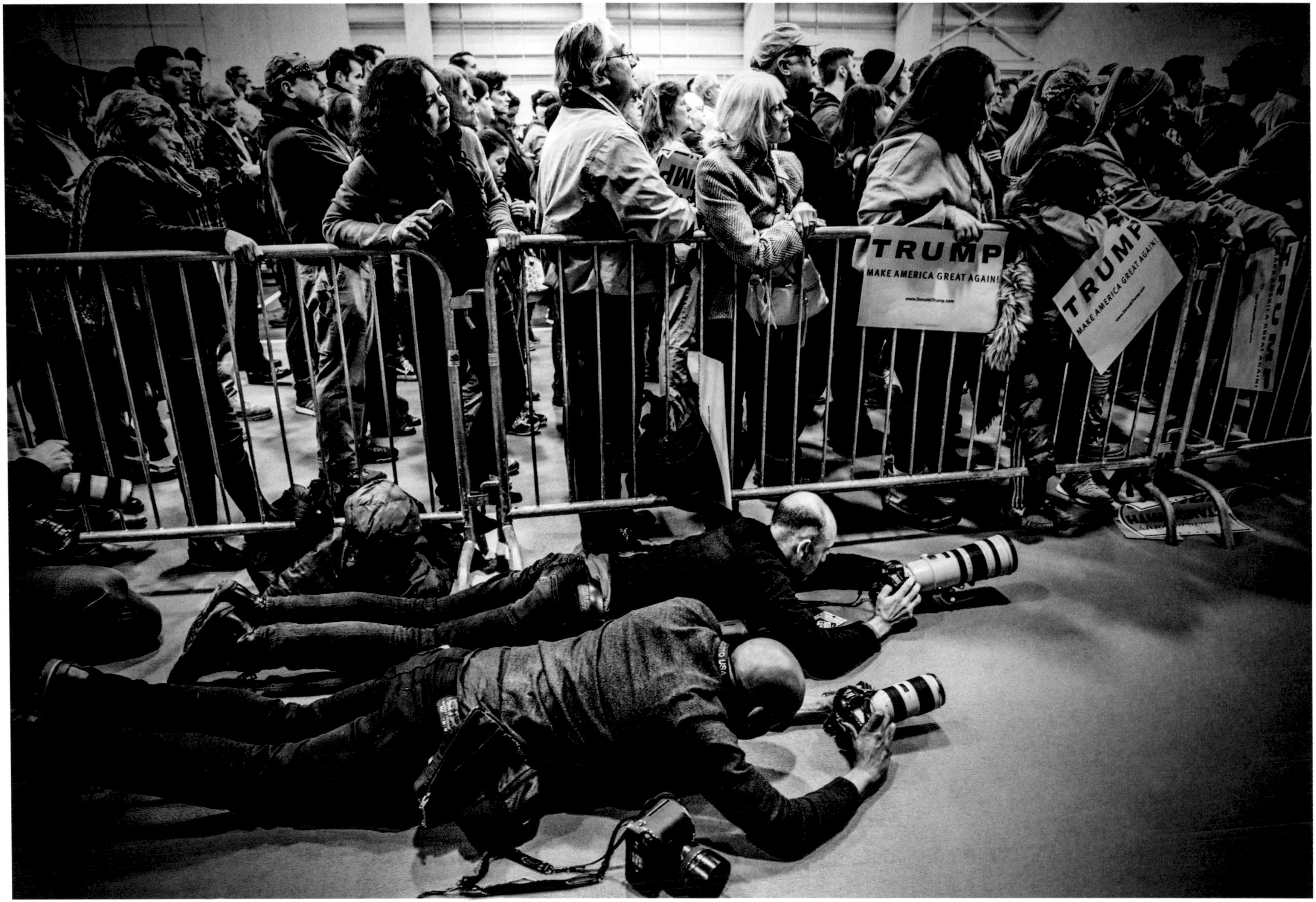
TRUMP
MAKE AMERICA GREAT AGAIN!
TRUMP
MAKE AMERICA GREAT AGAIN!

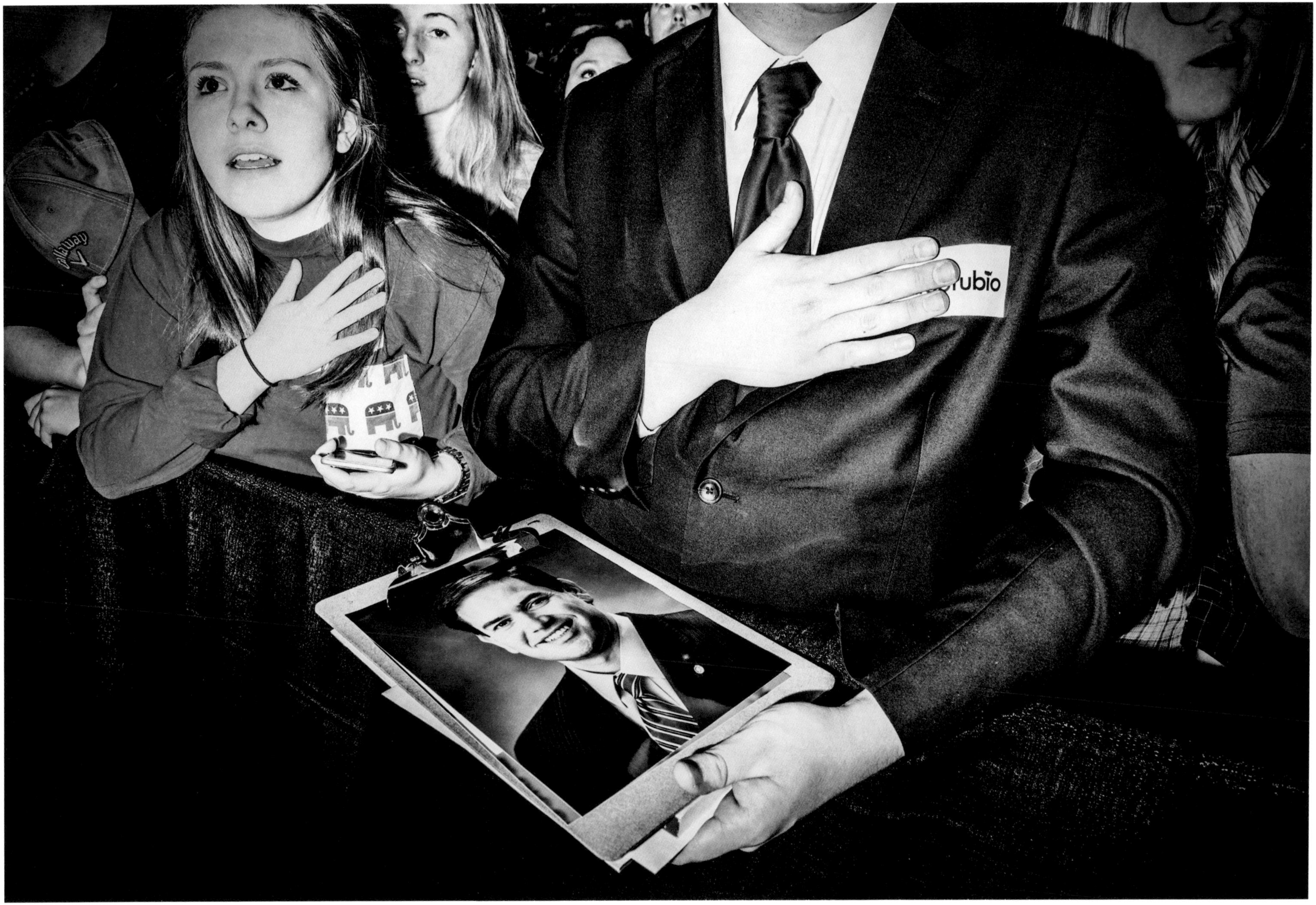
rubio

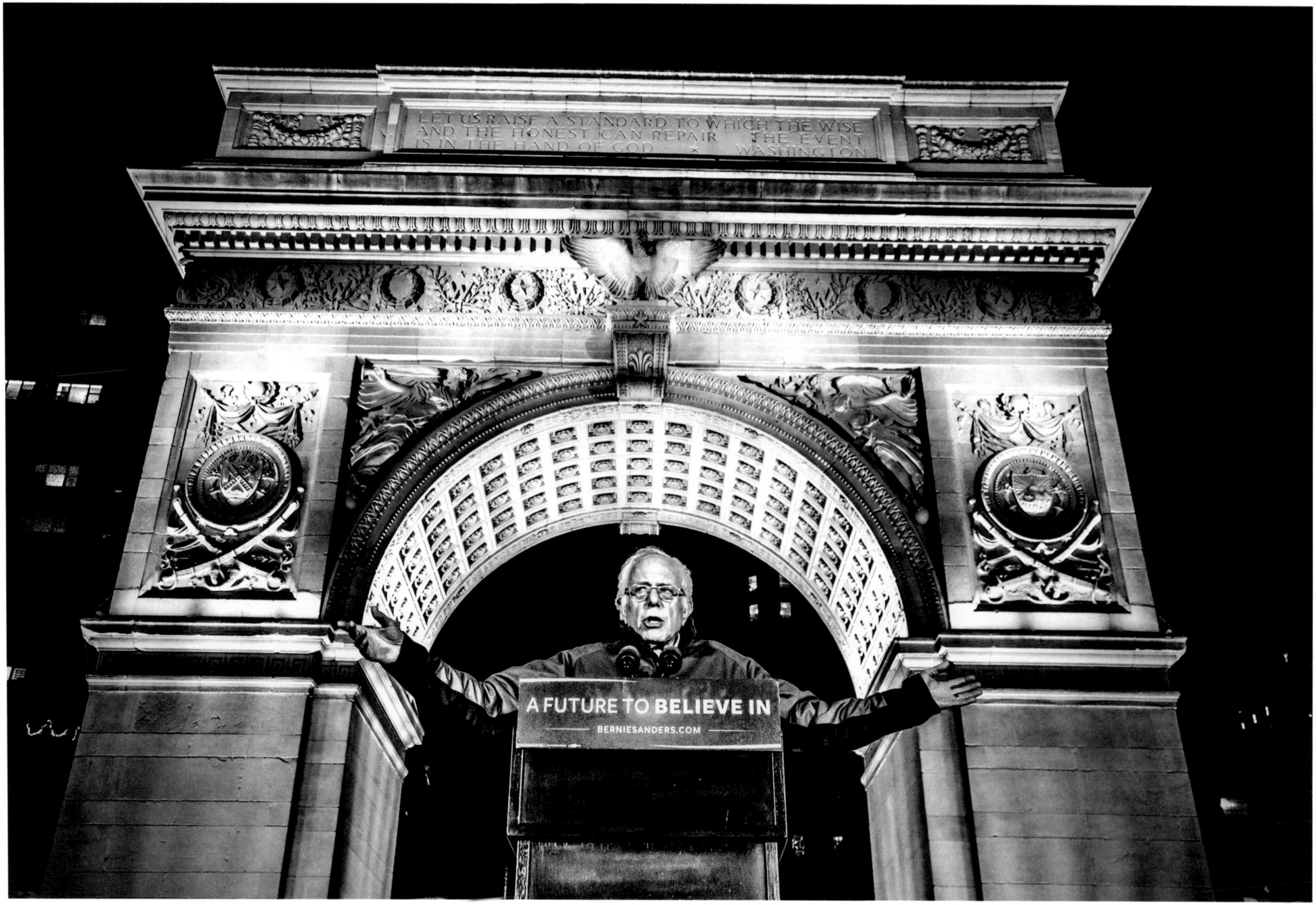
LET US RAISE A STANDARD TO WHICH THE WISE
AND THE HONEST CAN REPAIR THE EVENT
IS IN THE HAND OF GOD ★ WASHINGTON
A FUTURE TO BELIEVE IN
BERNIESANDERS.COM

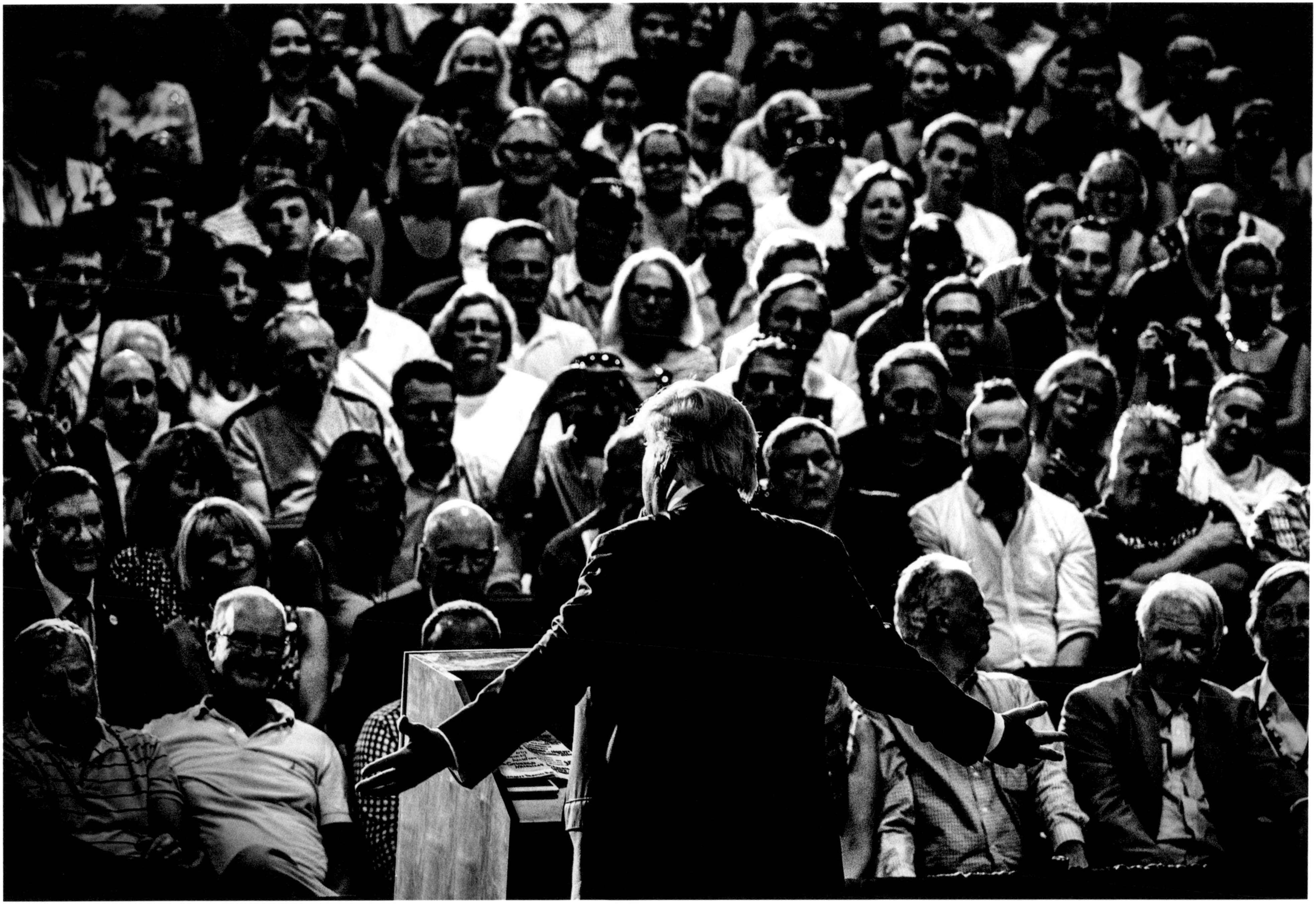

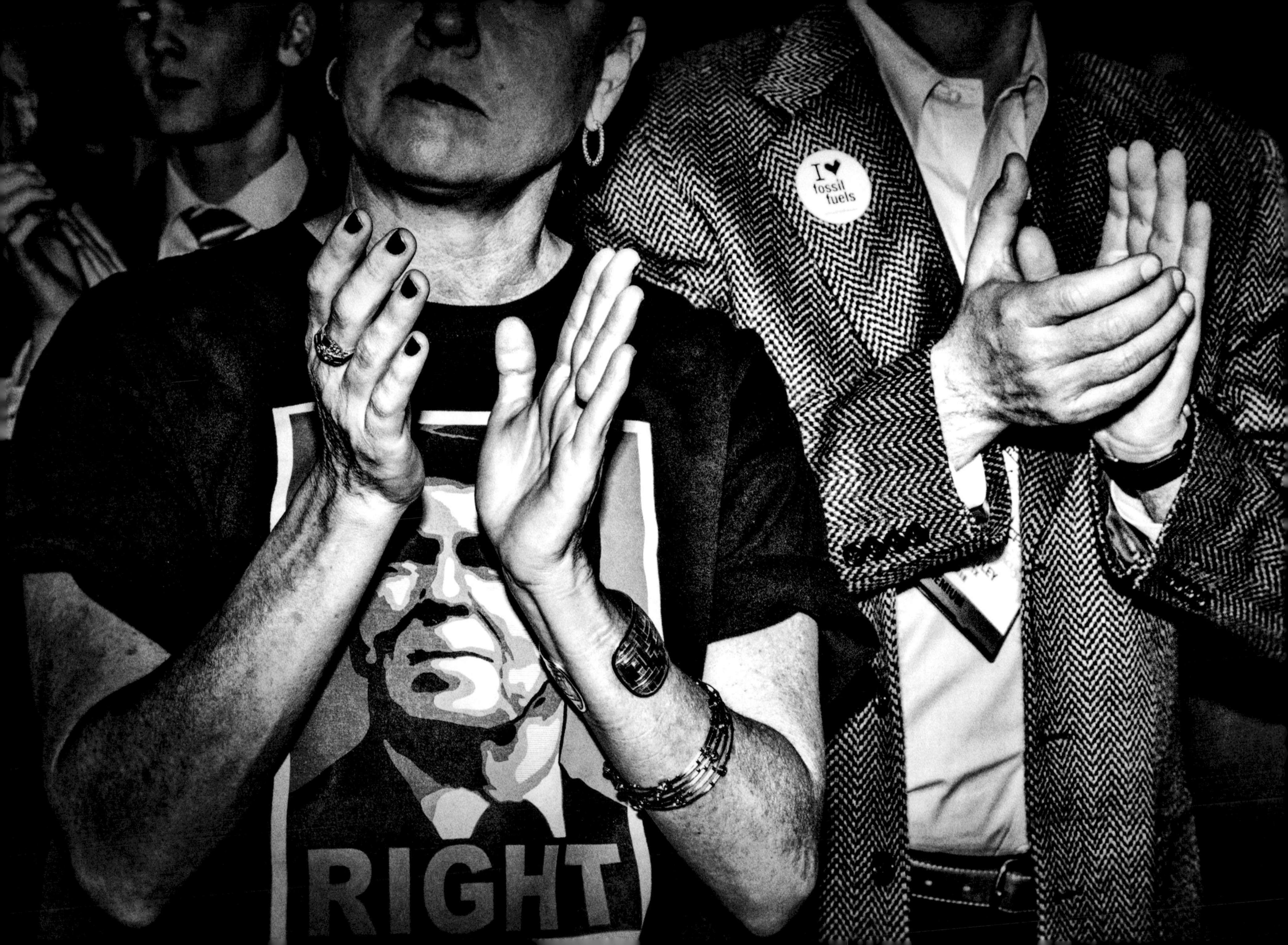
I ♥ fossil fuels
RIGHT

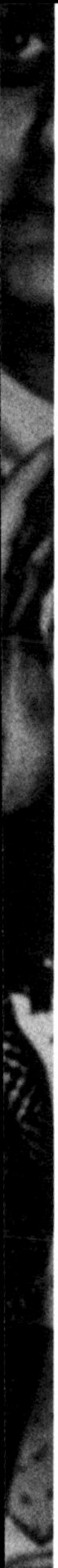

"How can a president not be an actor?"—**RONALD REAGAN**

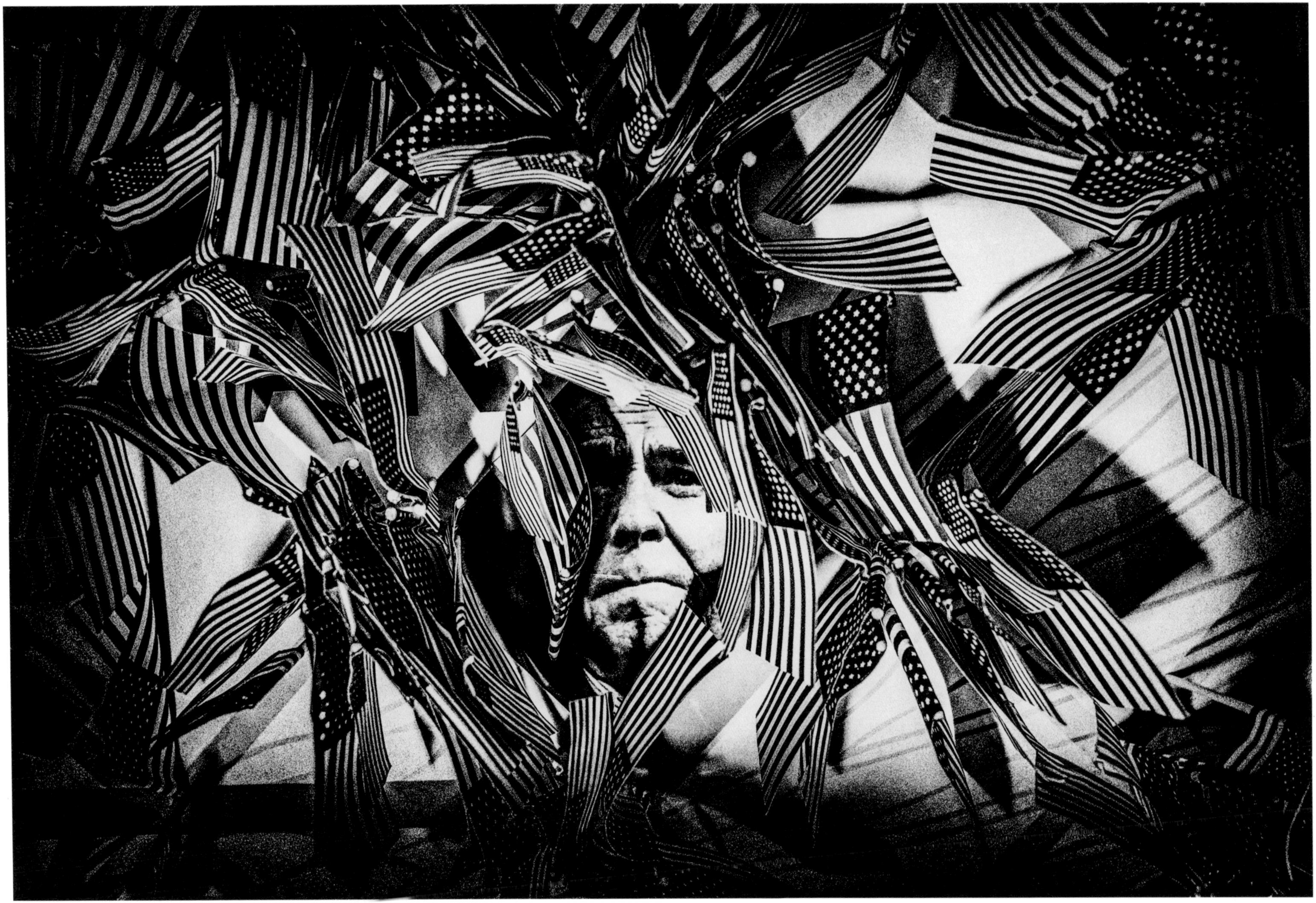

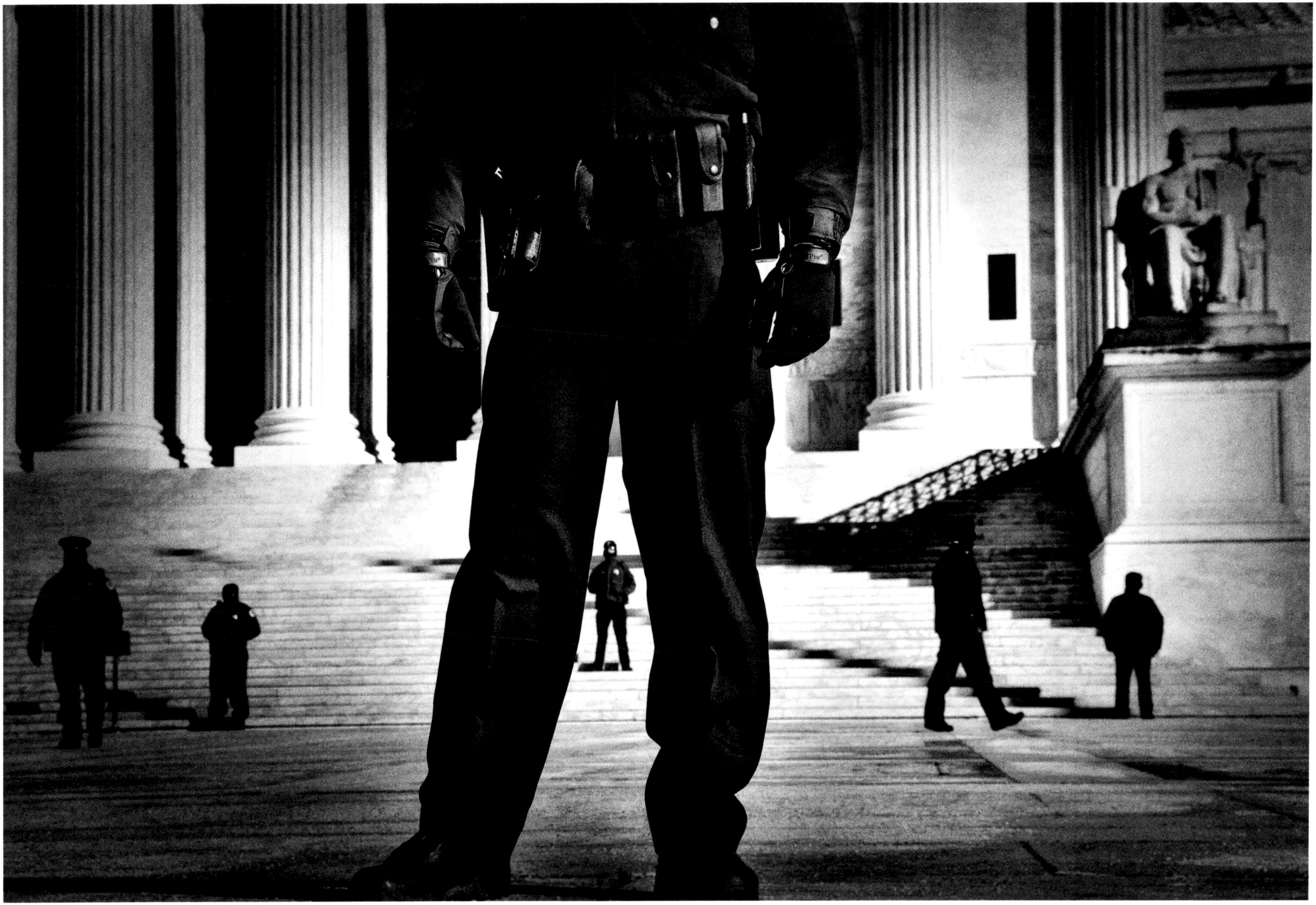

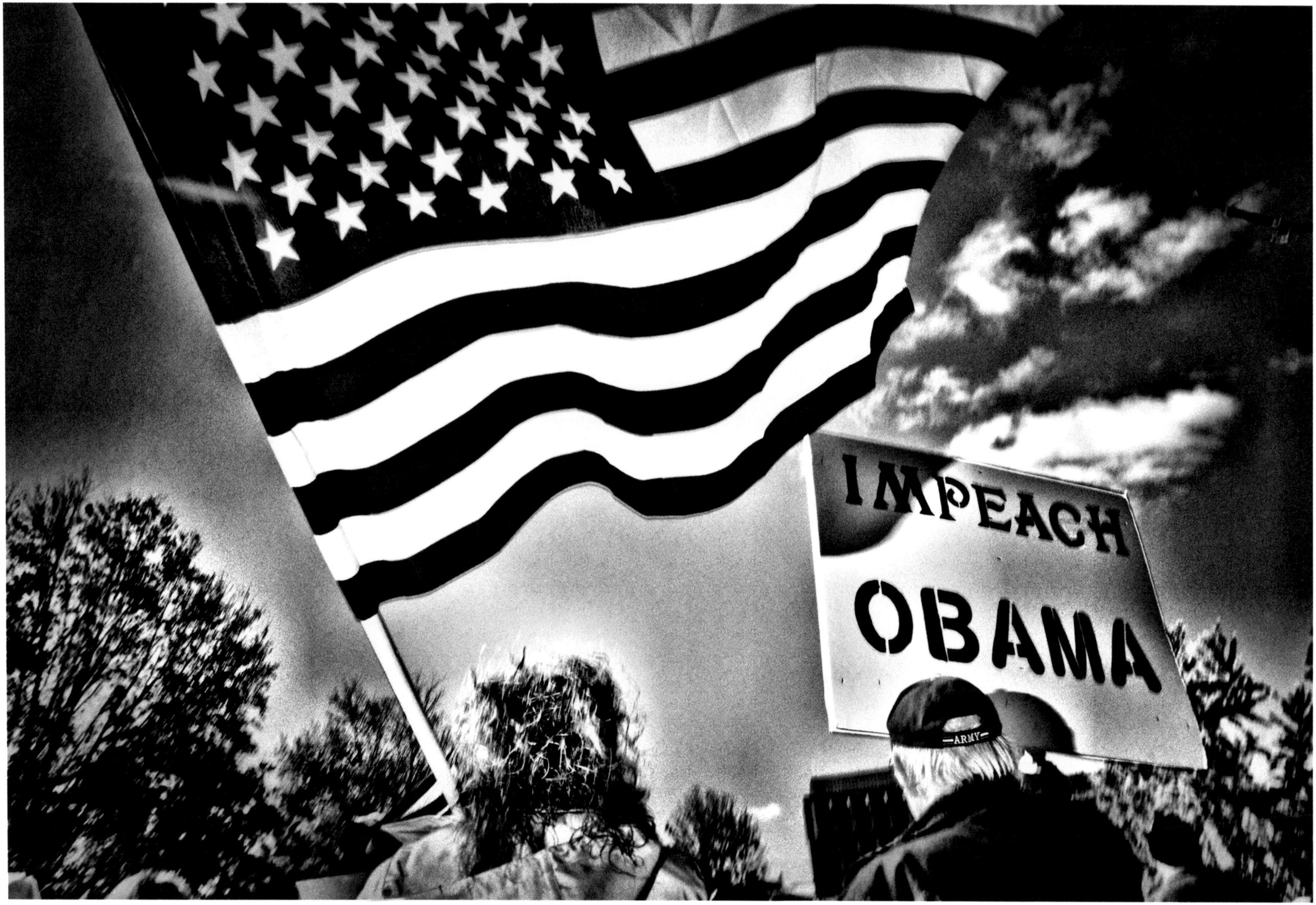
IMPEACH
OBAMA
ARMY

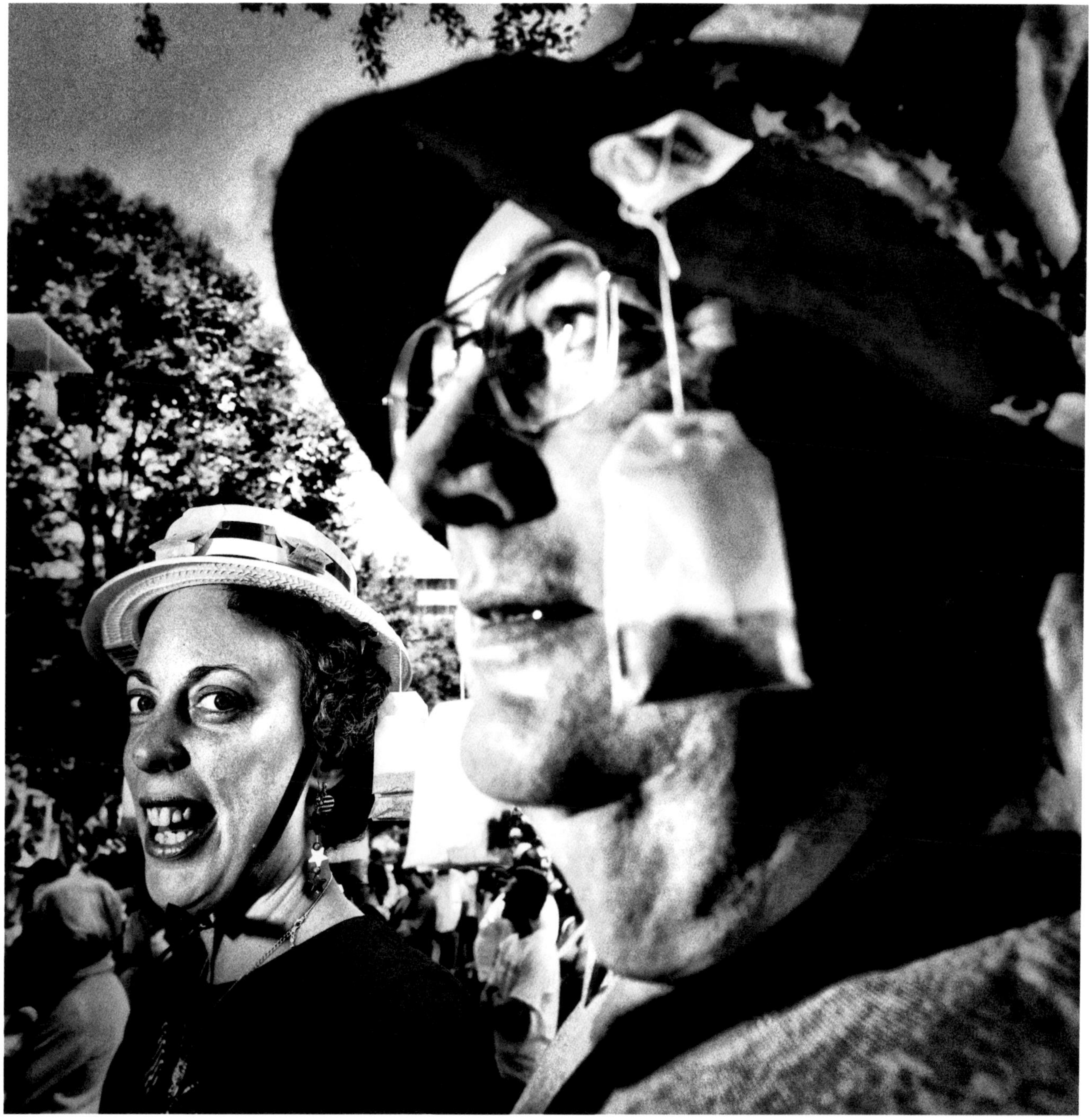

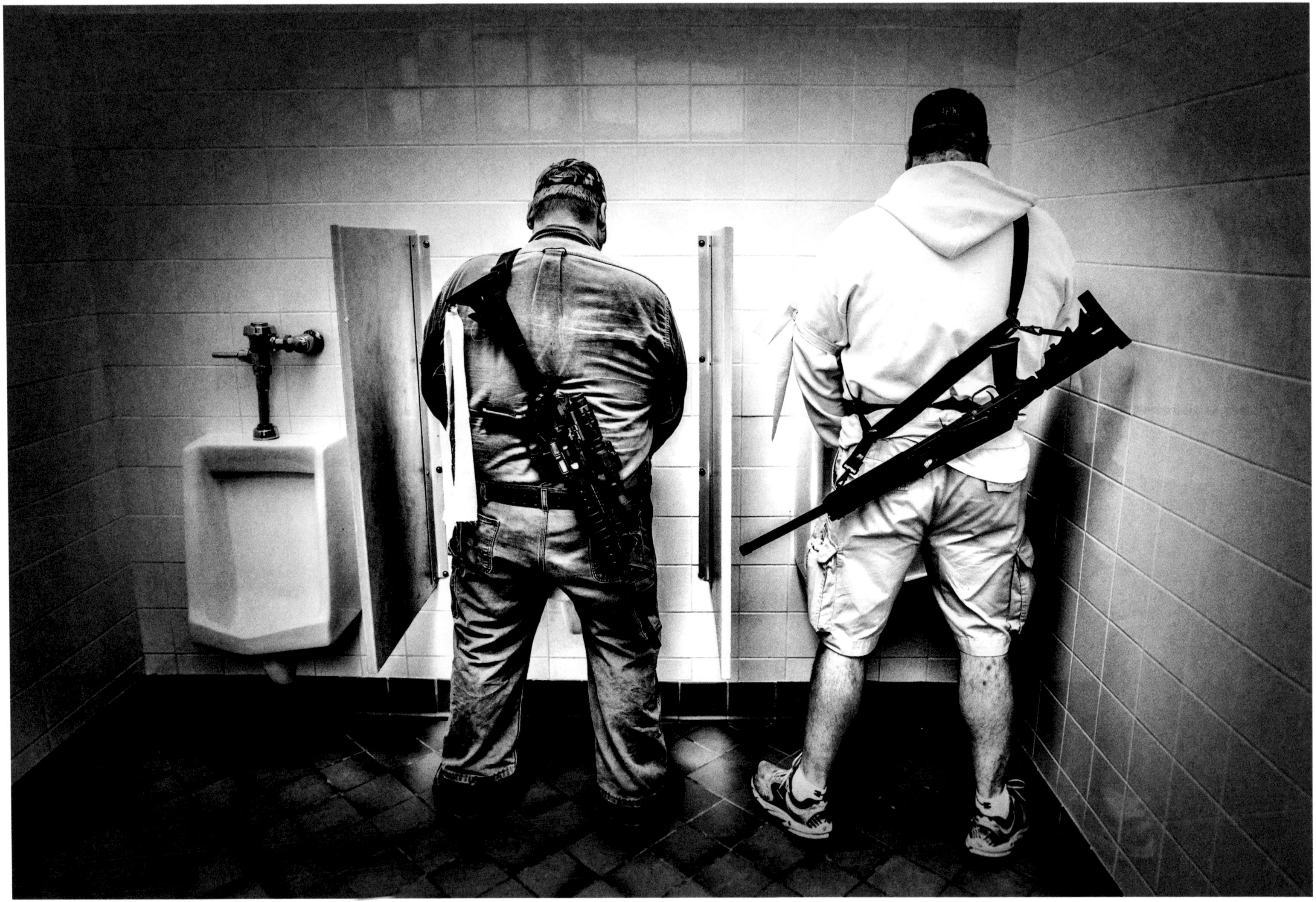

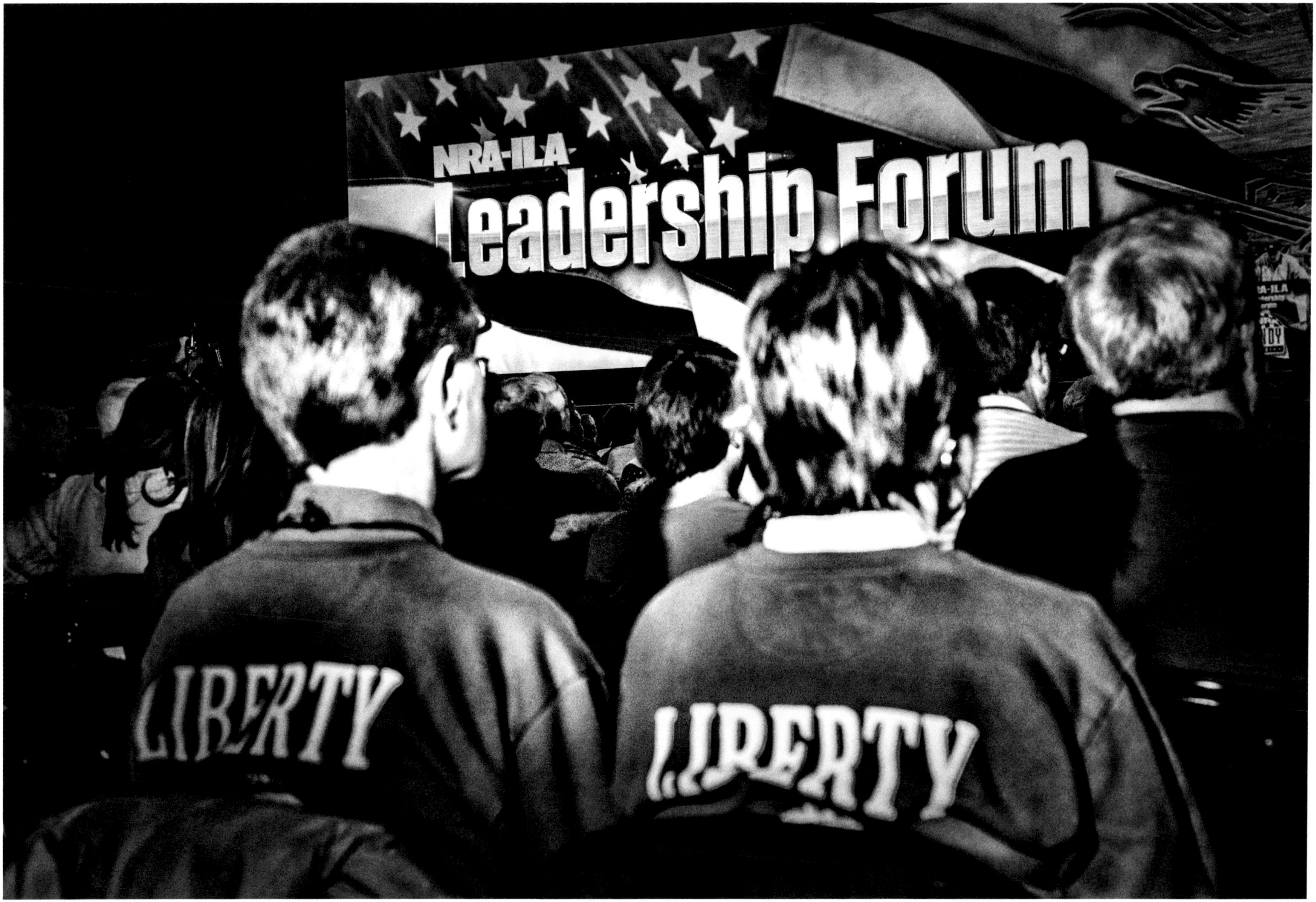
NRA-ILA
Leadership Forum
LIBERTY
LIBERTY

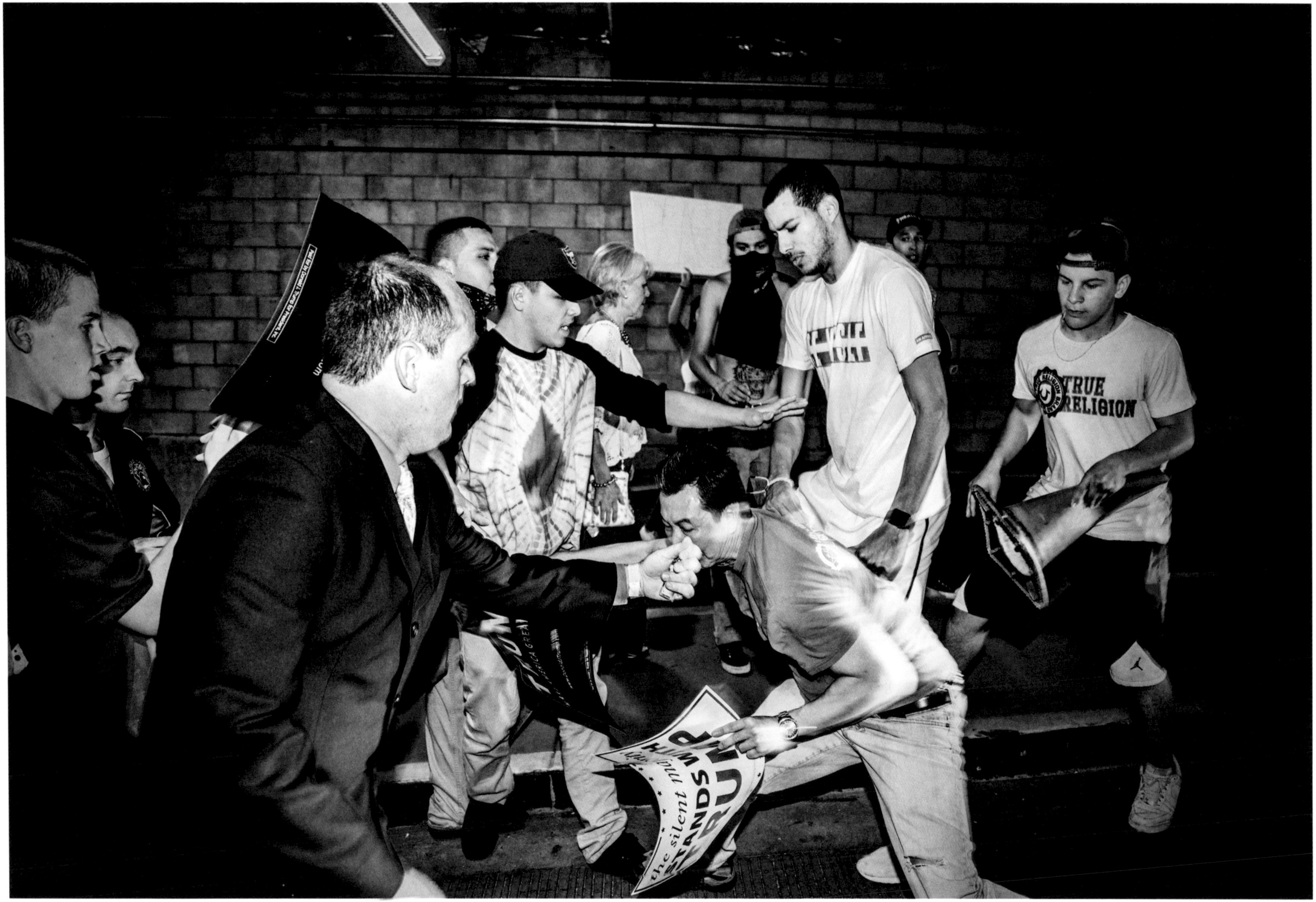
TRUE RELIGION

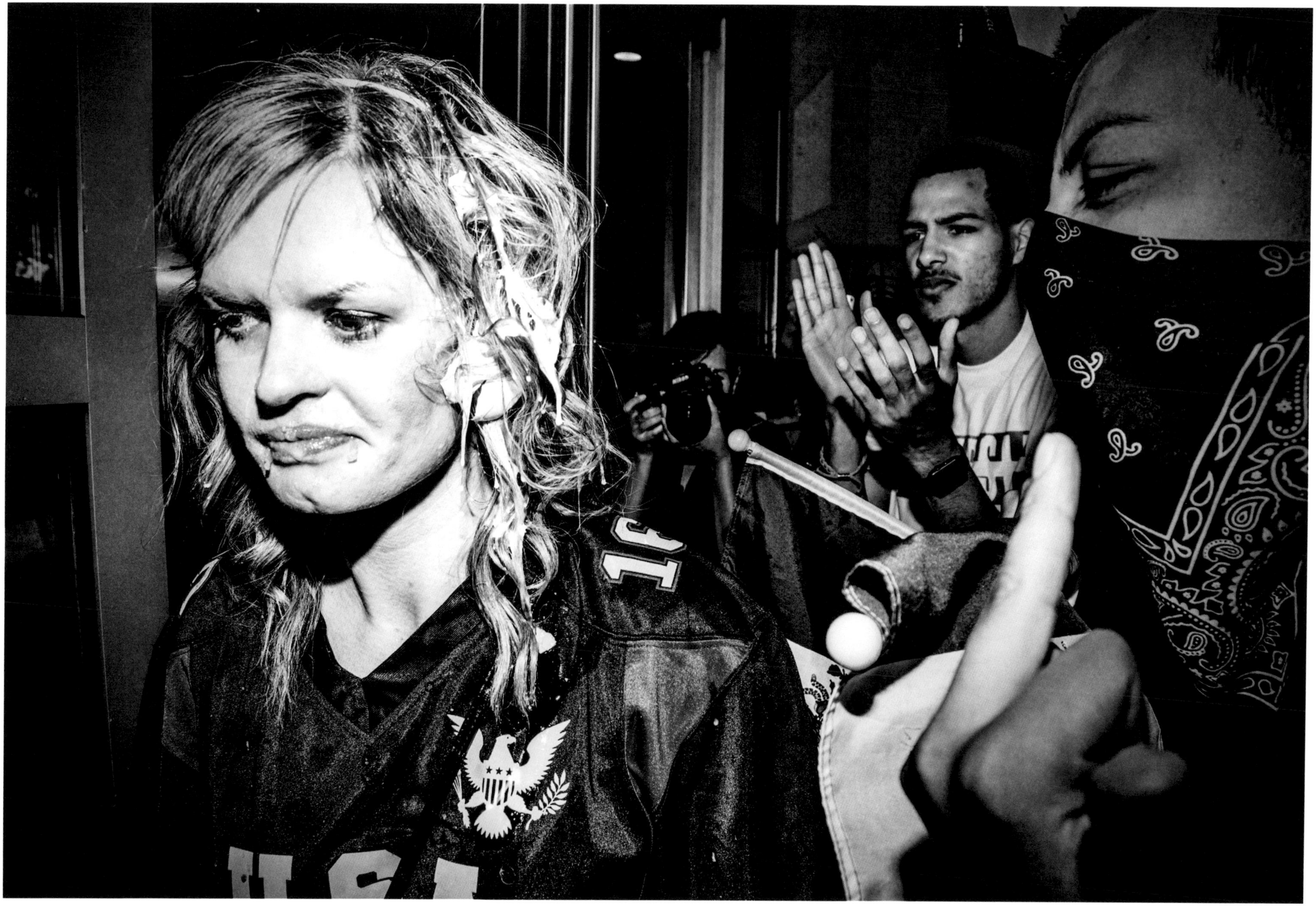

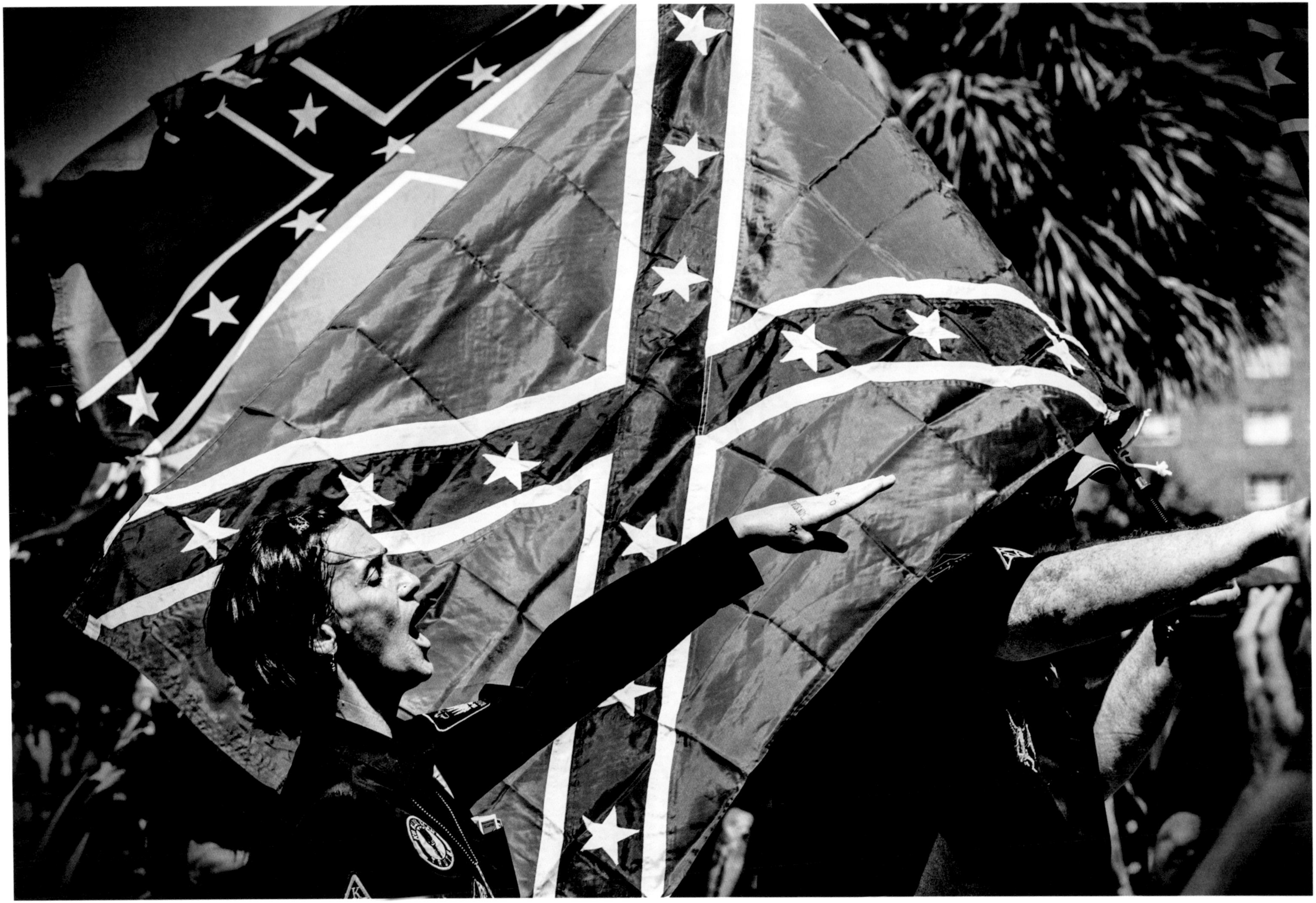

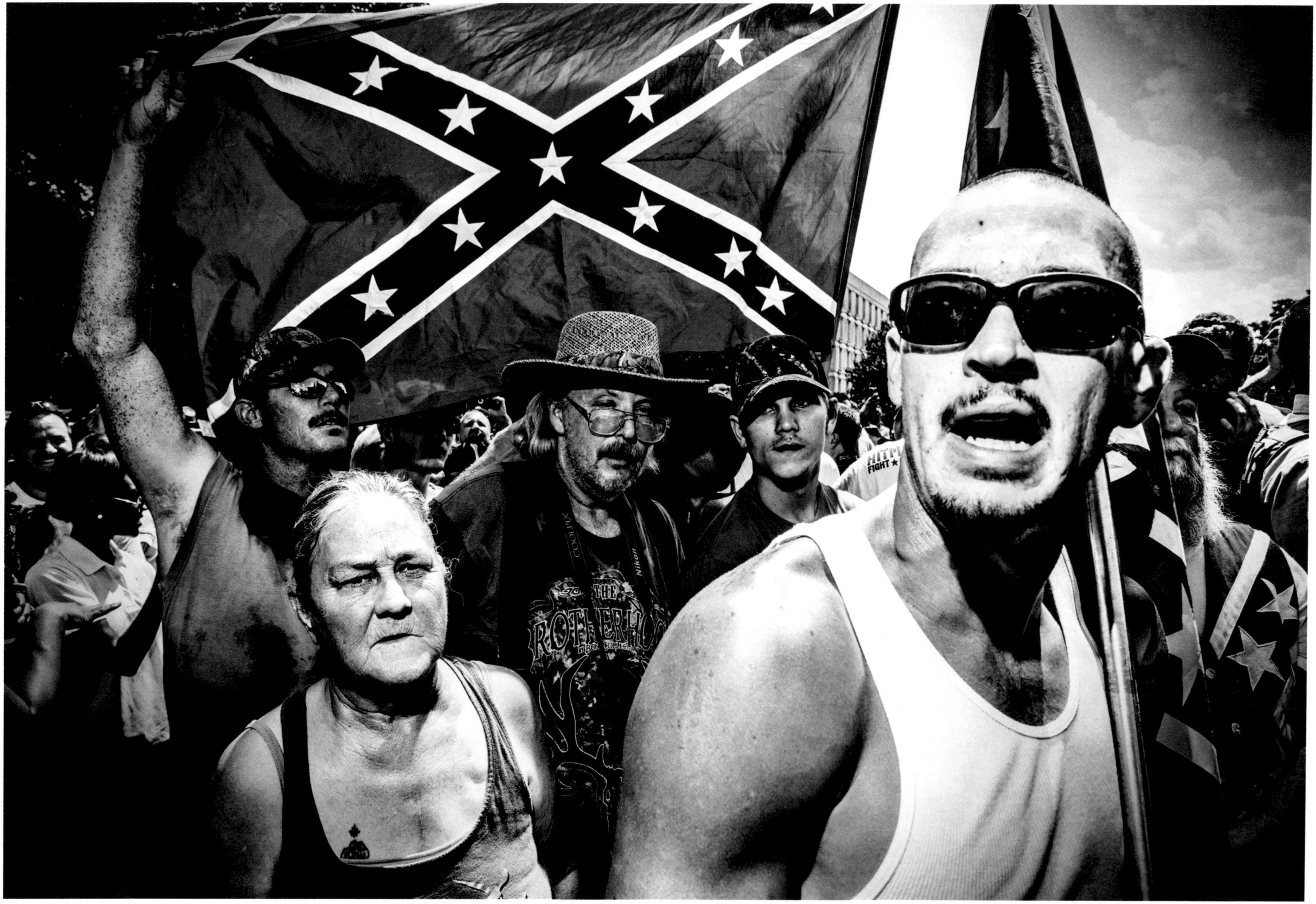
COOLPIX
Nikon
THE
FIGHT

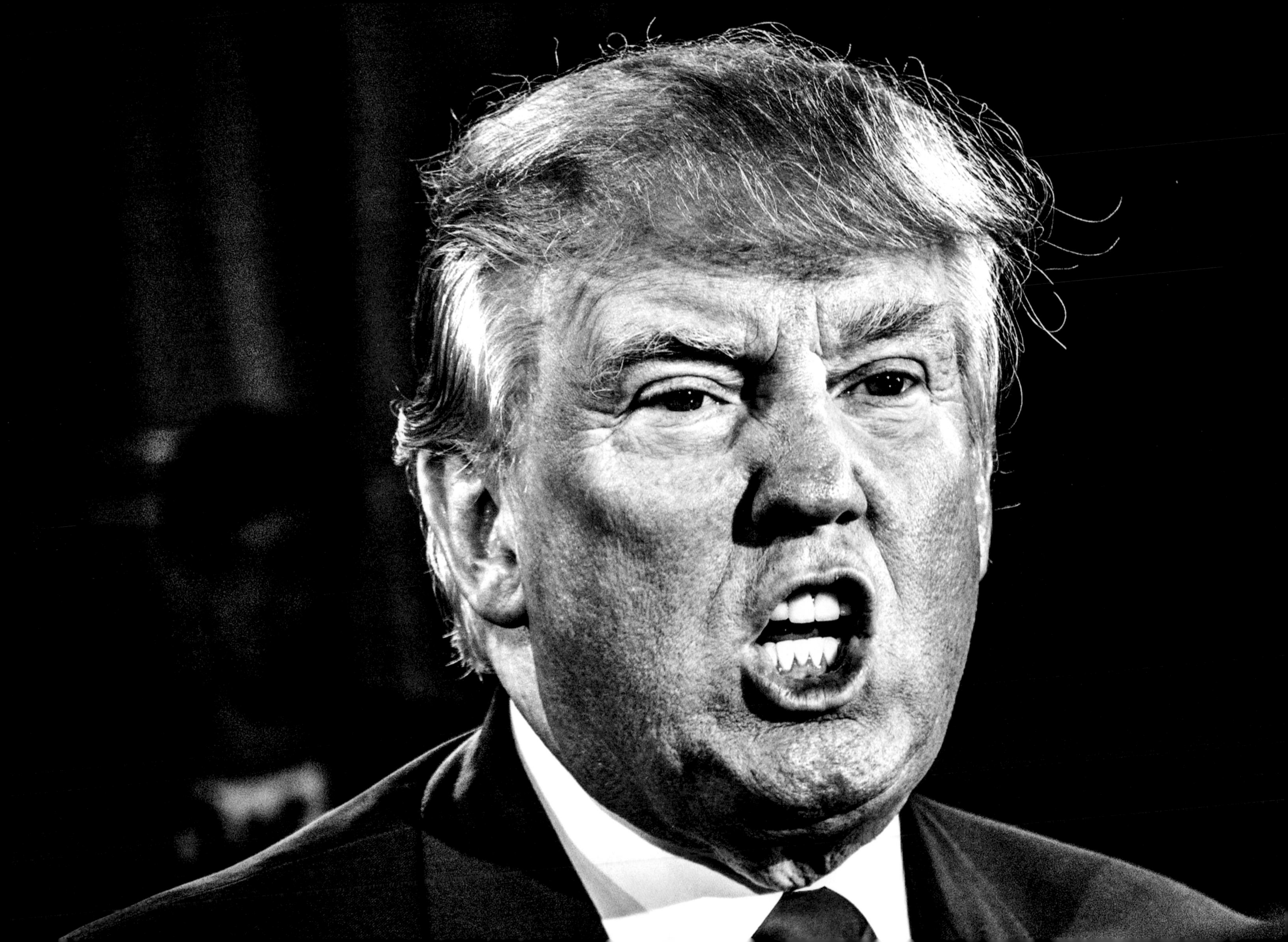

●●●○○ AT&T LTE 2:47 PM 95%

Hillary Clinton
6,134 Tweets

Tweets | Media | Likes

Hillary Clinton @HillaryClinton 1d
Trump has written a lot of books about business—but they all seem to end at Chapter 11.
15.8K 28.4K

Hillary Clinton @HillaryClinton 1d
"The last time we opted for Trump-style isolationism, it made the Great Depression longer and more painful." —Hillary
960 2,674

Hillary Clinton @HillaryClinton 1d
"He's giving more away to the 120,000 richest...families than he would to 120 million hardworking people." —Hillary on Trump's tax plan
1,065 2,690

Hillary Clinton @HillaryClinton 1d
"President Trump" would undo so much of the progress we've made over the past 8 years under President Obama.

Home Notifications 20+ Moments Messages Me

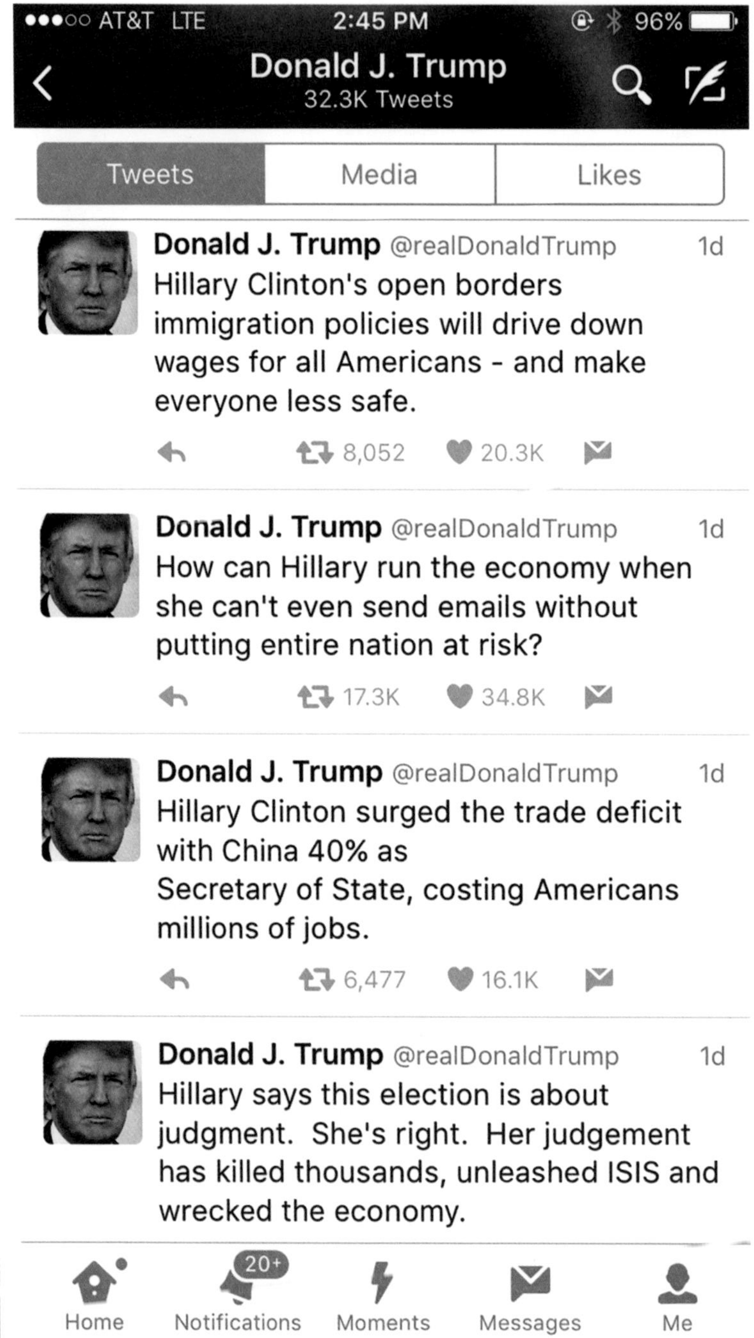
●●●○○ AT&T LTE
2:45 PM
96%
Donald J. Trump
32.3K Tweets
Tweets
Media
Likes
Donald J. Trump @realDonaldTrump 1d
Hillary Clinton's open borders immigration policies will drive down wages for all Americans - and make everyone less safe.
8,052
20.3K
Donald J. Trump @realDonaldTrump 1d
How can Hillary run the economy when she can't even send emails without putting entire nation at risk?
17.3K
34.8K
Donald J. Trump @realDonaldTrump 1d
Hillary Clinton surged the trade deficit with China 40% as Secretary of State, costing Americans millions of jobs.
6,477
16.1K
Donald J. Trump @realDonaldTrump 1d
Hillary says this election is about judgment. She's right. Her judgement has killed thousands, unleashed ISIS and wrecked the economy.
20+
Home
Notifications
Moments
Messages
Me

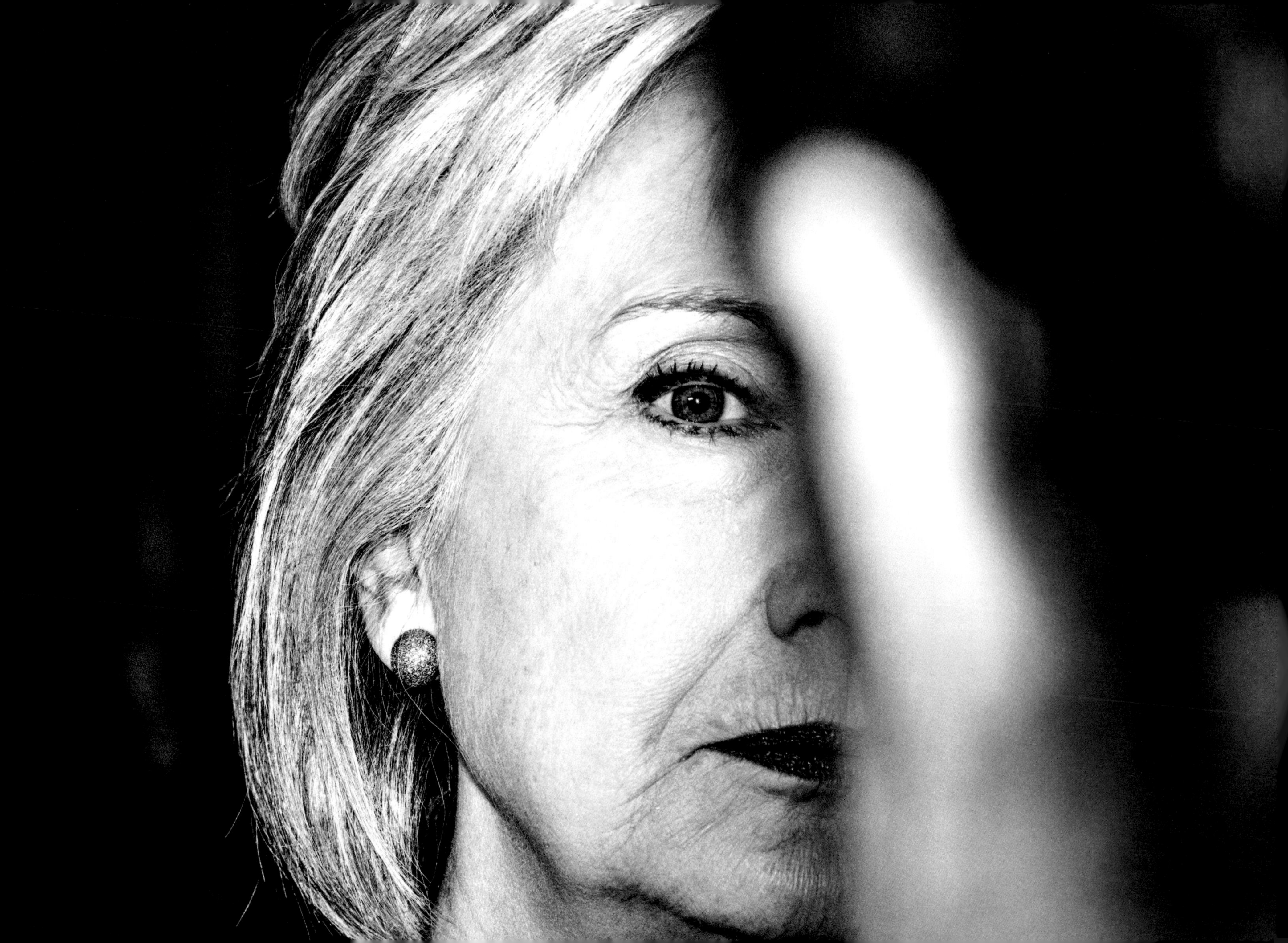

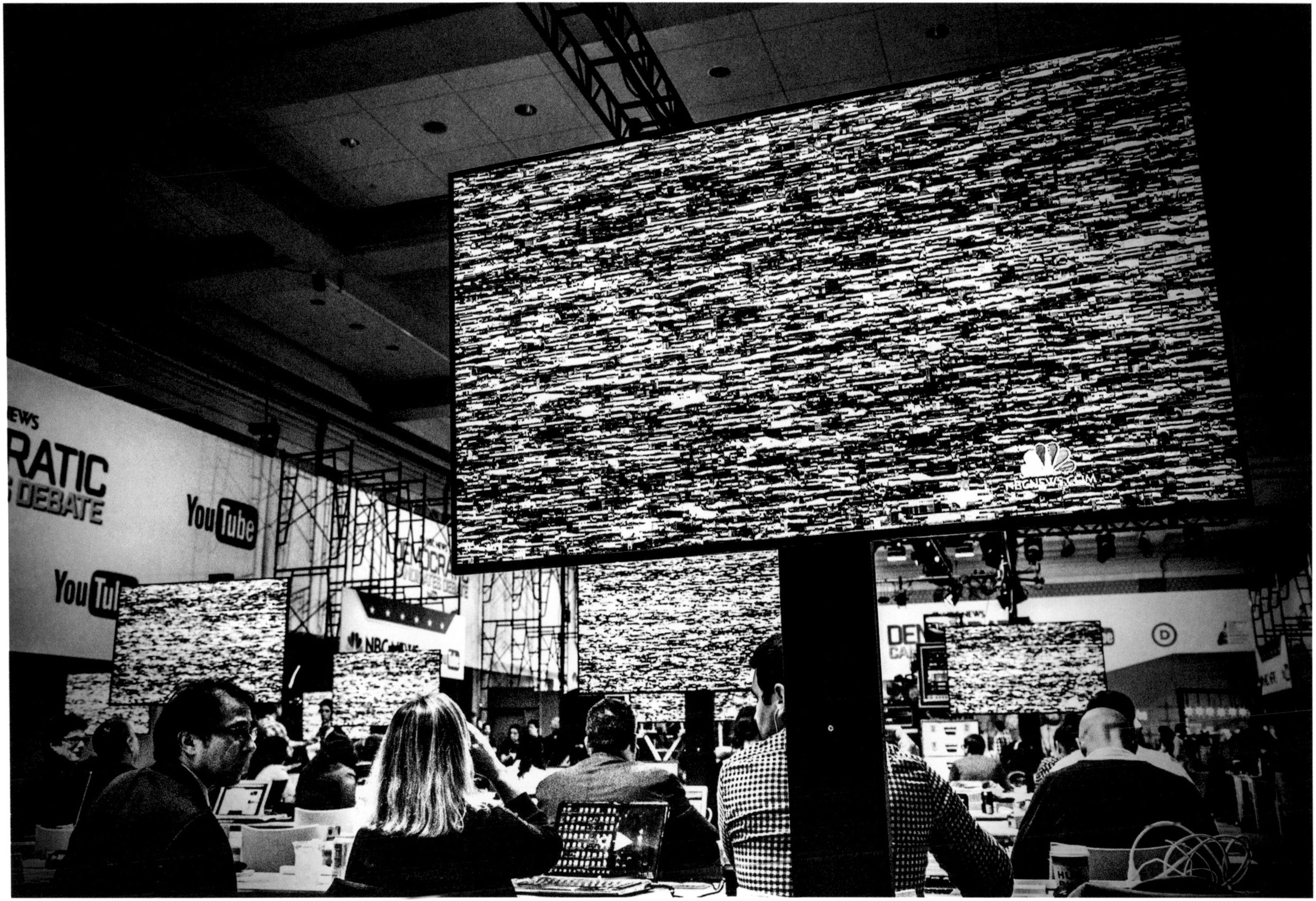
RATIC
DEBATE
YouTube

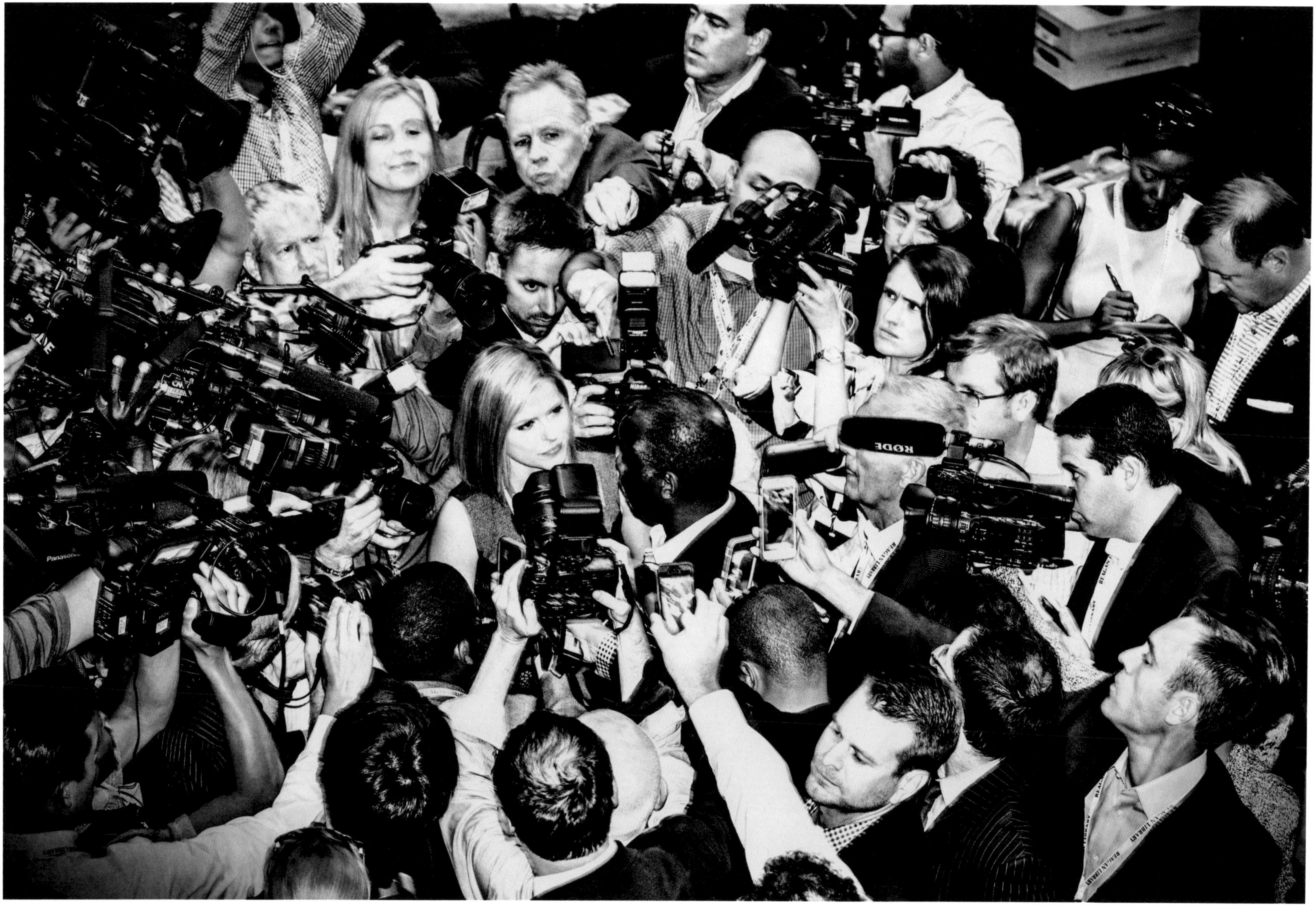
Panasonic
RØDE
REAGAN LIBRARY

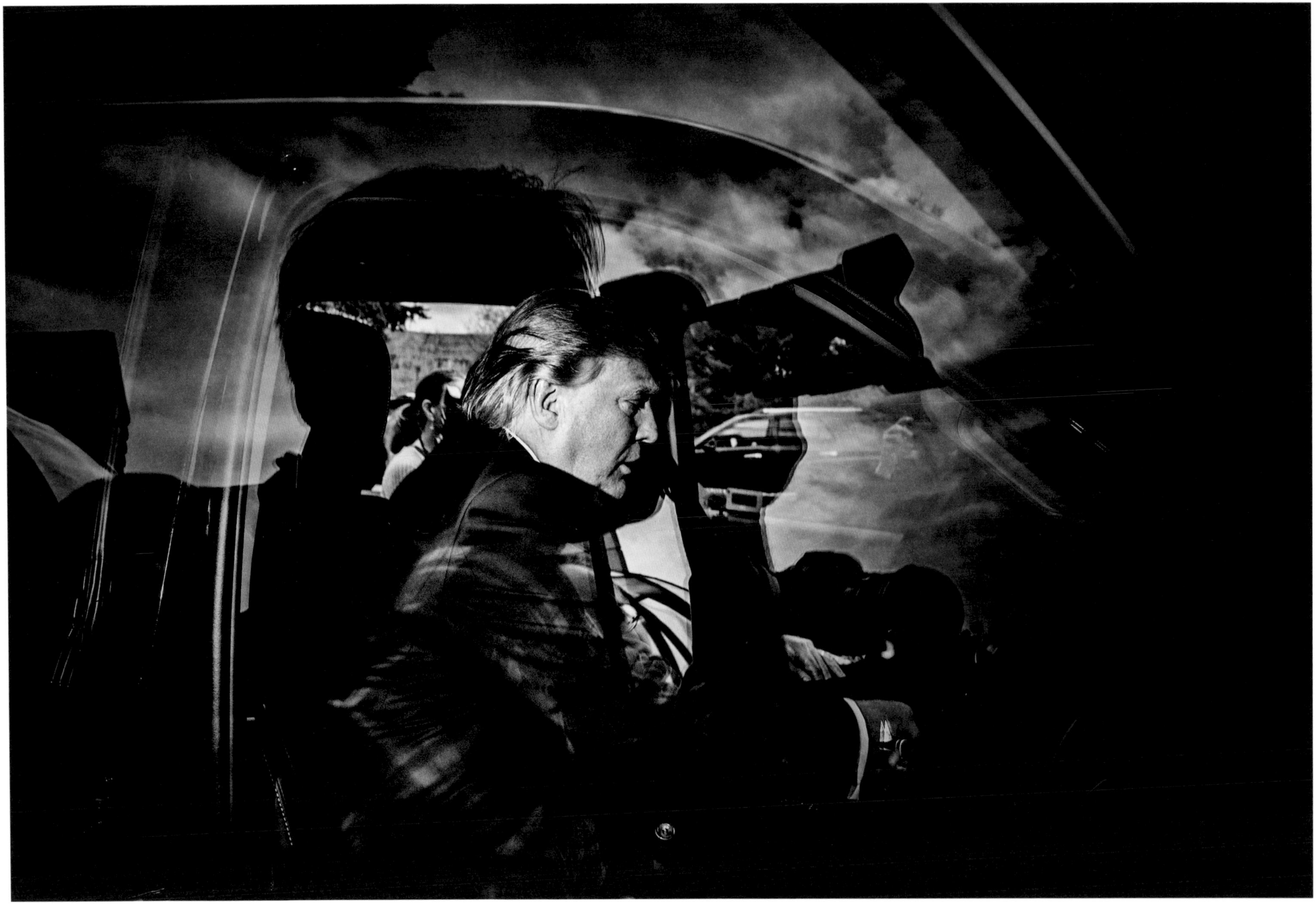

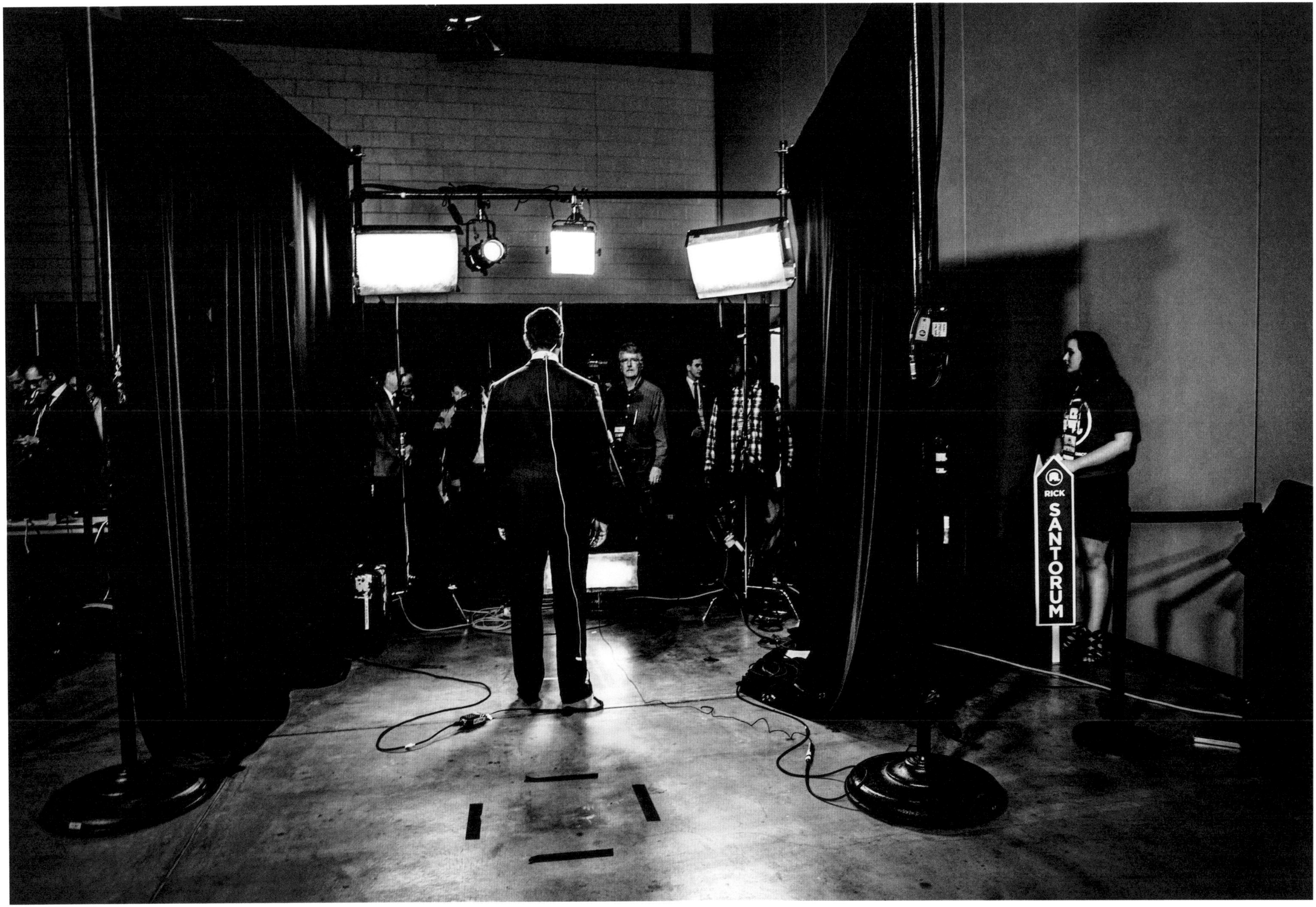
RICK
SANTORUM

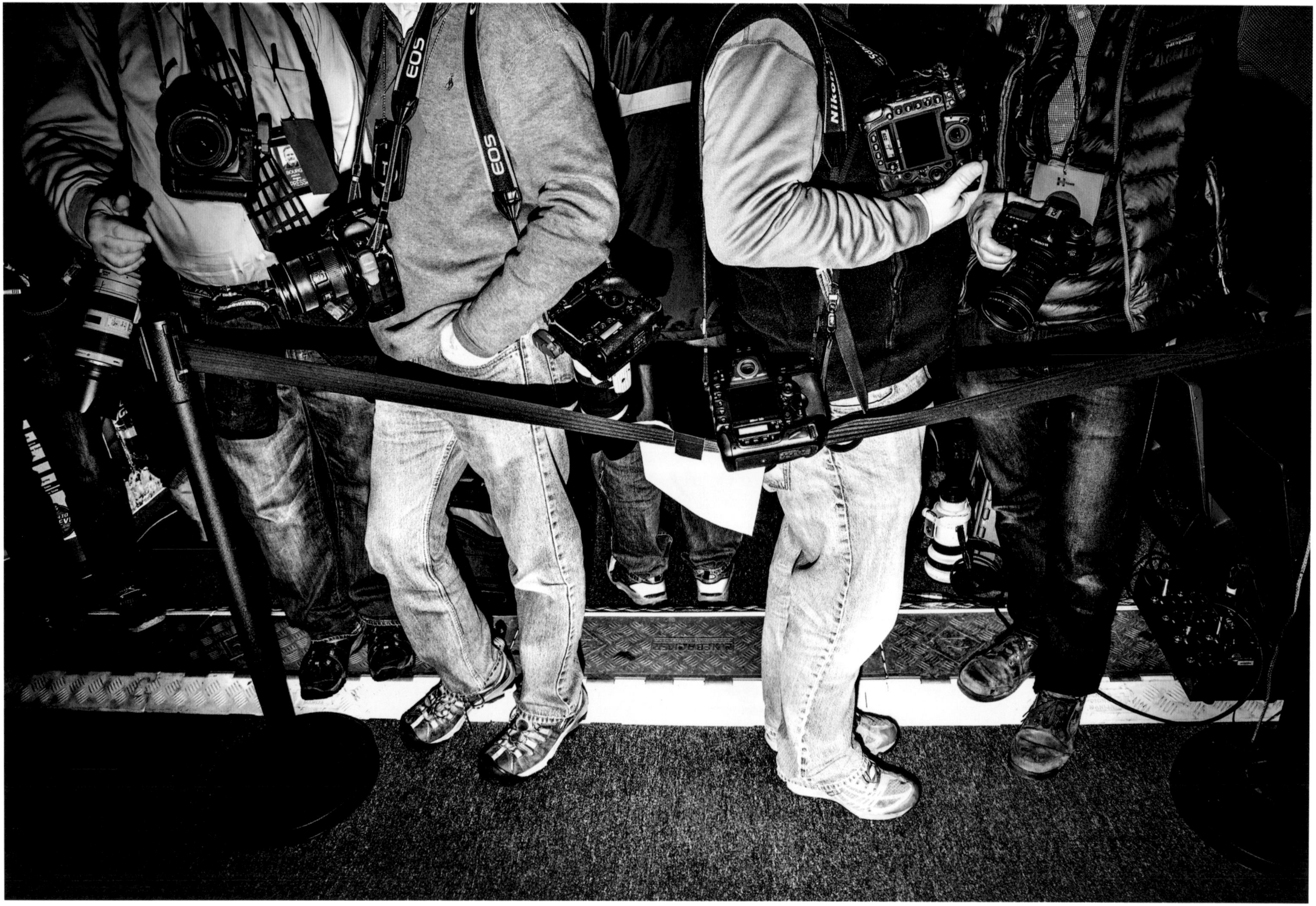
EOS
EOS
Nikon
PRESS

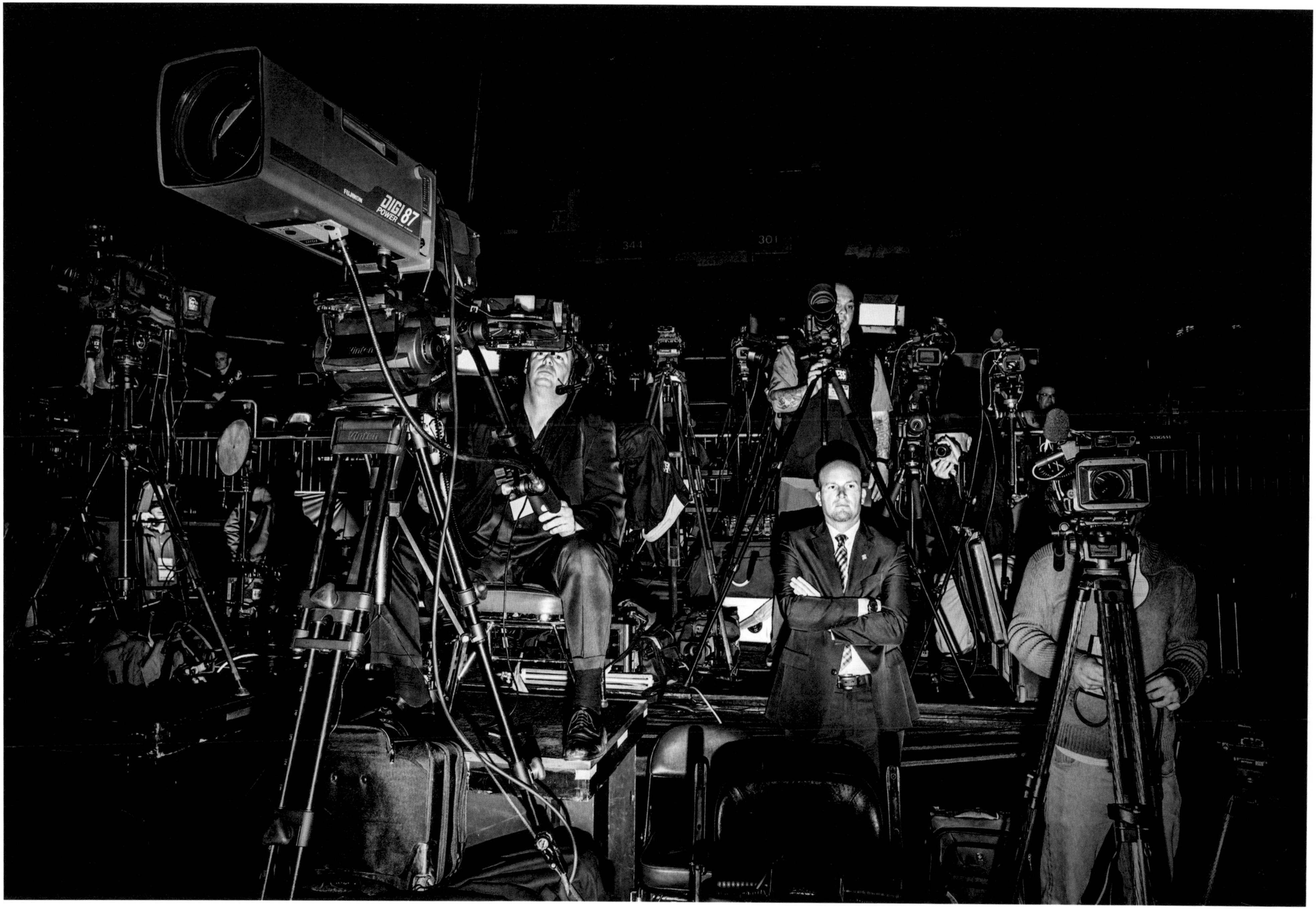
FUJINON
DIGI 87
POWER
344
301

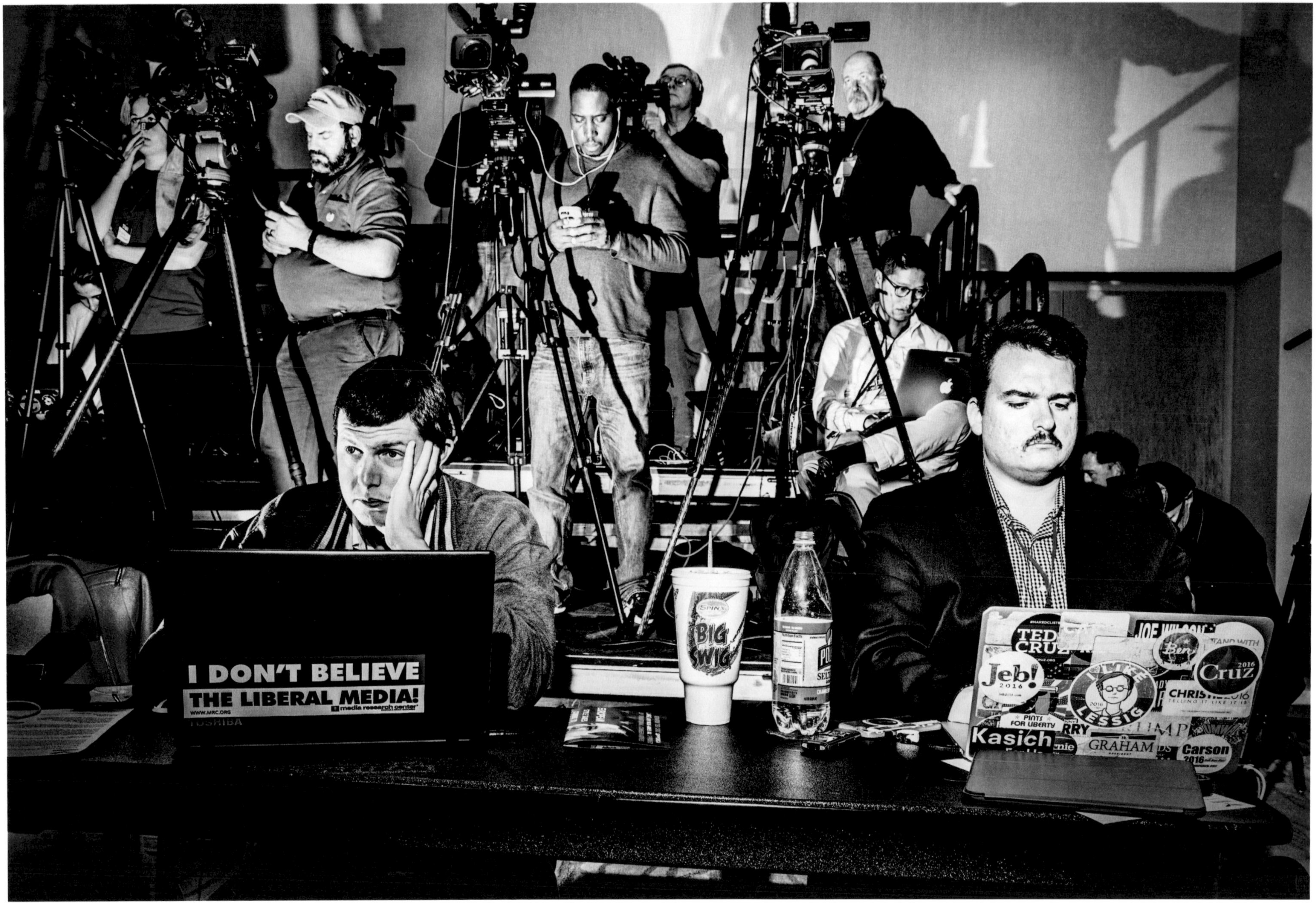
I DON'T BELIEVE
THE LIBERAL MEDIA!
WWW.MRC.ORG
media research center
BIG SWIG
TED CRUZ
JOE WILSON
Jeb! 2016
Cruz 2016
CHRISTIE 2016
TELLING IT LIKE IT IS
LESSIG
PINTS FOR LIBERTY
Kasich
GRAHAM
Carson 2016

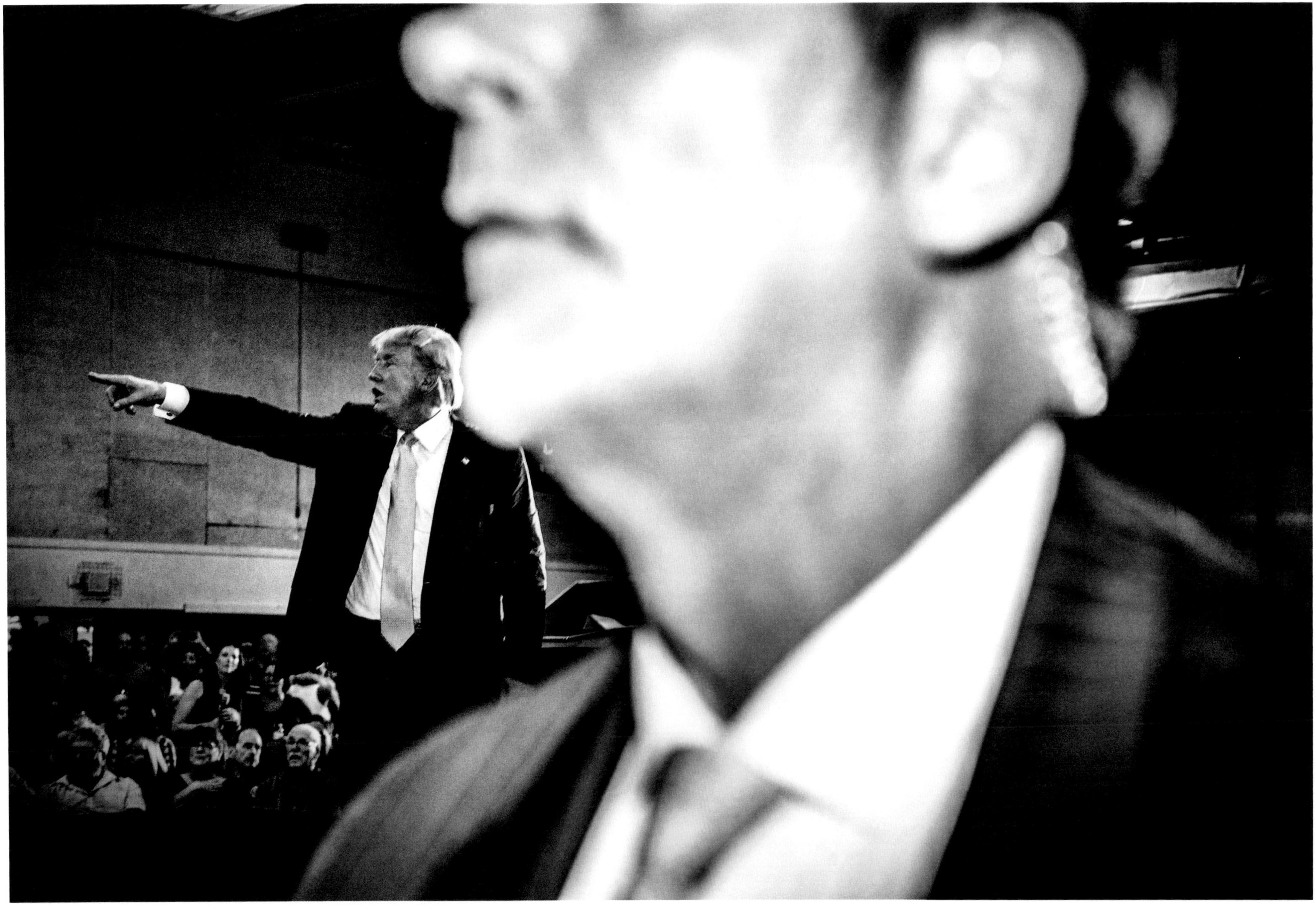

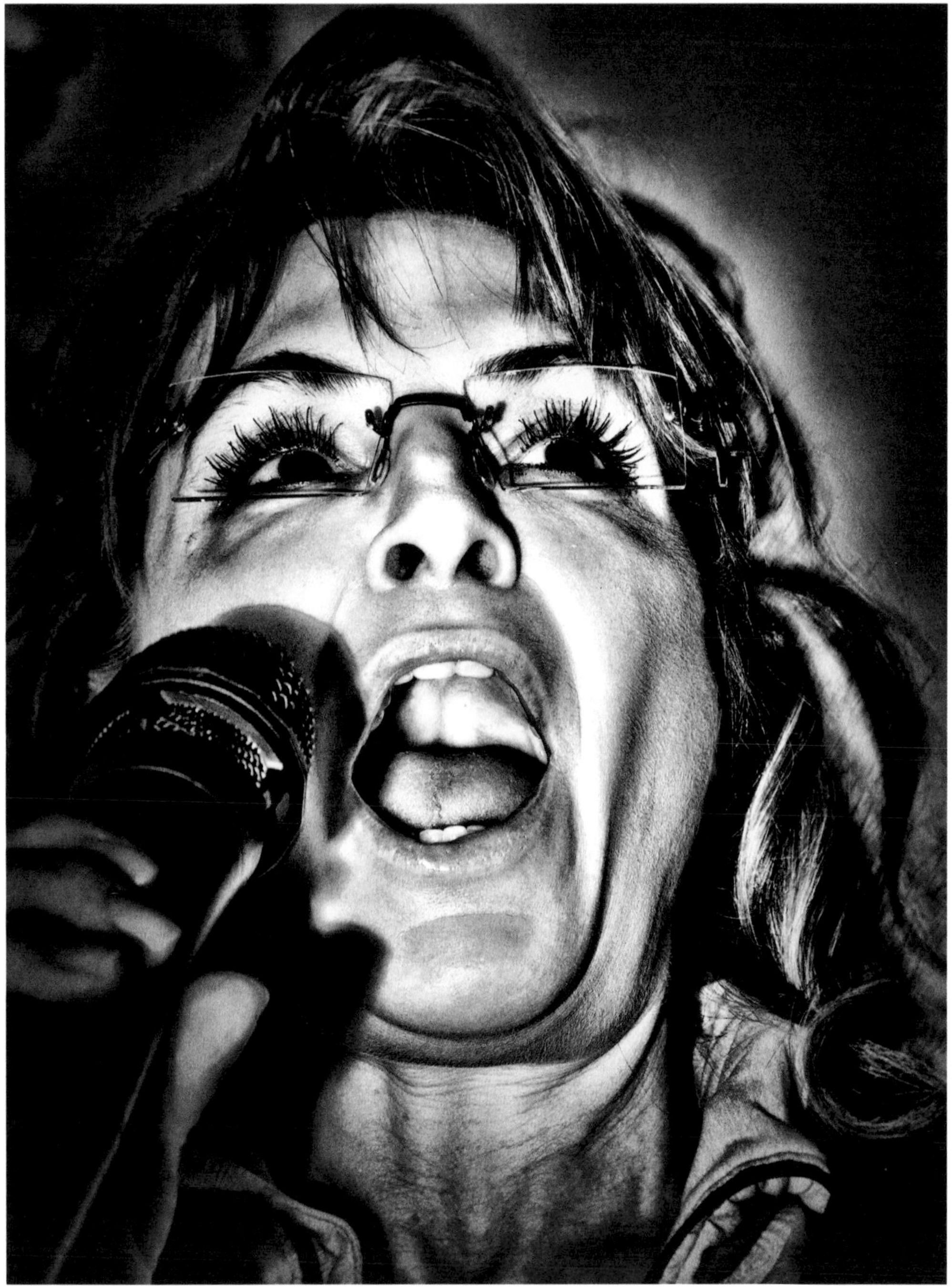

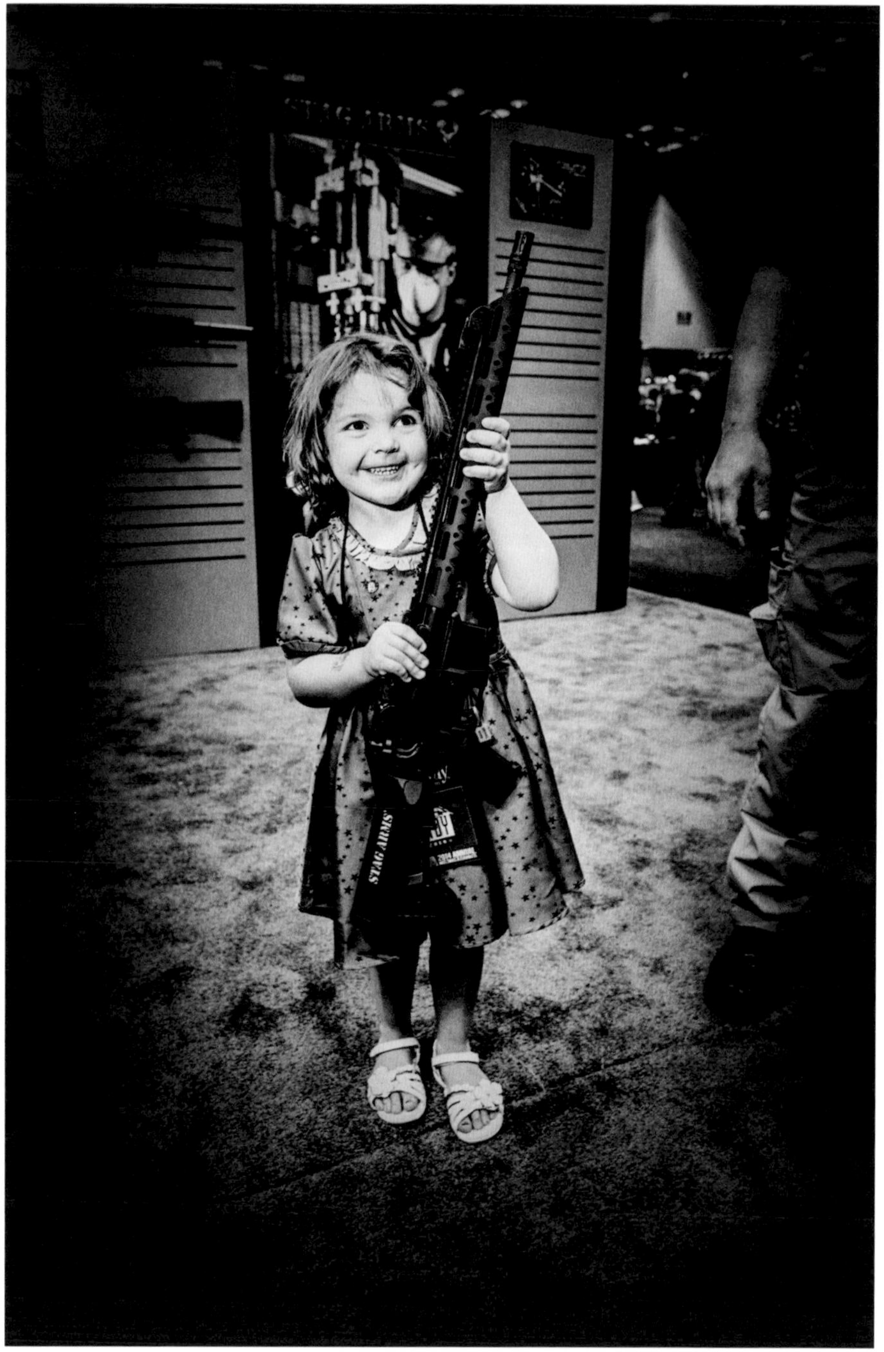
STAG ARMS

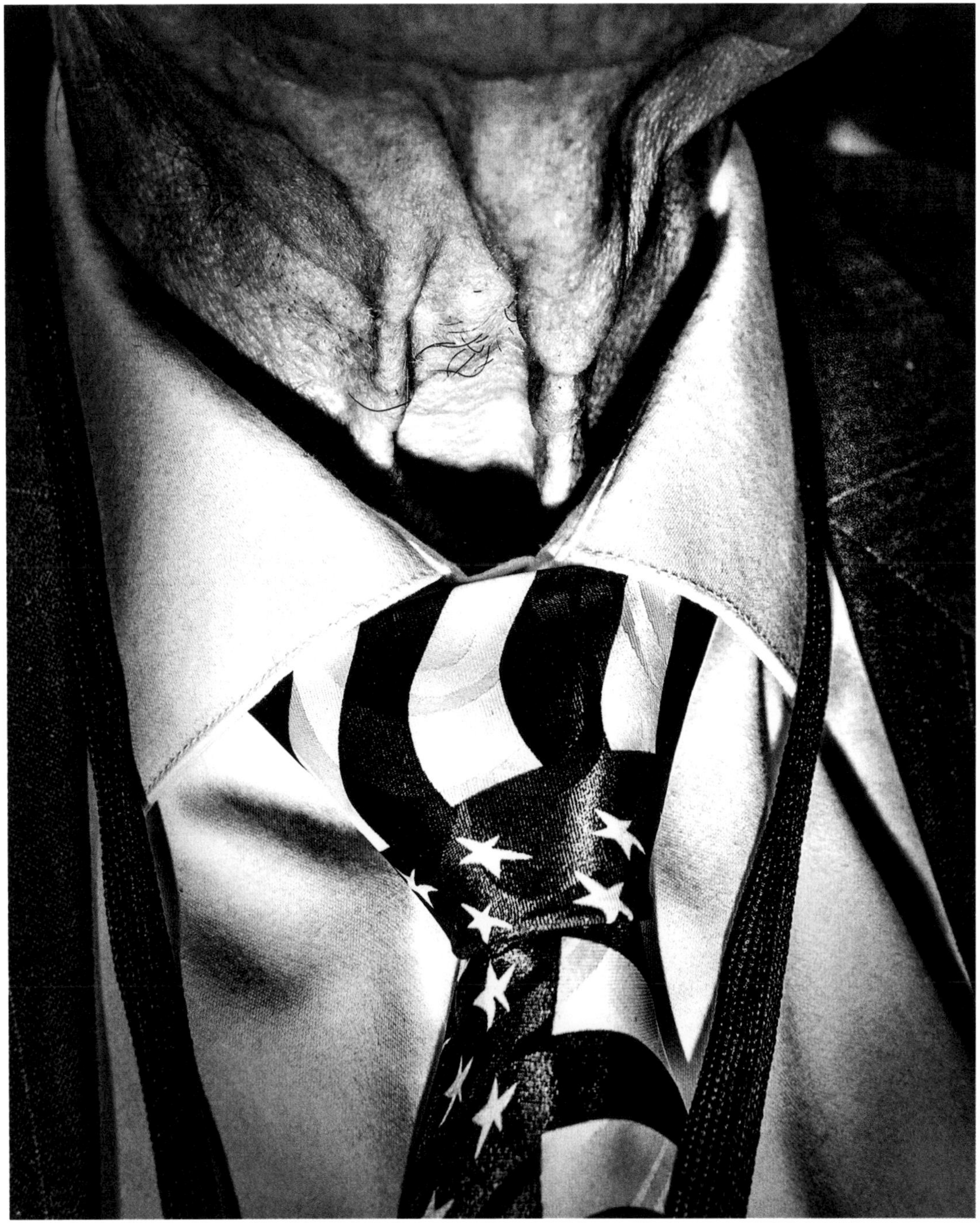

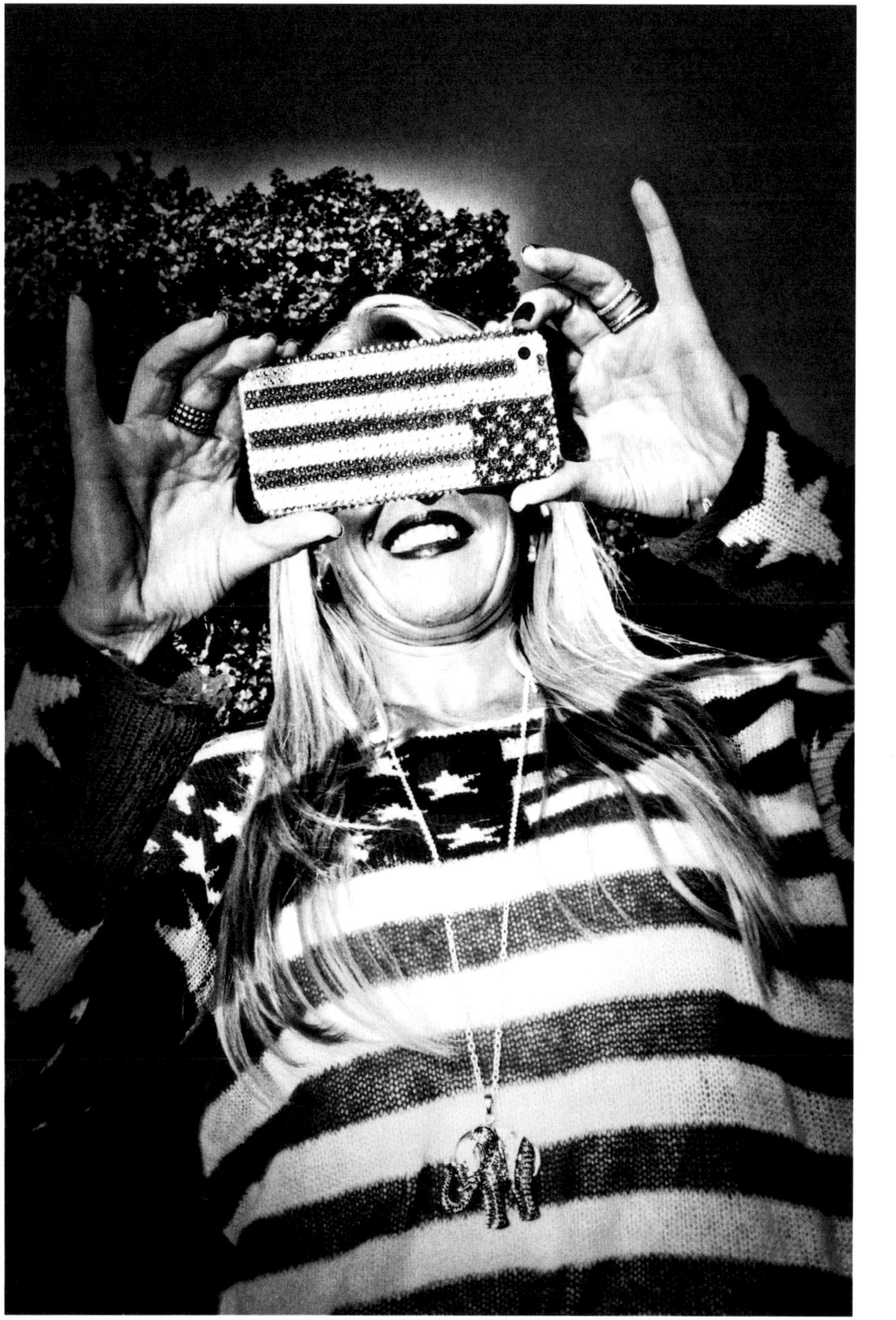

A little more than a year after the 2008 presidential election, I coauthored a book about it called *Game Change*. The subtitle of the book was *Obama and the Clintons, McCain and Palin, and the Race of a Lifetime*. At the time, there seemed scant risk in employing that final phrase. It was hard to imagine a subsequent campaign being more of a white-knuckle rollercoaster ride than one that had featured a freshman senator with the middle name Hussein defeating a former First Lady of the United States for the Democratic nomination, a moose-hunting Alaskan plucked from obscurity and put on the Republican ticket, and a global financial crisis threatening to unleash a second Great Depression—and had ended with the elevation of the country's first African American president. How on earth could a future battle for the White House be more mind-blowing than that?

Eight years later, we found out how. The 2016 presidential campaign has had little of the uplift or inspiration of its predecessor eight years ago. But it has been, in its own way, every bit as unexpected and unprecedented, as astonishing and operatic, as eye-popping and jaw-dropping—and, to countless voters, vastly more alarming.

The source of much of the shocking surreality of the 2016 election can be easily and precisely identified: Donald J. Trump. The rise to political prominence and power of the billionaire real-estate mogul, reality-TV star, and self-branding virtuoso was not only a development unforeseen but deemed beyond the realm of possibility by virtually every Establishment politician, analyst, and pundit. By any conventional metric, Trump was plainly unqualified to be president; he possessed neither the resume, the knowledge of domestic and foreign policy, nor the temperament ordinarily required to occupy the Oval Office. His suitability even to be the Republican nominee was just as dubious. He held an array of positions at odds with the party's long-held orthodoxies; indeed, for most of his life, he had been a member of the Democratic Party. Once Trump launched his campaign, these strikes against him were magnified by his outlandish behavior: a seemingly endless string of political and personal provocations and offenses; policy proposals that ranged from the obviously implausible (building a giant wall along the Mexican border, financed by Mexico) to the clearly unconstitutional (banning all Muslims from entering the United States); his routine and gleeful incitement of violence at his rallies; and a consistent and overt appeal to the racist, nativist, xenophobic elements within the Republican Party.

And yet, despite (or maybe, more troublingly, because of) all of this, Trump led the Republican race from its outset to its conclusion, secured the GOP nomination with relative ease, and, as the homestretch of the general election loomed, found himself in a dead heat with Hillary Clinton. The odds were still against Trump emerging victorious on Election Day—but they were undeniably shrinking. The possibility of a President Trump was no longer dauntingly or comfortingly (depending on your point of view) farfetched.

Trump's triumph, however, was not the only shock of the 2016 campaign. On the Democratic side, there was the startling and unpredicted ascendance of Bernie Sanders. In the early months of 2015, the proposition that a 74-year-old, self-described Socialist from Vermont would ultimately pose an existential threat to Clinton—with her enormous financial and organizational advantages, her robust support among the most crucial Democratic constituencies, and her historic claim to be the first female President of the United States—would have been dismissed as a fantasy as pure as it was absurd. But Sanders did just that. By attracting an army of young supporters and others dismayed by the levels of economic inequality in America, the outsized influence of monied interests

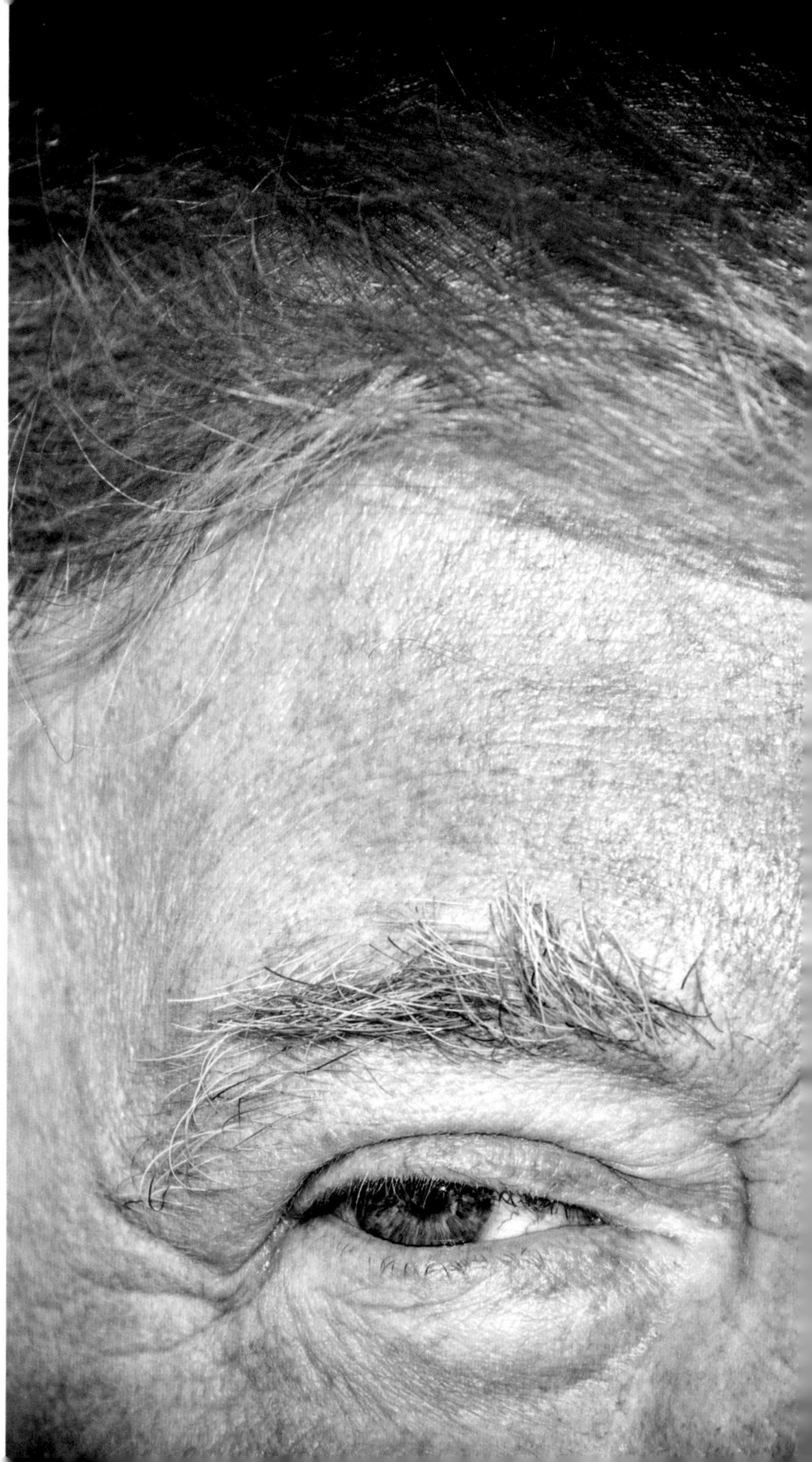

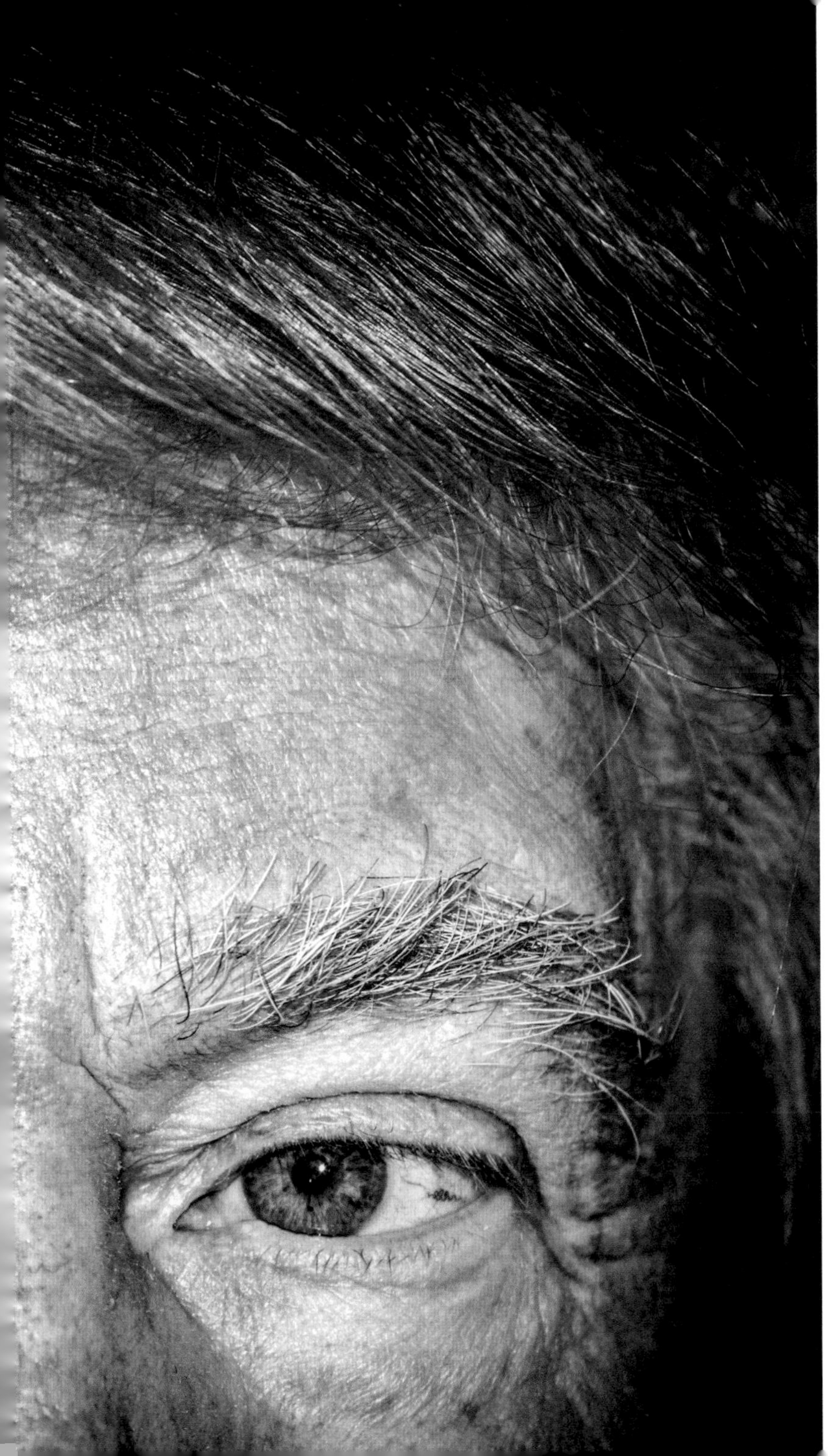

in the nation's politics, and what his adherents saw as the corruption of the ideals and ambitions of the Democratic Party, Sanders prevailed in 23 primaries or caucuses and won more than 13 million votes (out of roughly 30 million cast). He pushed Clinton to the left on many issues, from foreign trade to criminal justice. His adamant attacks on the billionaire class, his acid description of the country's ruling class an "oligarchy," and his passionate call for a "political revolution" struck loud and resonant chords not just among progressive Democrats but across the ideological spectrum.

The Trump and Sanders phenomena were, of course, animated by radically divergent convictions and worldviews. But both reflected a profound disruption taking place outside the confines of Washington, DC. For at least the past 30 years, the central twin dynamics in U.S. politics have been an increasingly bitter and paralyzing degree of partisan polarization and an incipient populist impulse among millions of ordinary voters. On the one hand, the Republican Party has lurched further and further to the right, while the Democratic Party has moved further and further to the left. On the other, the distrust of and anger towards established institutions of all kinds—the federal government, Wall Street, big business, big labor, the mainstream media—has grown pervasive and feral. This populism is bipartisan and ecumenical, and is undergirded by an inchoate but not unfounded sense that the essential American promise that each successive generation will inherit a better life than its predecessors is no longer operative; that the old economic, social, cultural, and demographic orders are inexorably unraveling.

Fueled by decades of stagnant incomes and living standards, and exacerbated by the lingering aftereffects of the 2008 financial crisis, in 2016 the simmering frustrations and resentments of a broad swath of the American electorate reached a roiling boil. And from that seething stew arose the appeal and potency of Trump and Sanders.

No journalist covering the 2016 election in any medium has more beautifully and harrowingly captured the campaign and our politics more generally than Mark Peterson. In *Political Theatre,* Peterson presents the drama and comedy, the transparent fakery and moments of accidental authenticity, and the abject chaos that has transfixed and often mortified anyone paying attention. What makes *Political Theatre* so compelling is that Peterson trains his lens with equal acuity on the action playing out on stage and in the audience. Using techniques inspired, fittingly, by *Citizen Kane,* Peterson's focus on the candidates exposes and then strips away their and their handlers' relentless efforts to craft prettified, prefabricated personas for public consumption. He lays bare Trump, Clinton, Sanders, and the rest for what they are: impressive but flawed, confident but vulnerable, idealistic but narcissistic human beings consumed by a fierce and unyielding hunger for power. When Peterson turns his camera from the proscenium and towards the voters, he casts a wide and withering but finally sympathetic eye on an electorate in the throes of an upheaval that few of them (which is to say, few of us) fully comprehend.

The result is a series of images that are vivid, stunning, surprising, and searingly revealing. They are also deeply true. In this, *Political Theatre* is something more than a captivating collection of photographs. Peterson has given us an indispensable record of an election at once more raw, divisive, and shot through with a sense of desperation—and, perhaps, for good or ill, more lastingly consequential—than any in our lifetime..

JOHN HEILEMANN
Author of "Game Change" and "Double Down"
Brooklyn, New York, September 2016

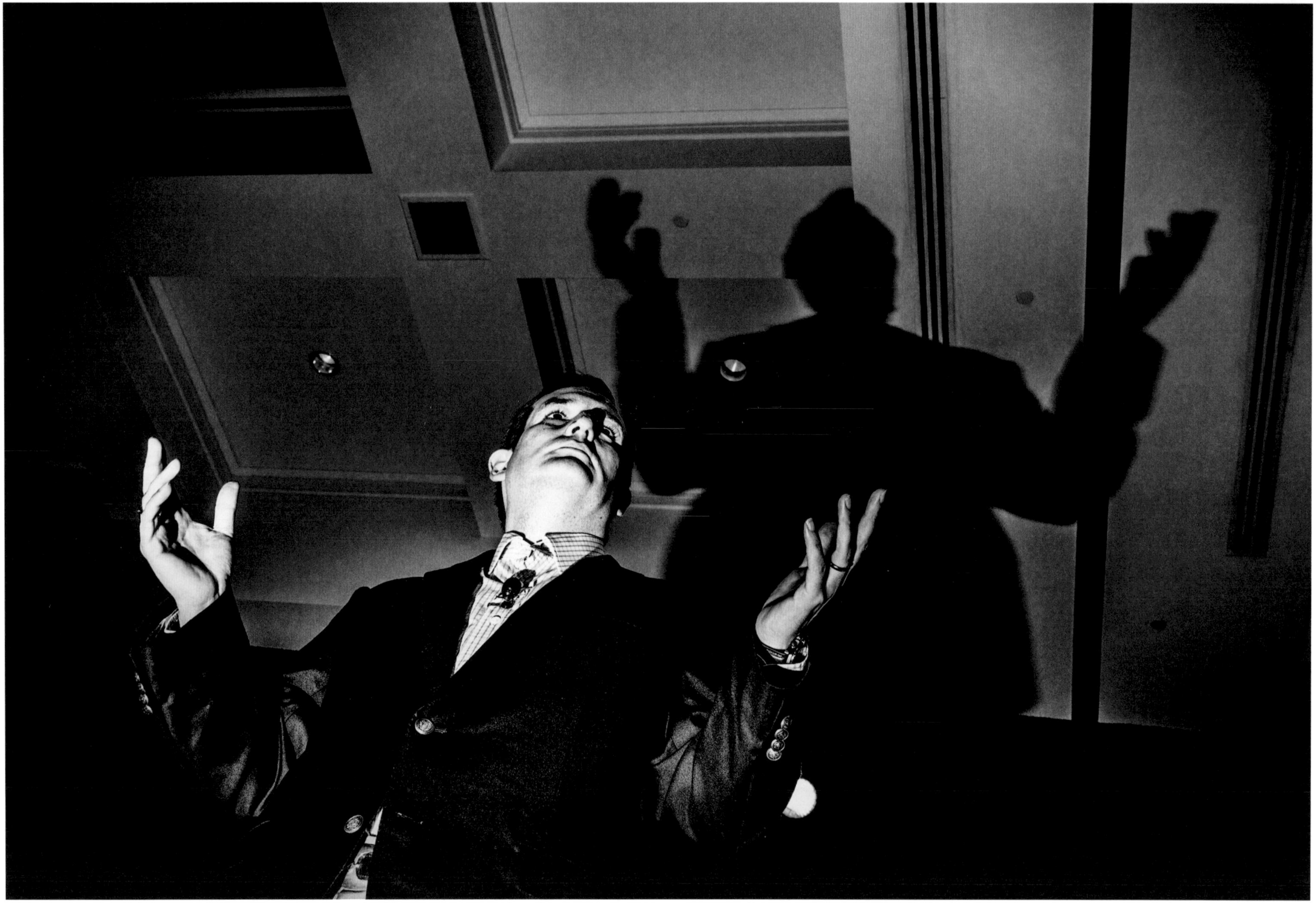

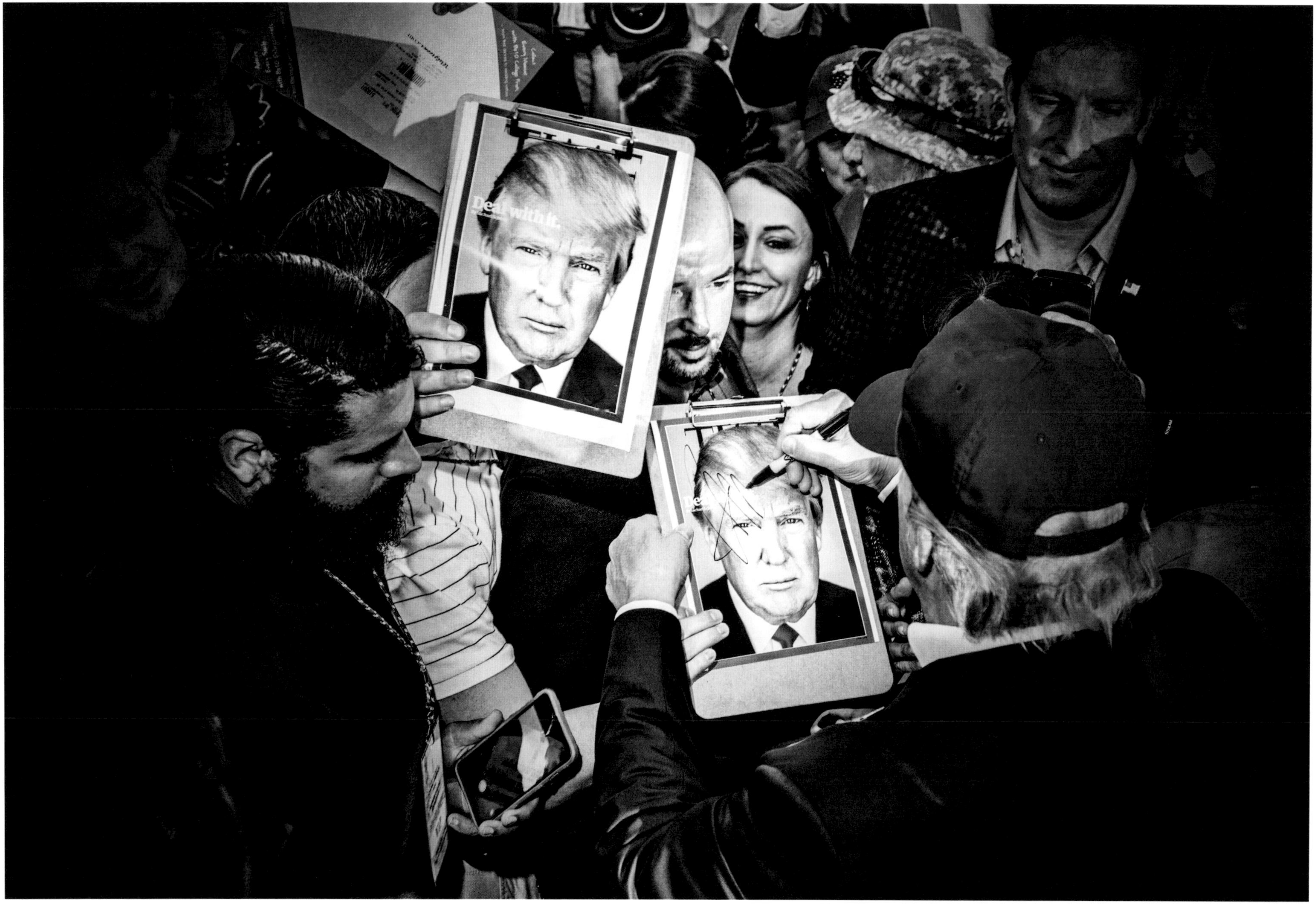
Deal with it.

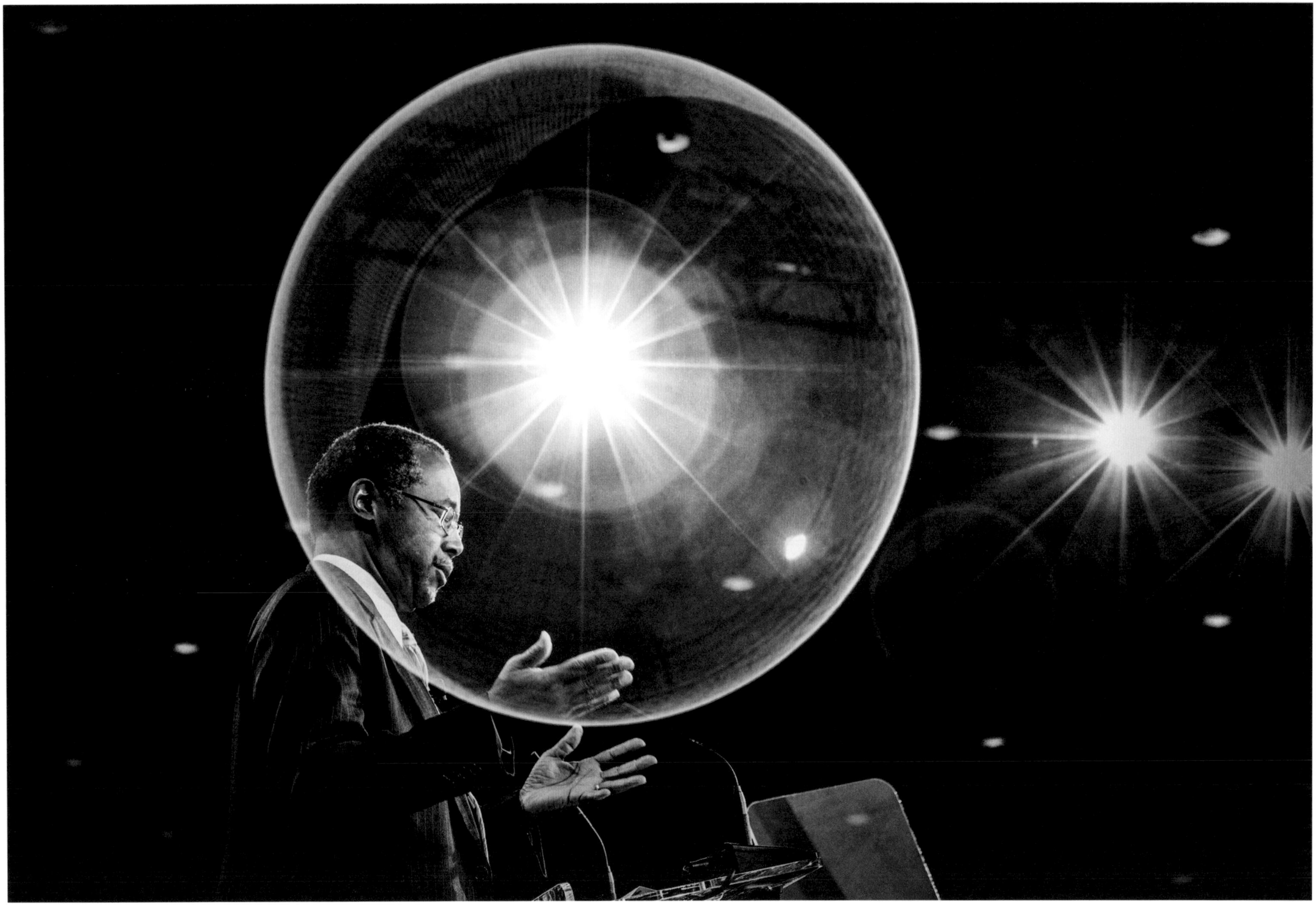

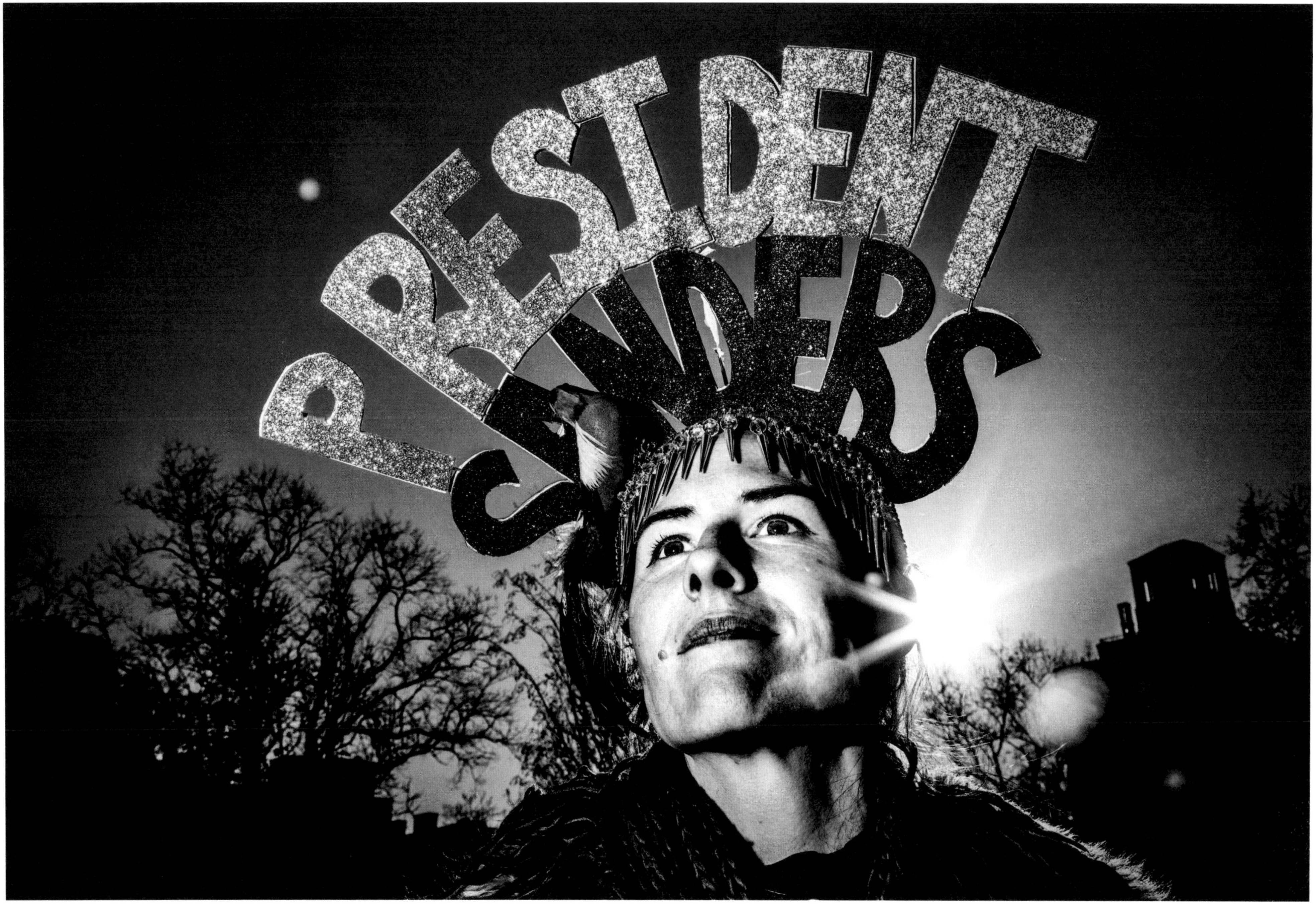
PRESIDENT
SANDERS

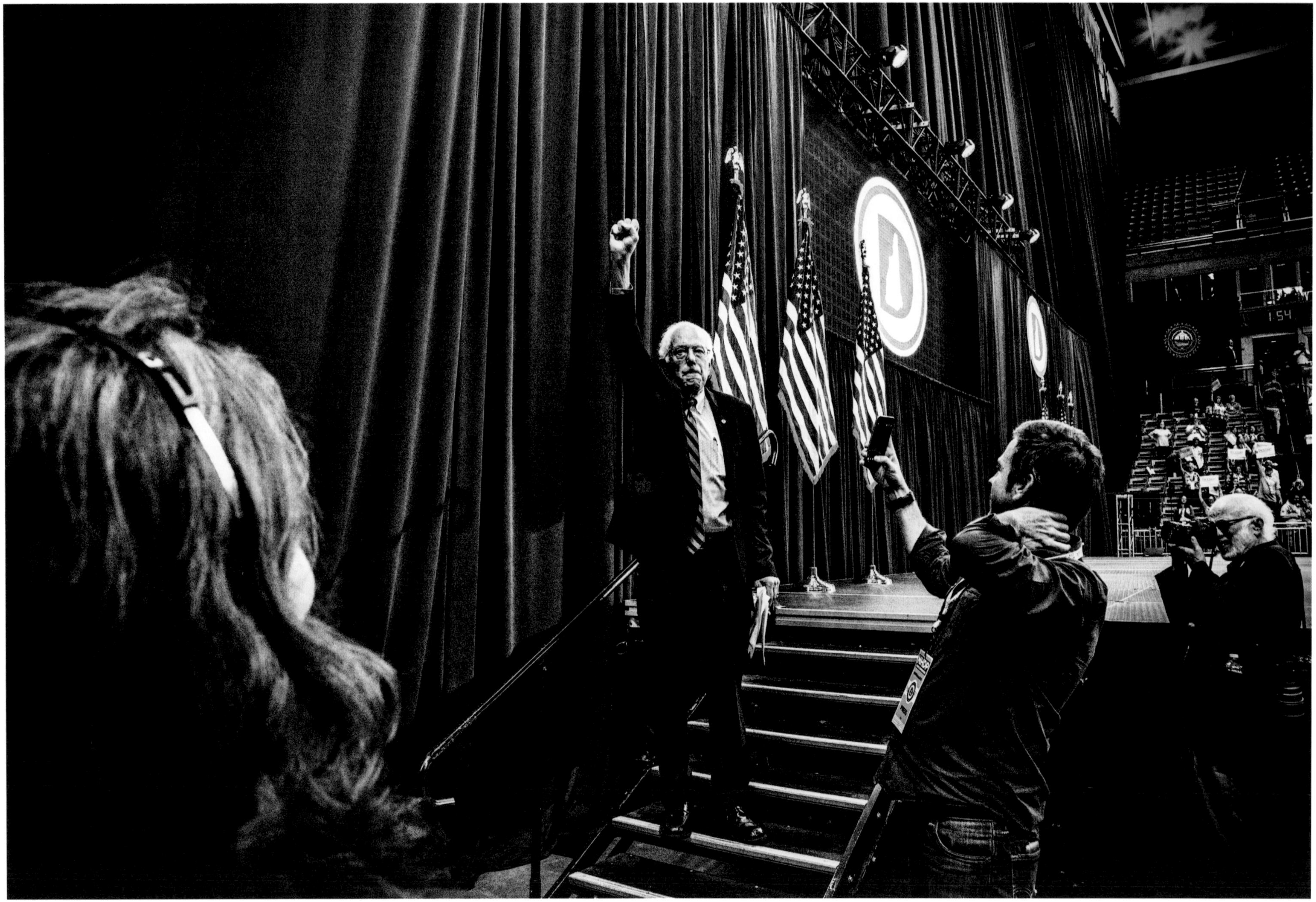

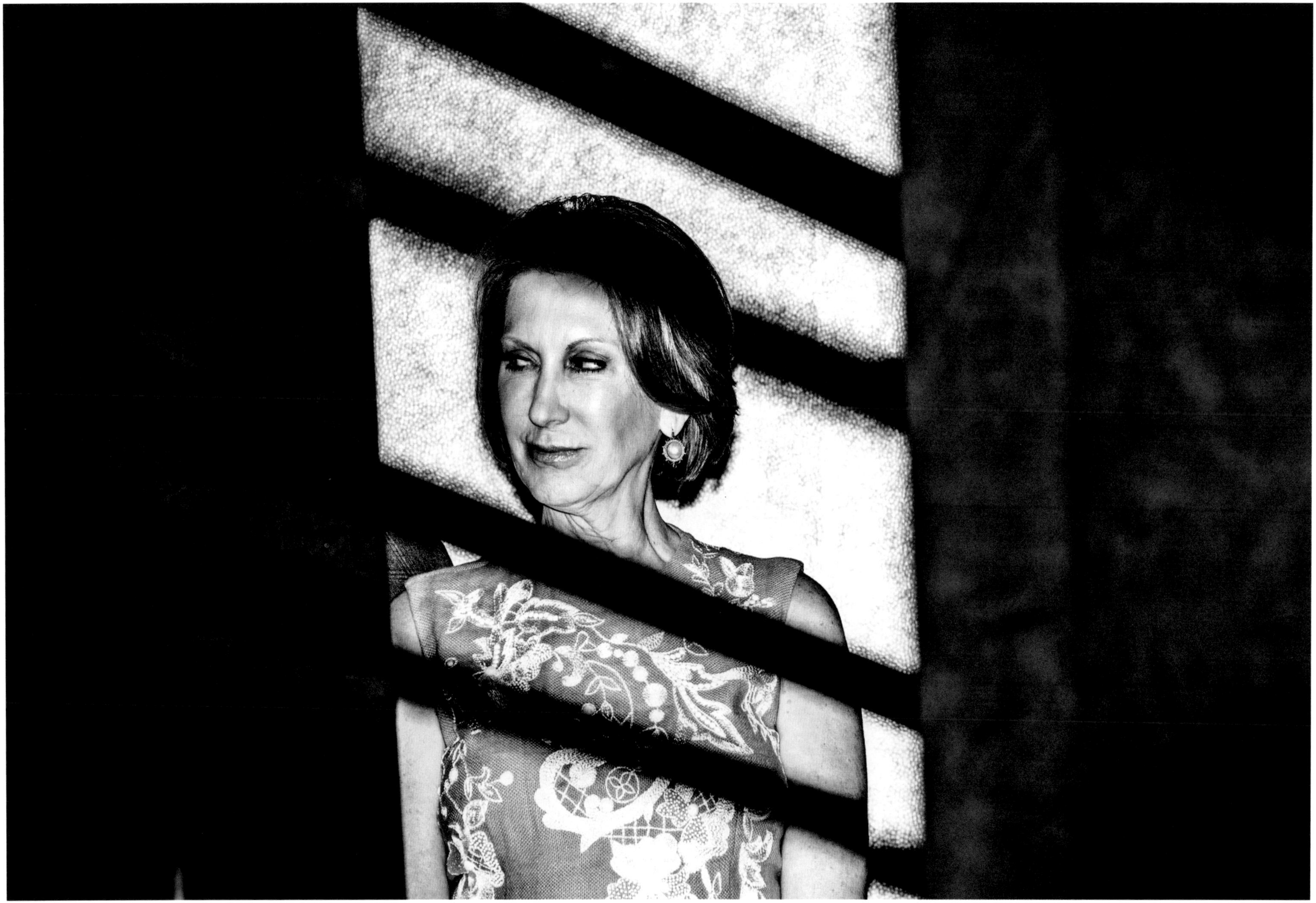

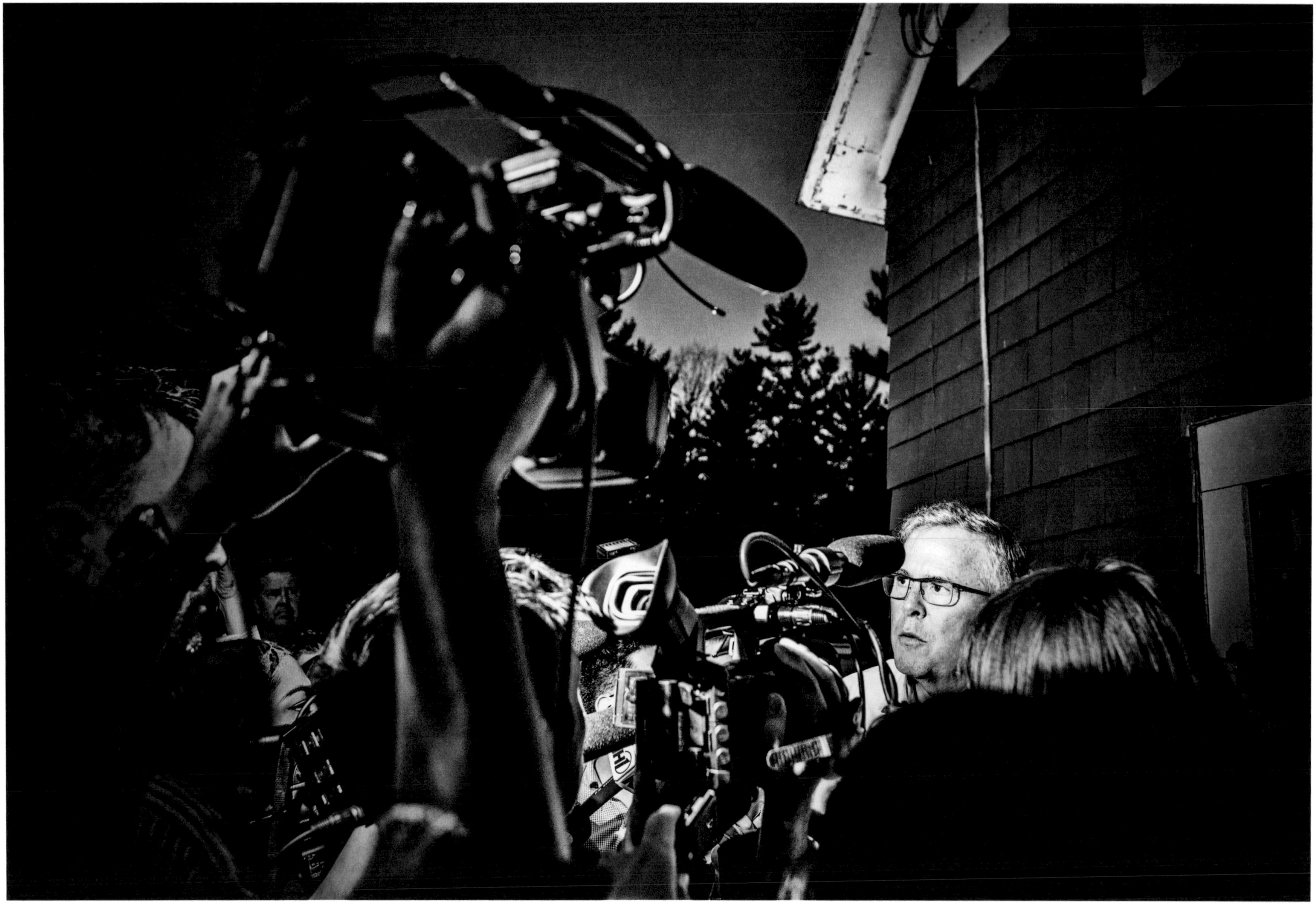

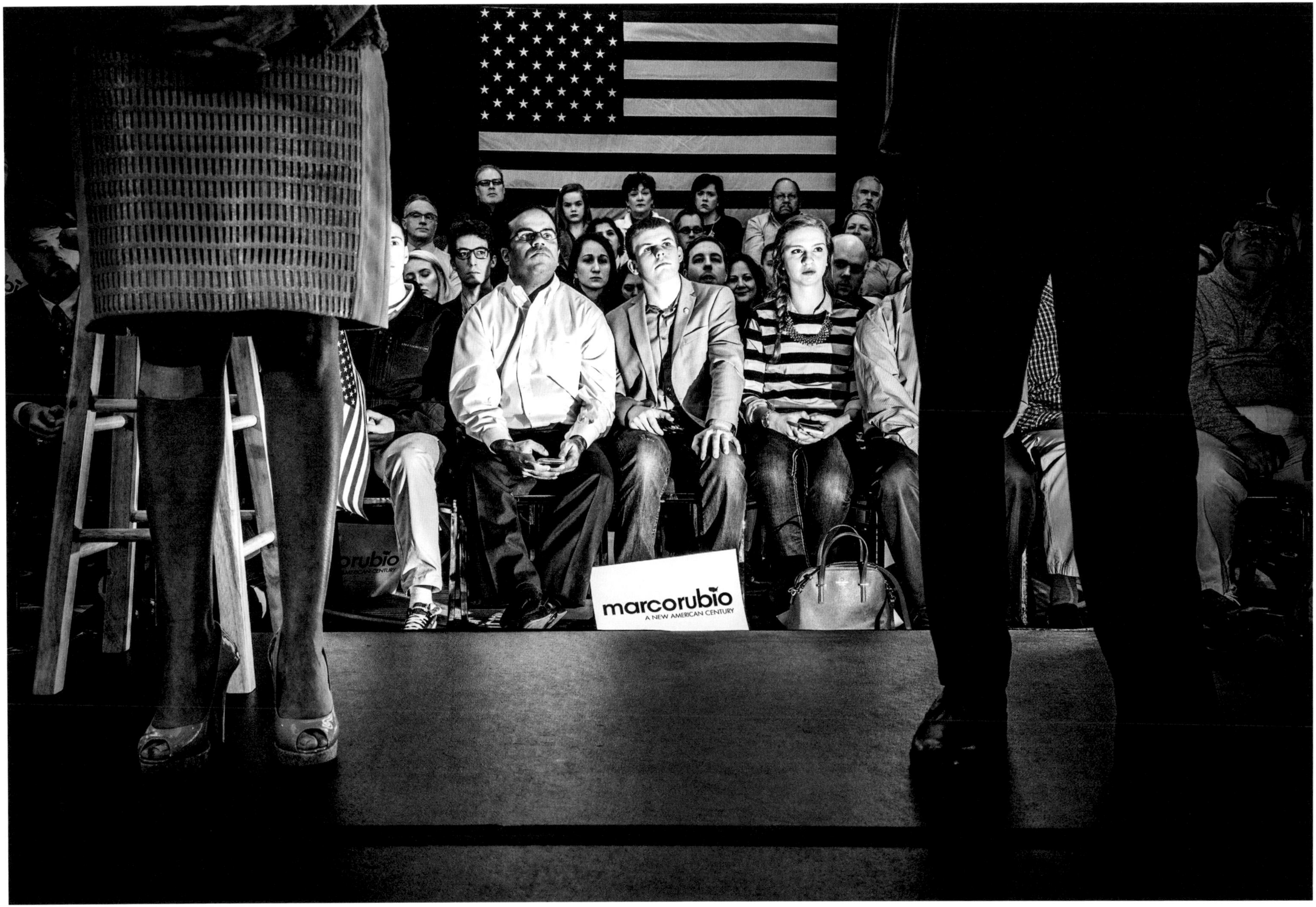
marcorubio
A NEW AMERICAN CENTURY

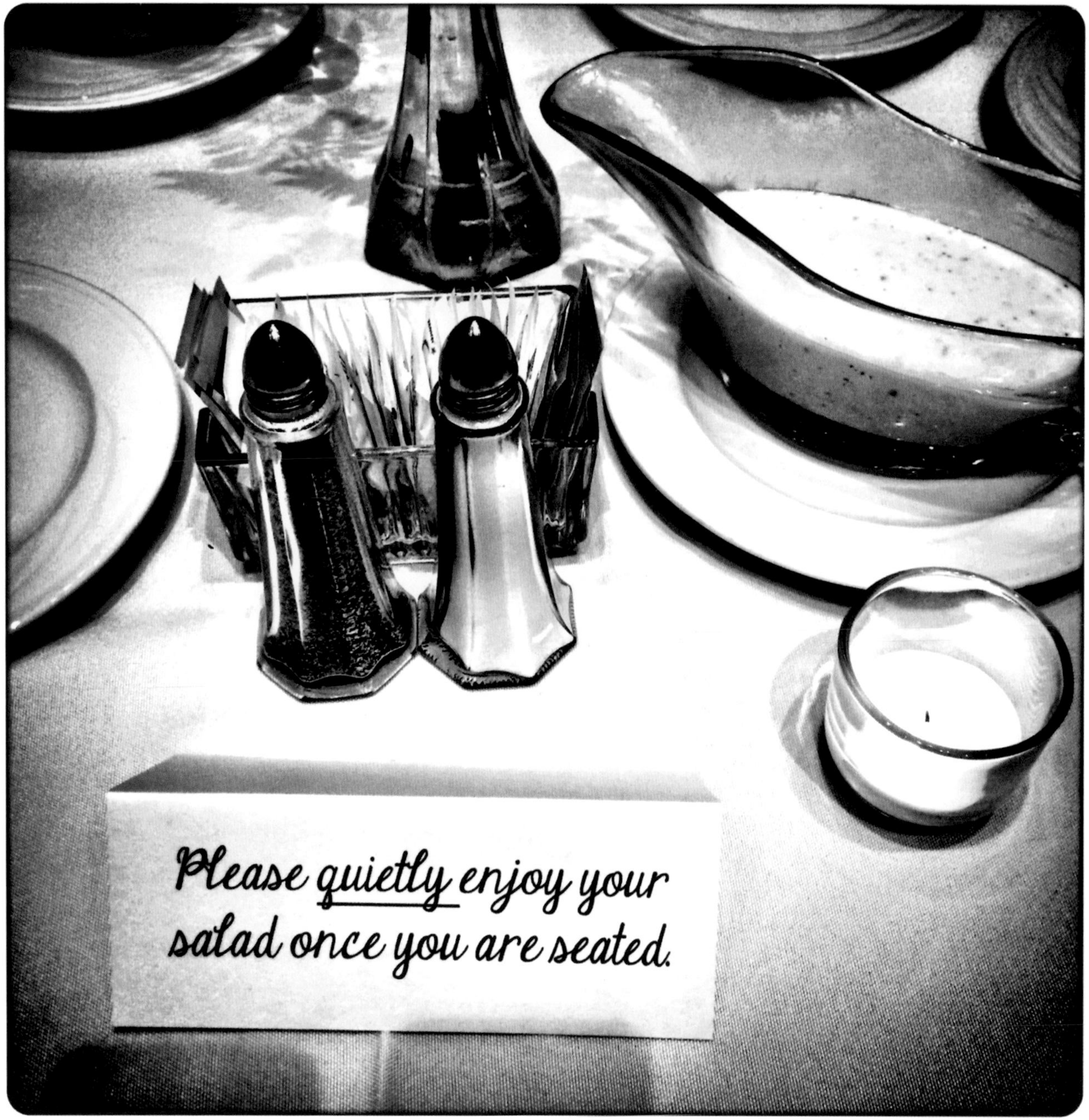
Please quietly enjoy your
salad once you are seated.

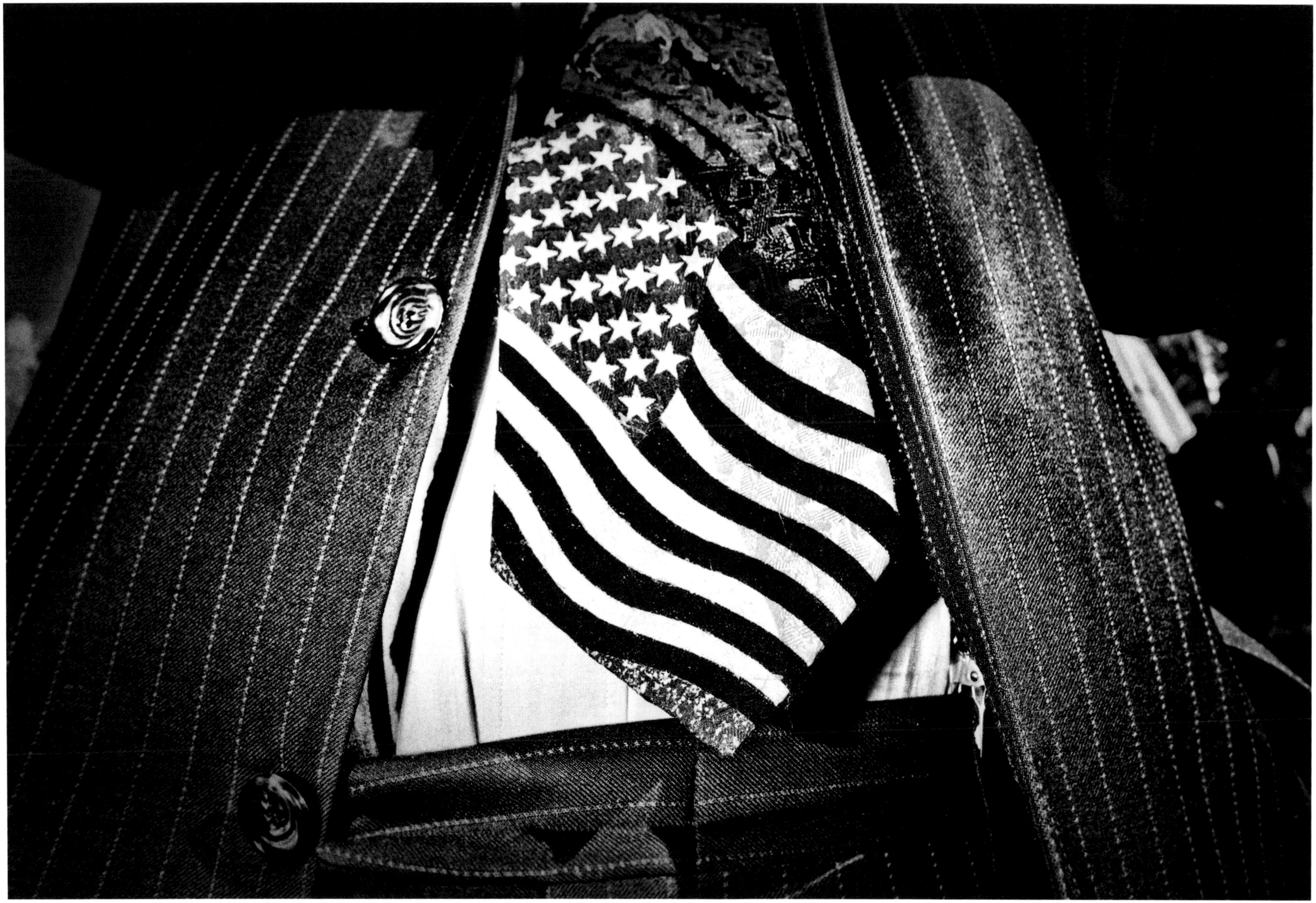

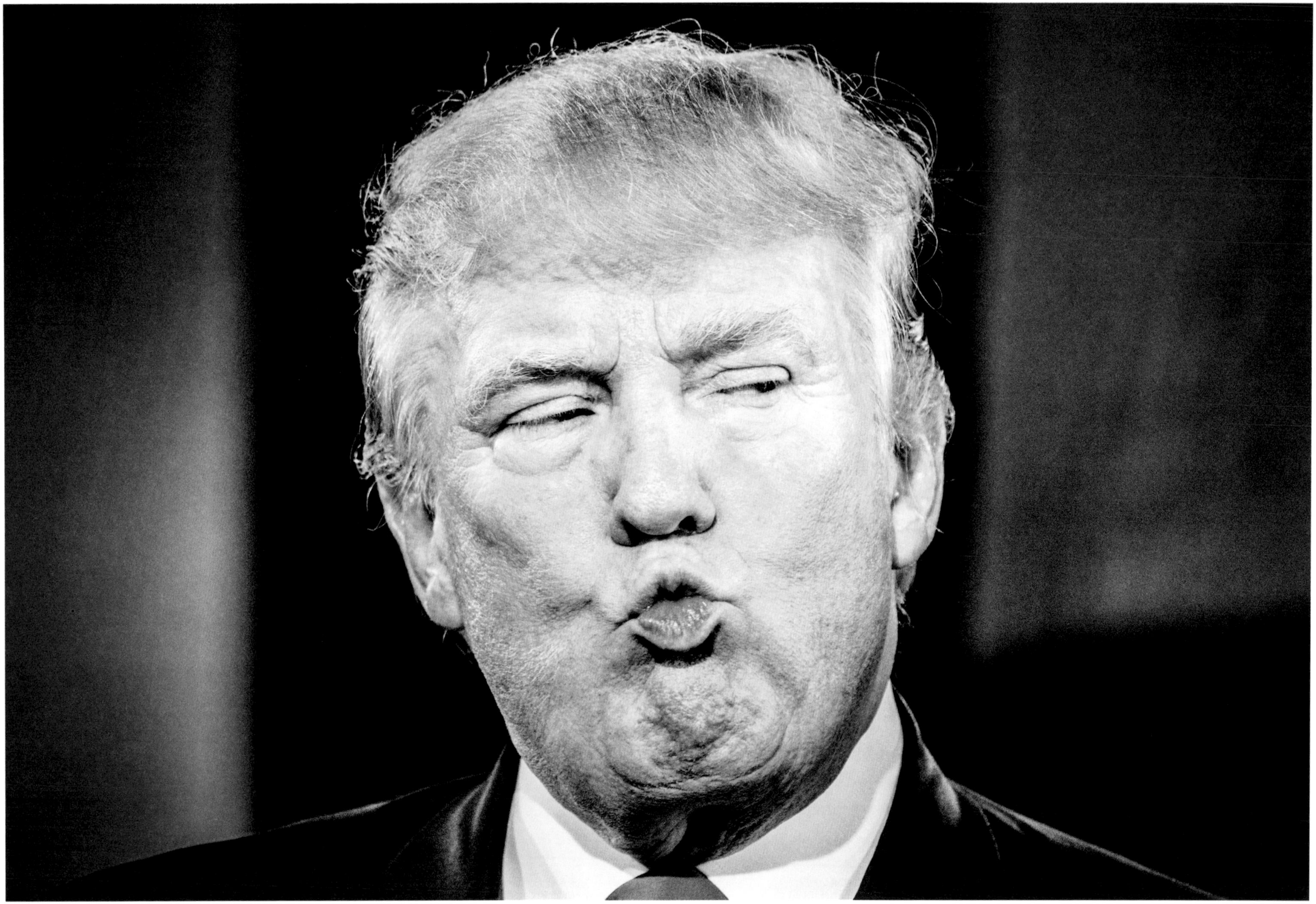

"It's true. I'm a supermodel. I'm on the cover of these magazines—I'm on the cover of the biggest magazines. I don't even know about it. I can't even read the story, because if I did, I wouldn't get any work done." —**DONALD TRUMP**

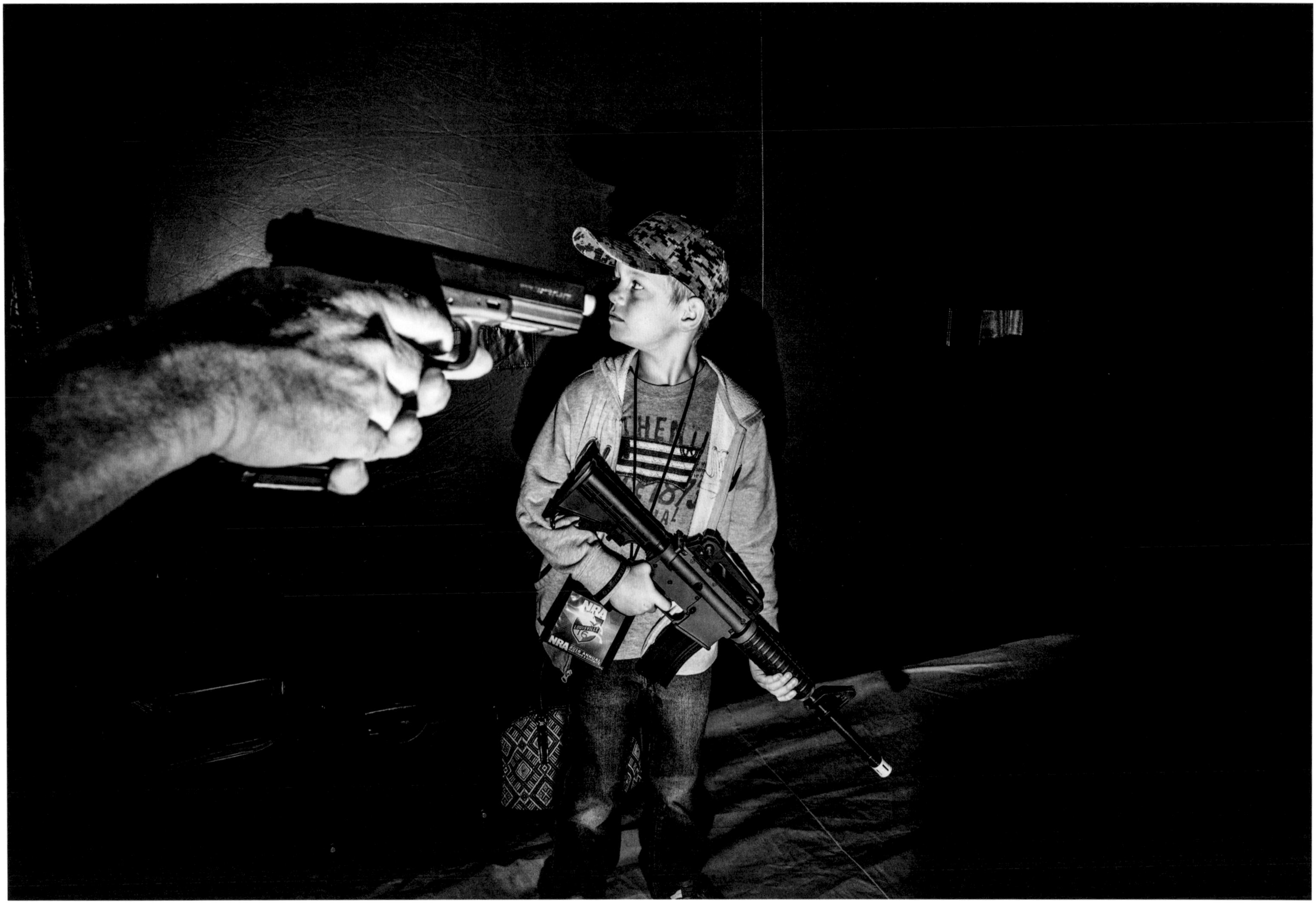
NRA
LOUISVILLE 16
NRA 2016 ANNUAL

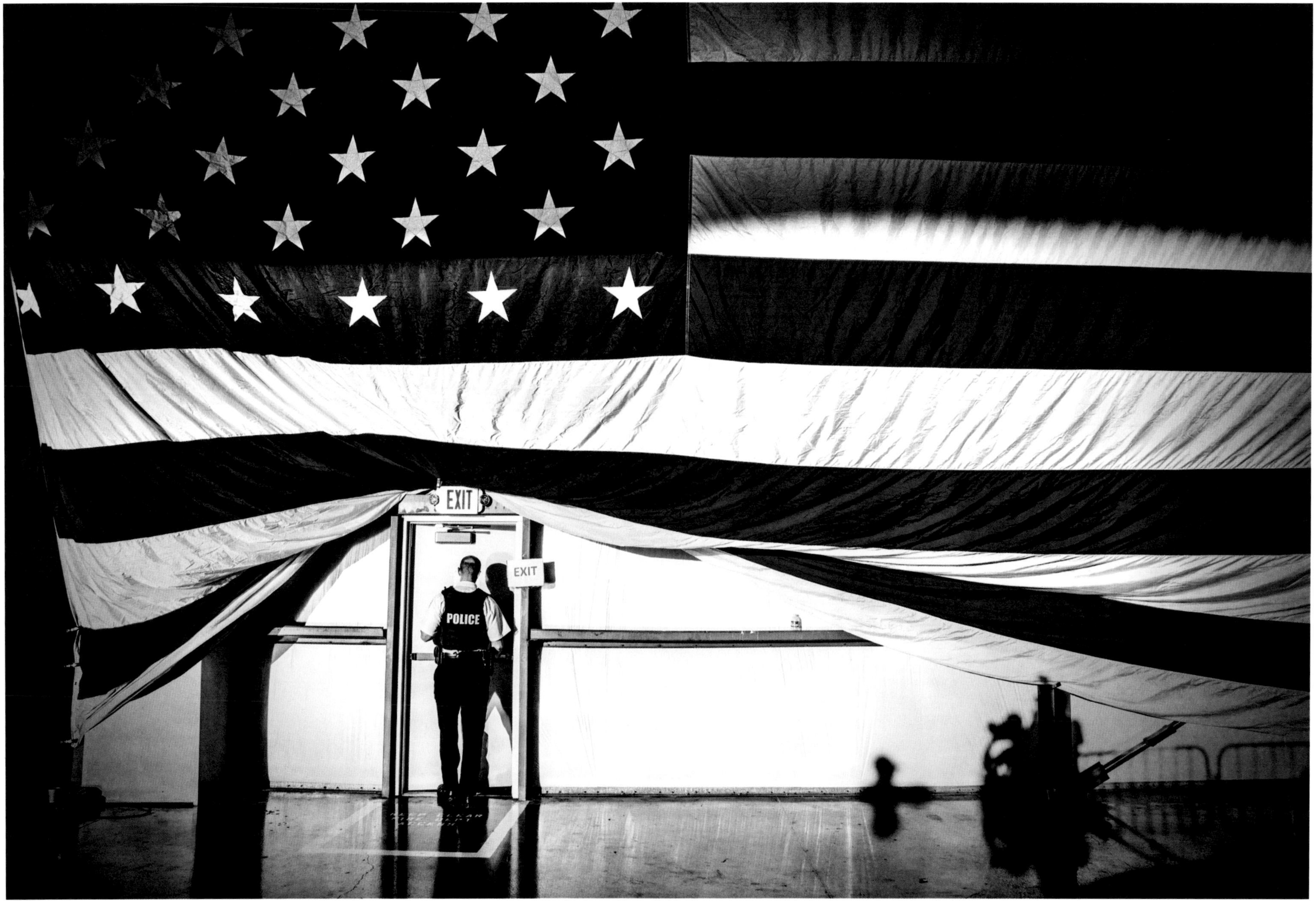
EXIT
EXIT
POLICE

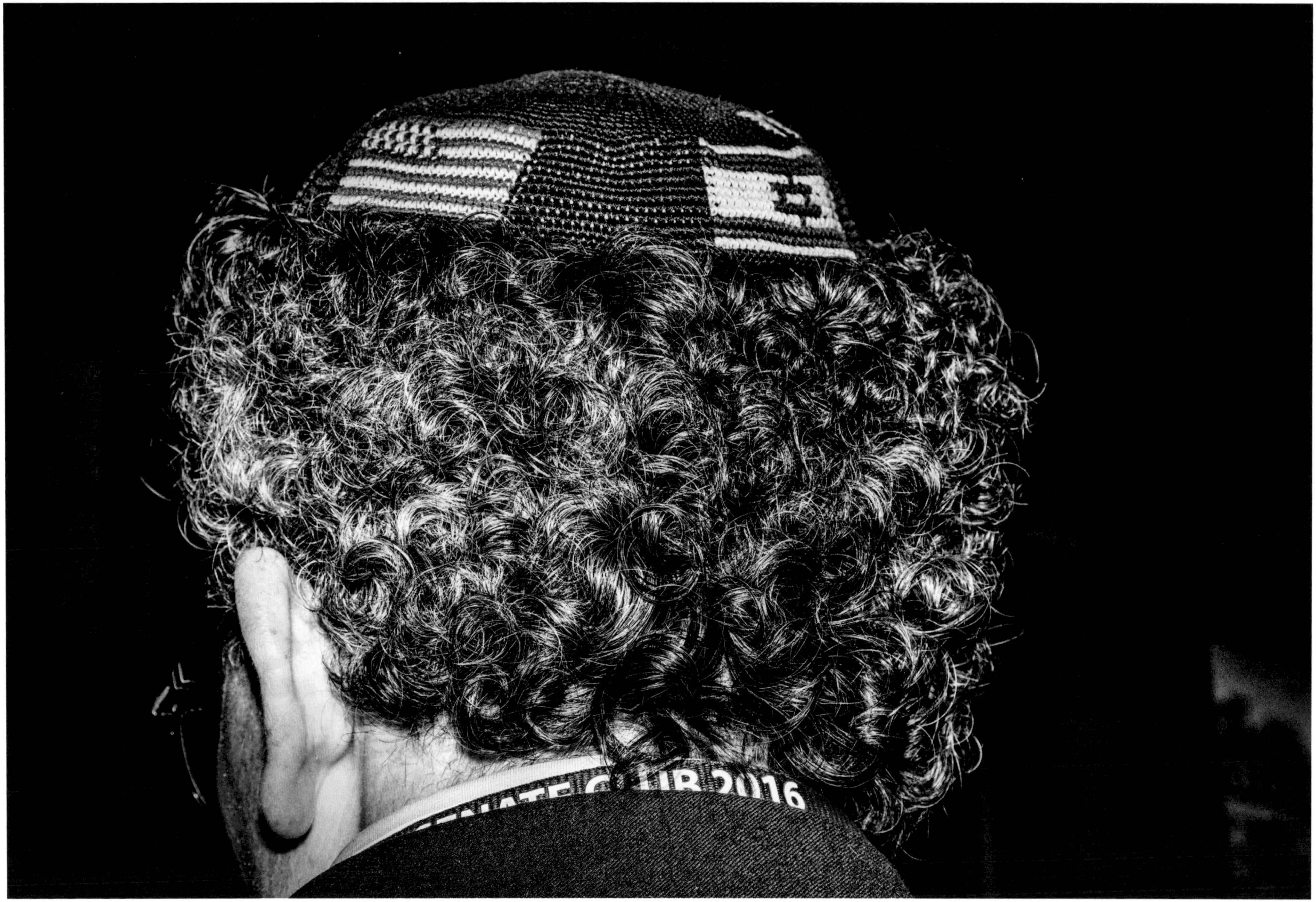
2016

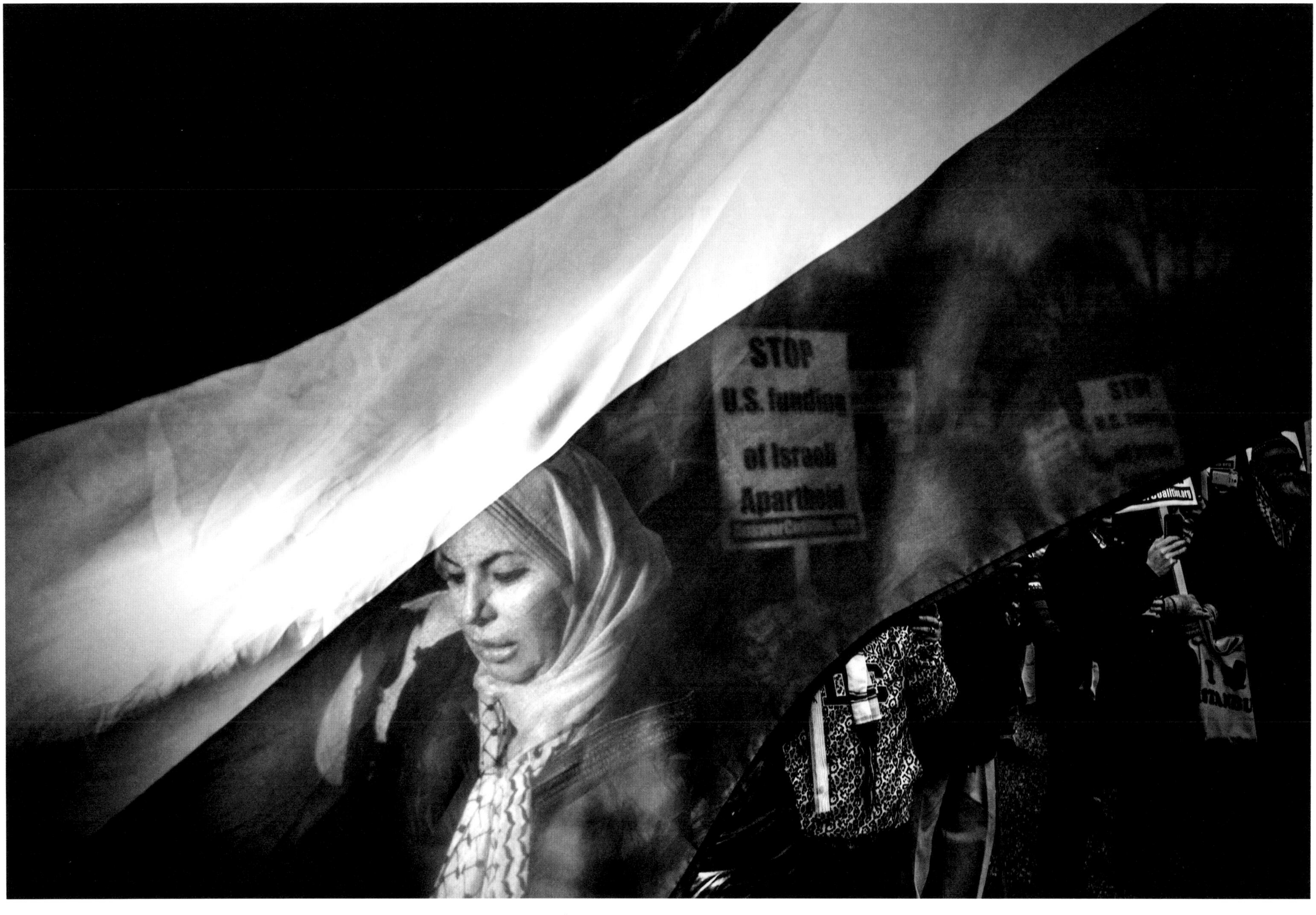
STOP
U.S. funding
of Israeli
Apartheid

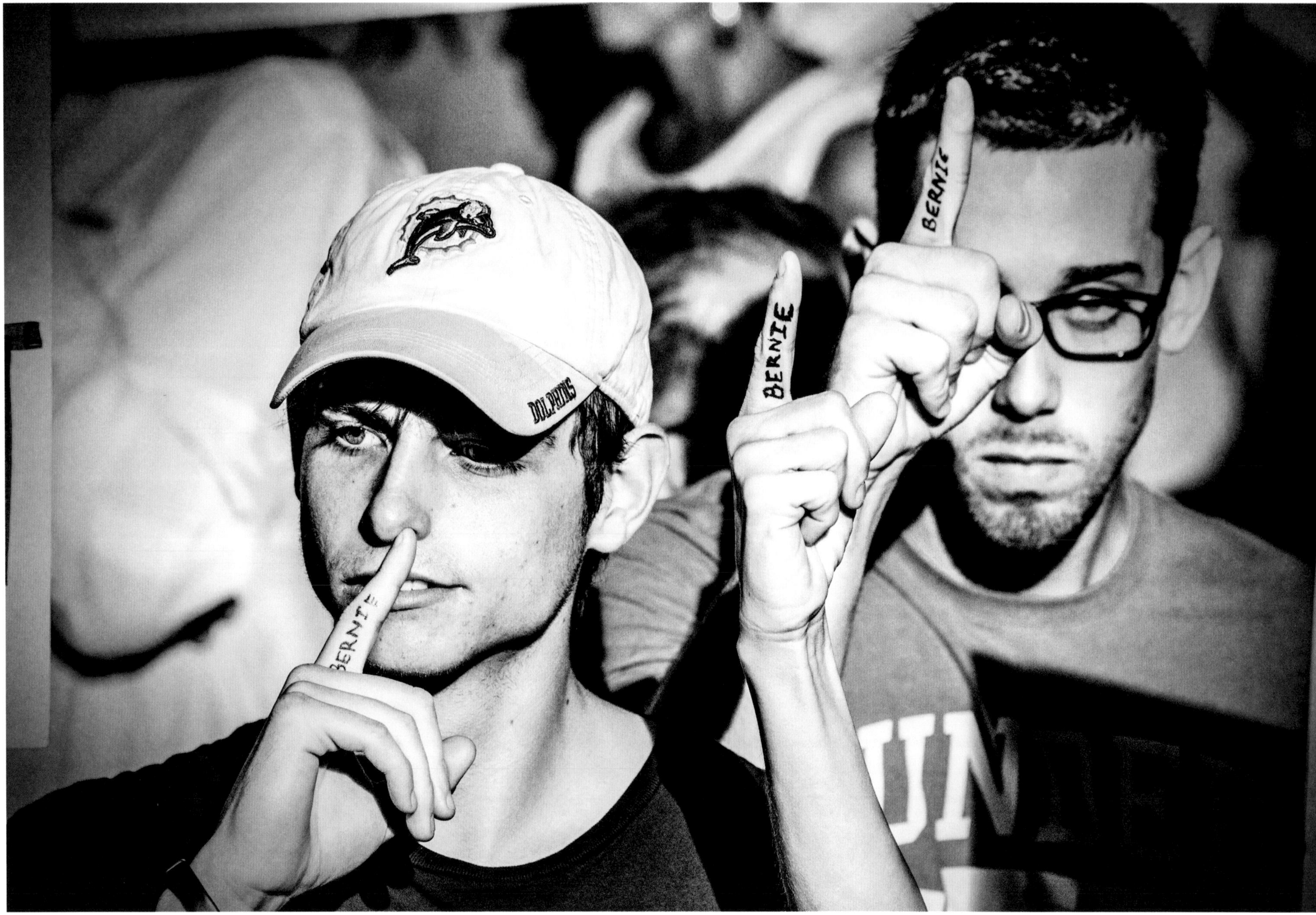
DOLPHINS
BERNIE
BERNIE
BERNIE

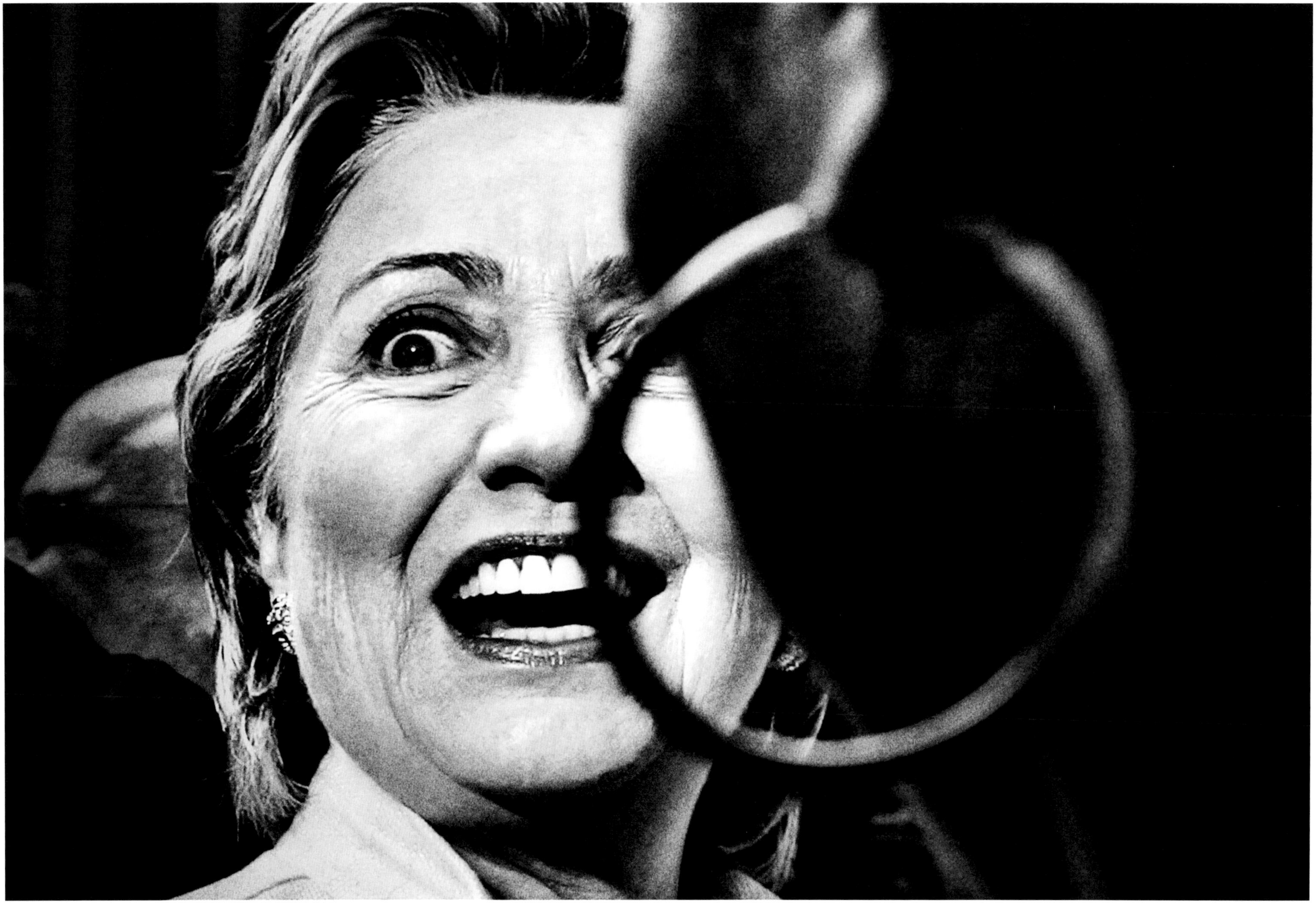

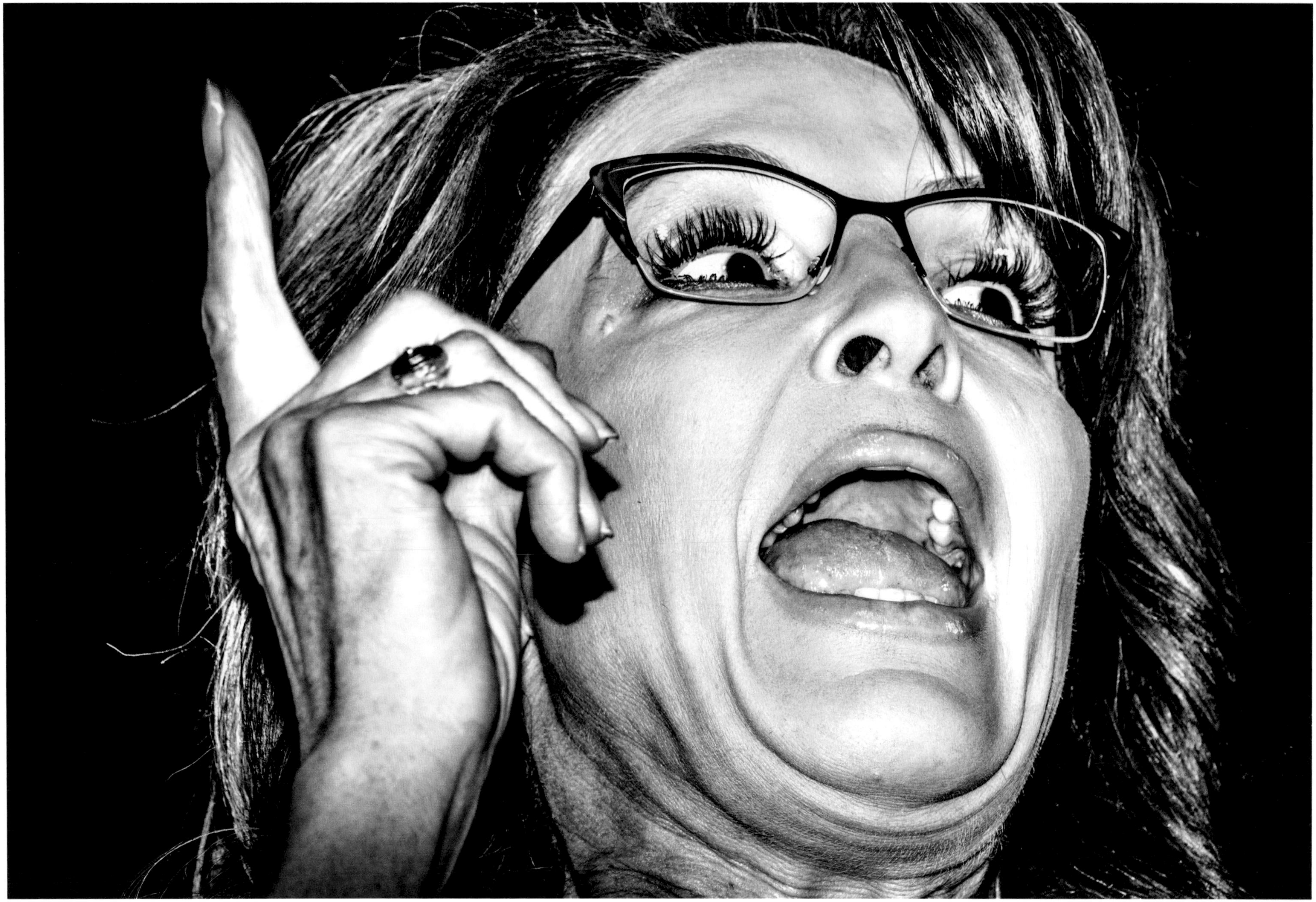

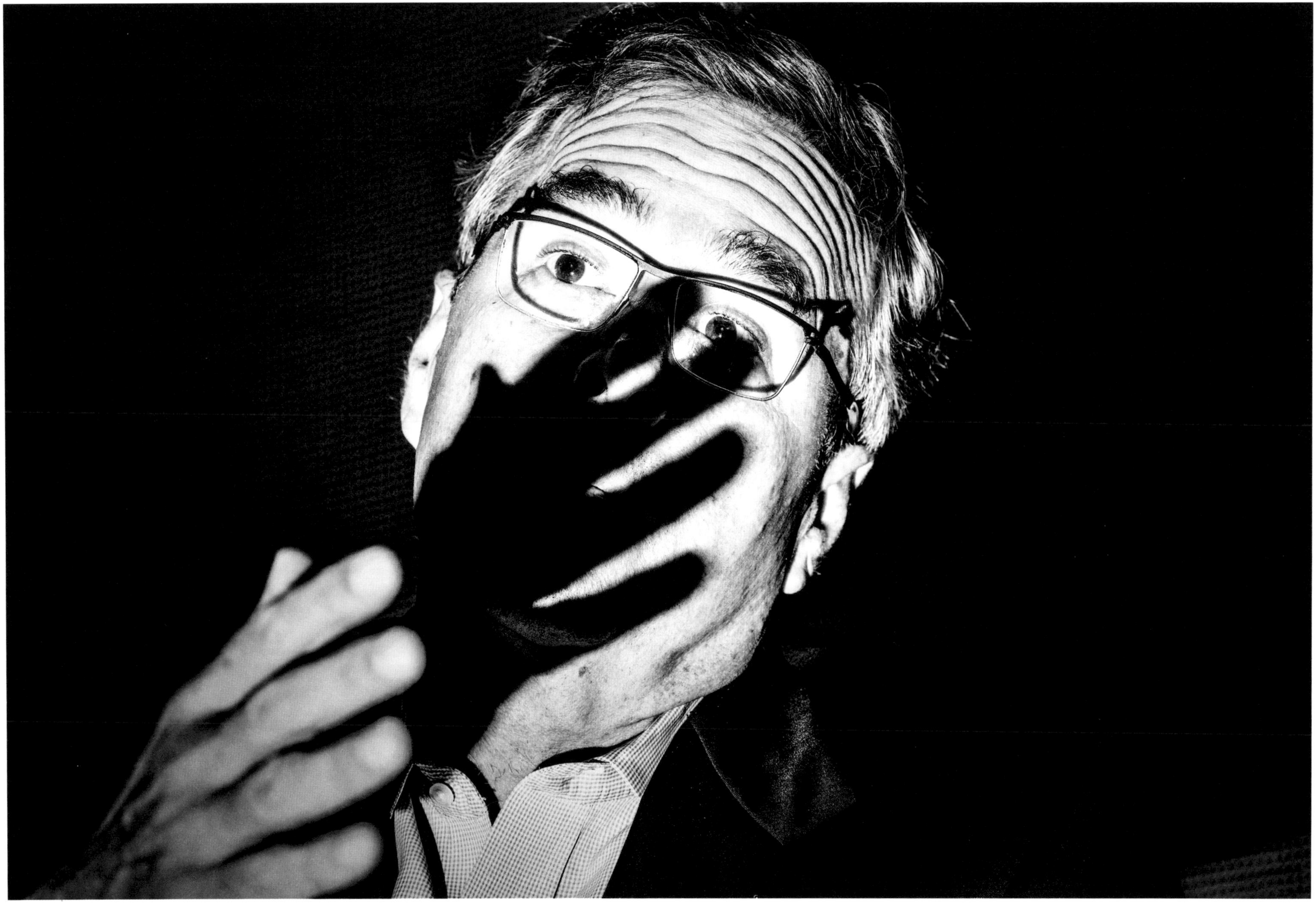

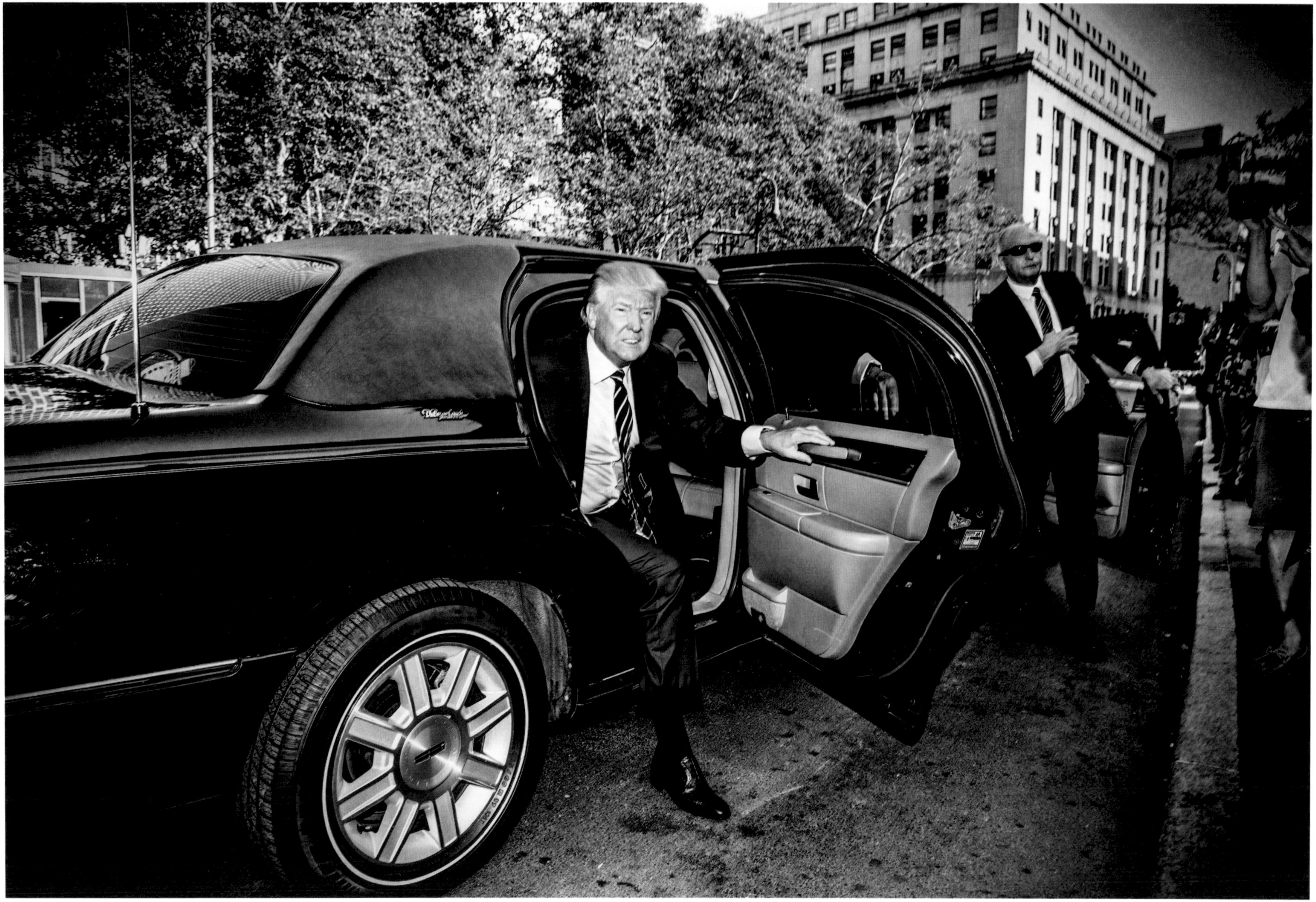

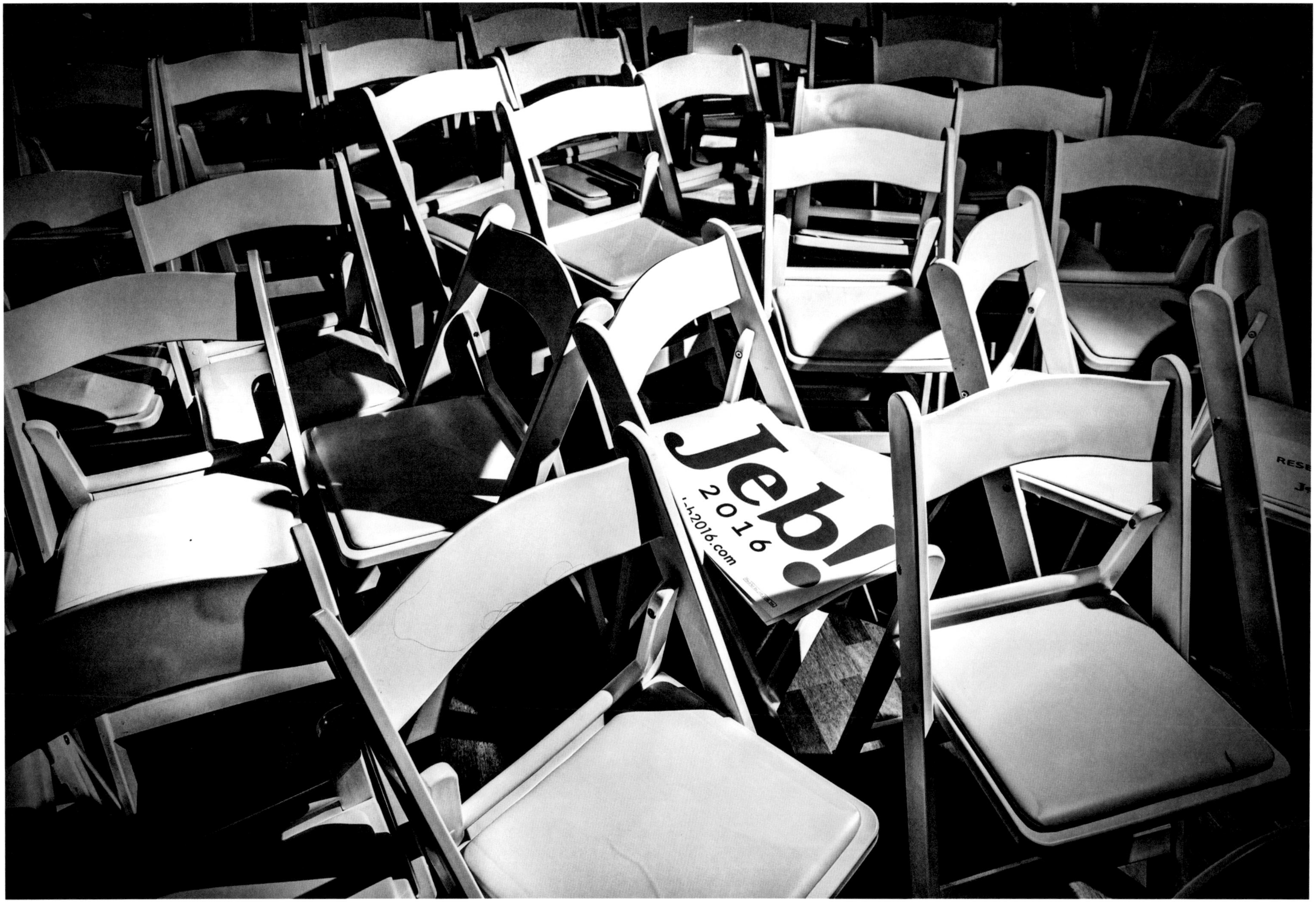
Jeb!
2016

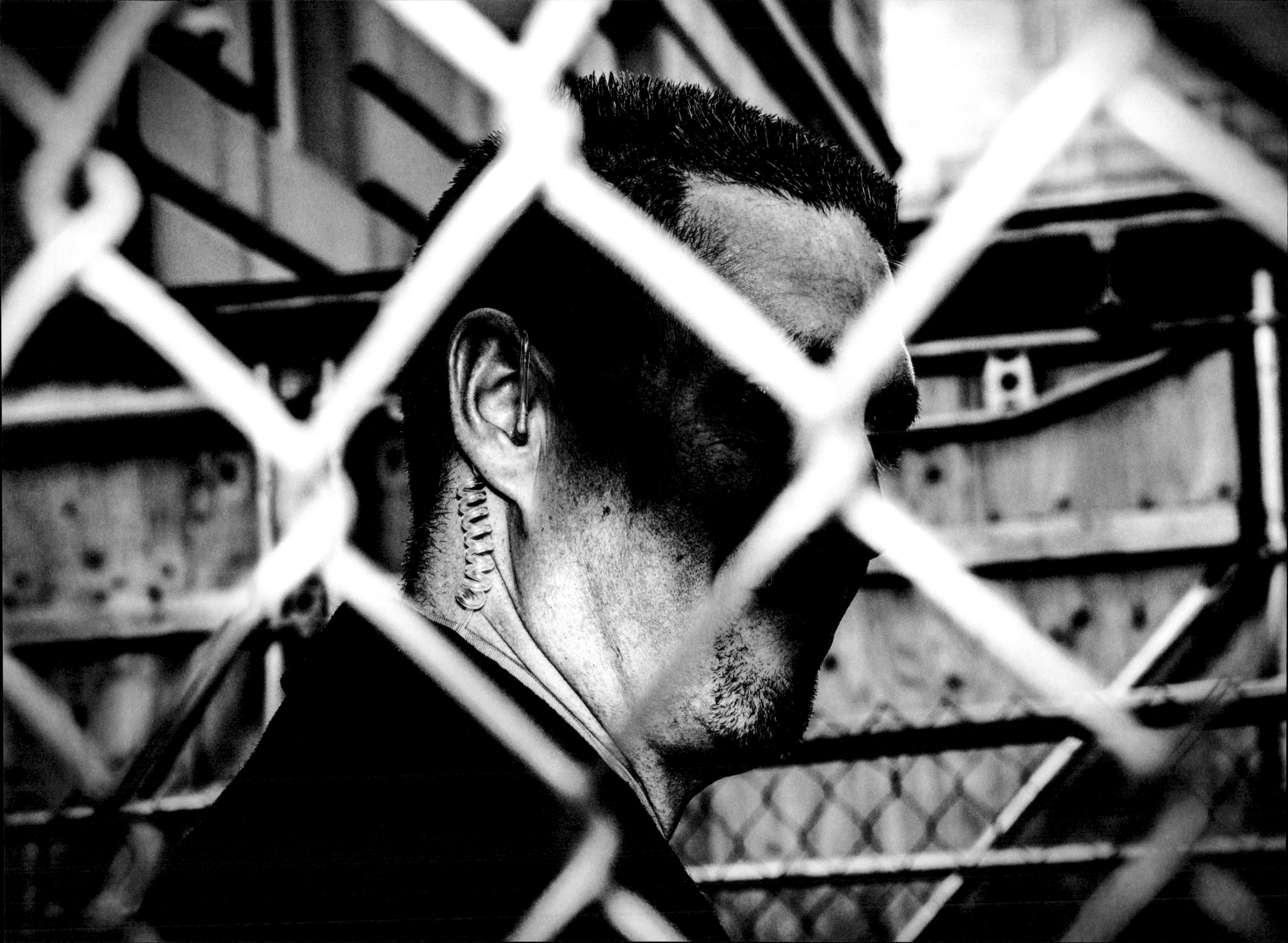

"I will build a great wall—and nobody builds walls better than me, believe me—and I'll build them very inexpensively. I will build a great, great wall on our southern border, and I will make Mexico pay for that wall. Mark my words."—**DONALD TRUMP**

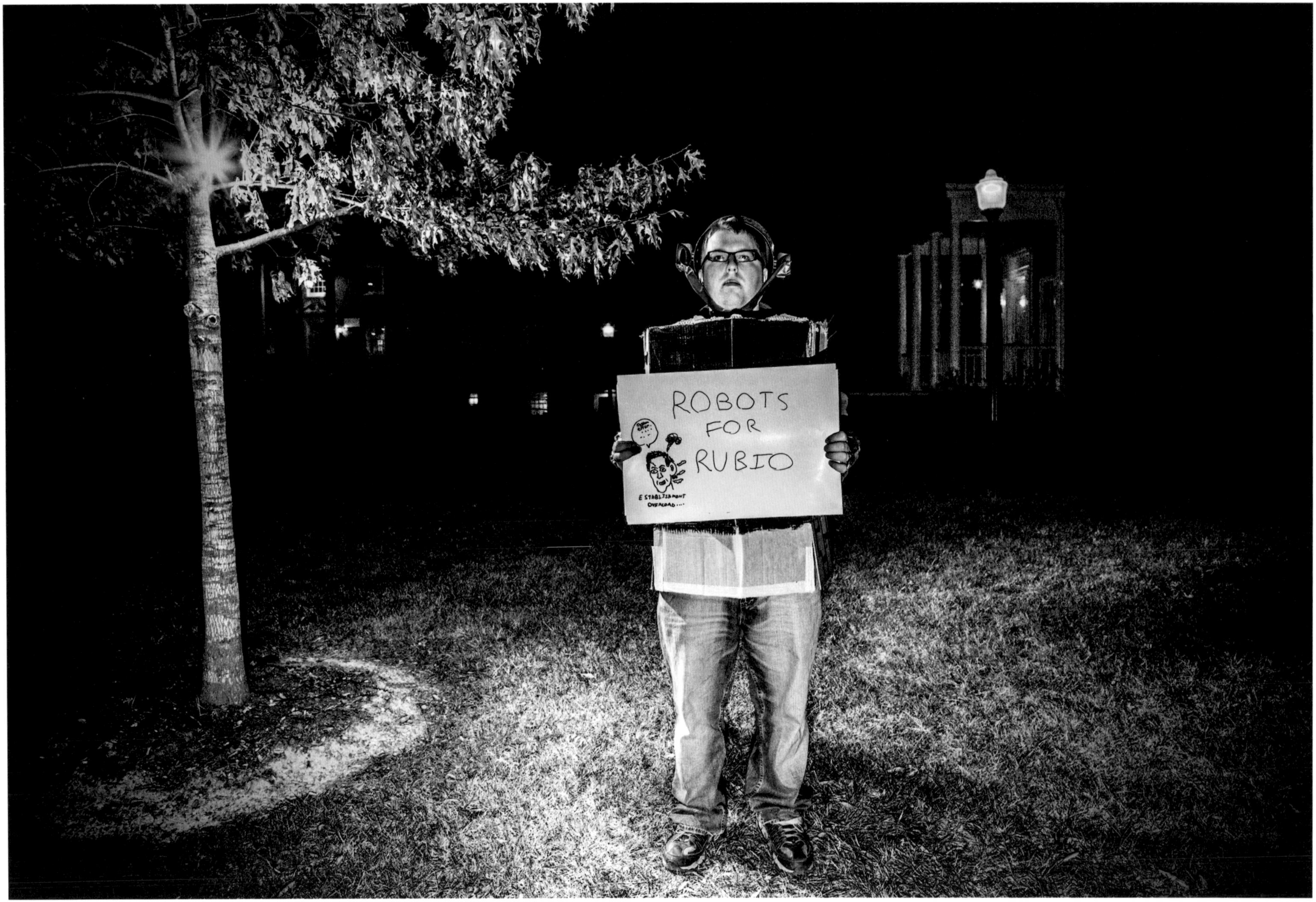
ROBOTS
FOR
RUBIO

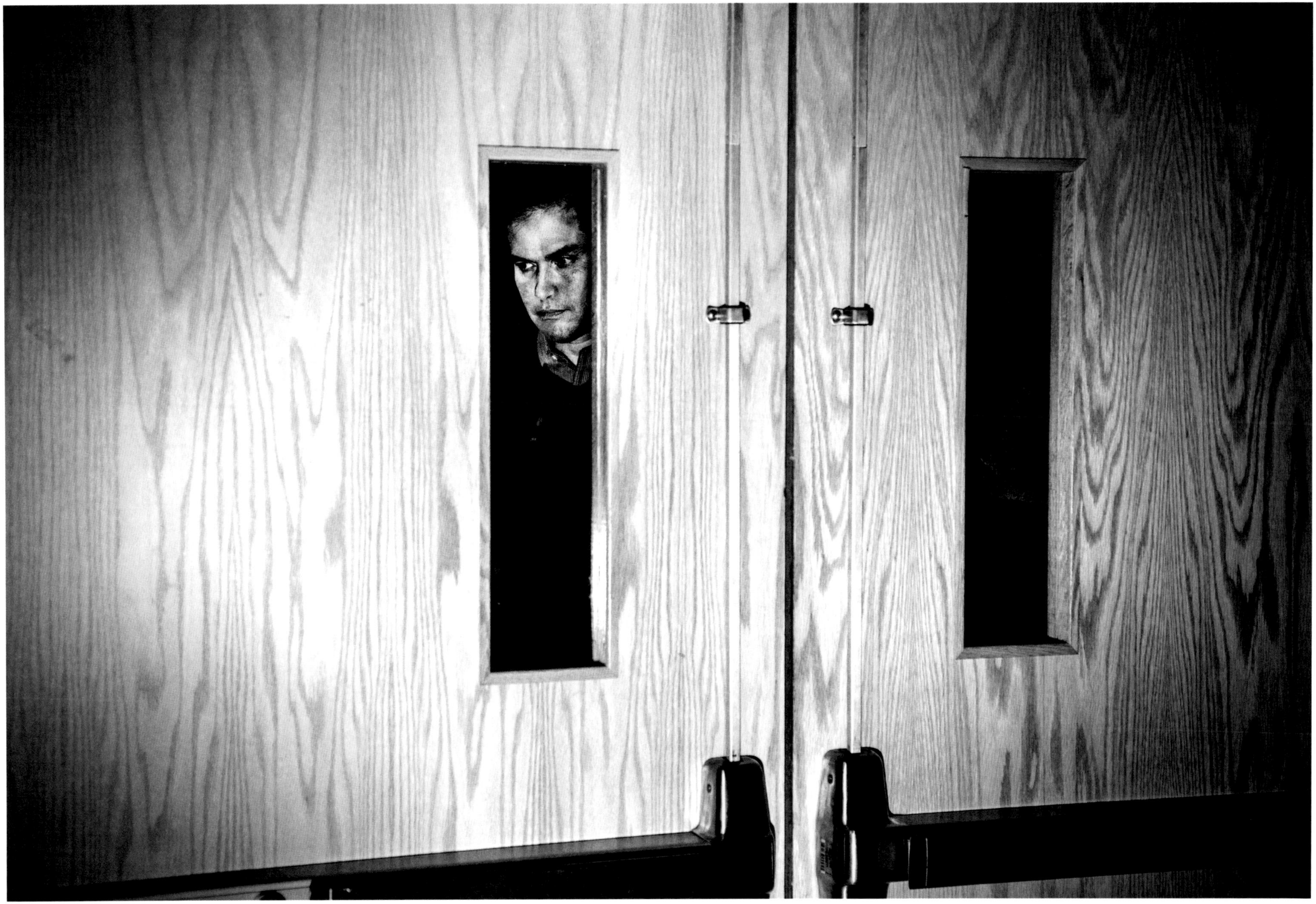

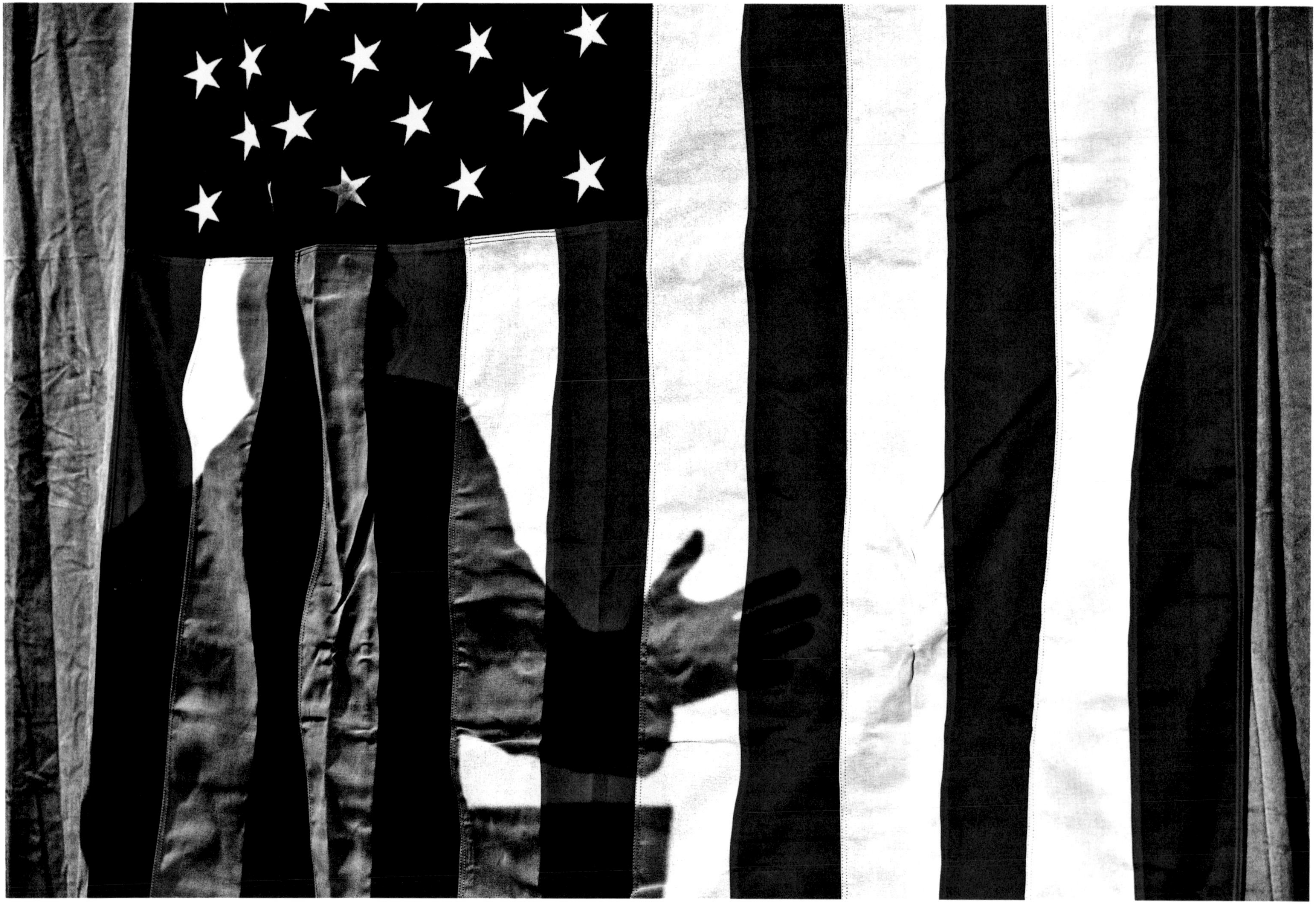

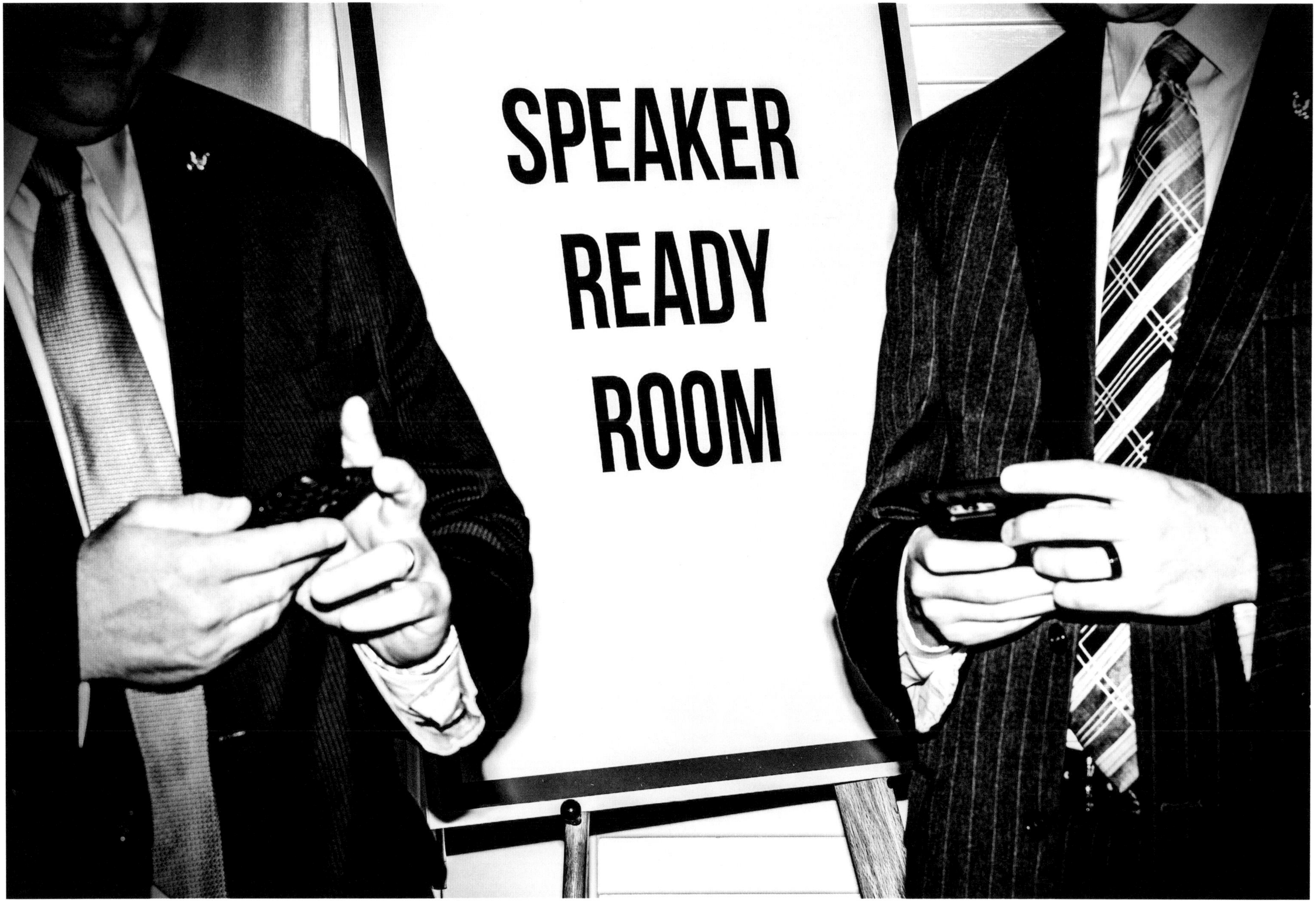
SPEAKER
READY
ROOM

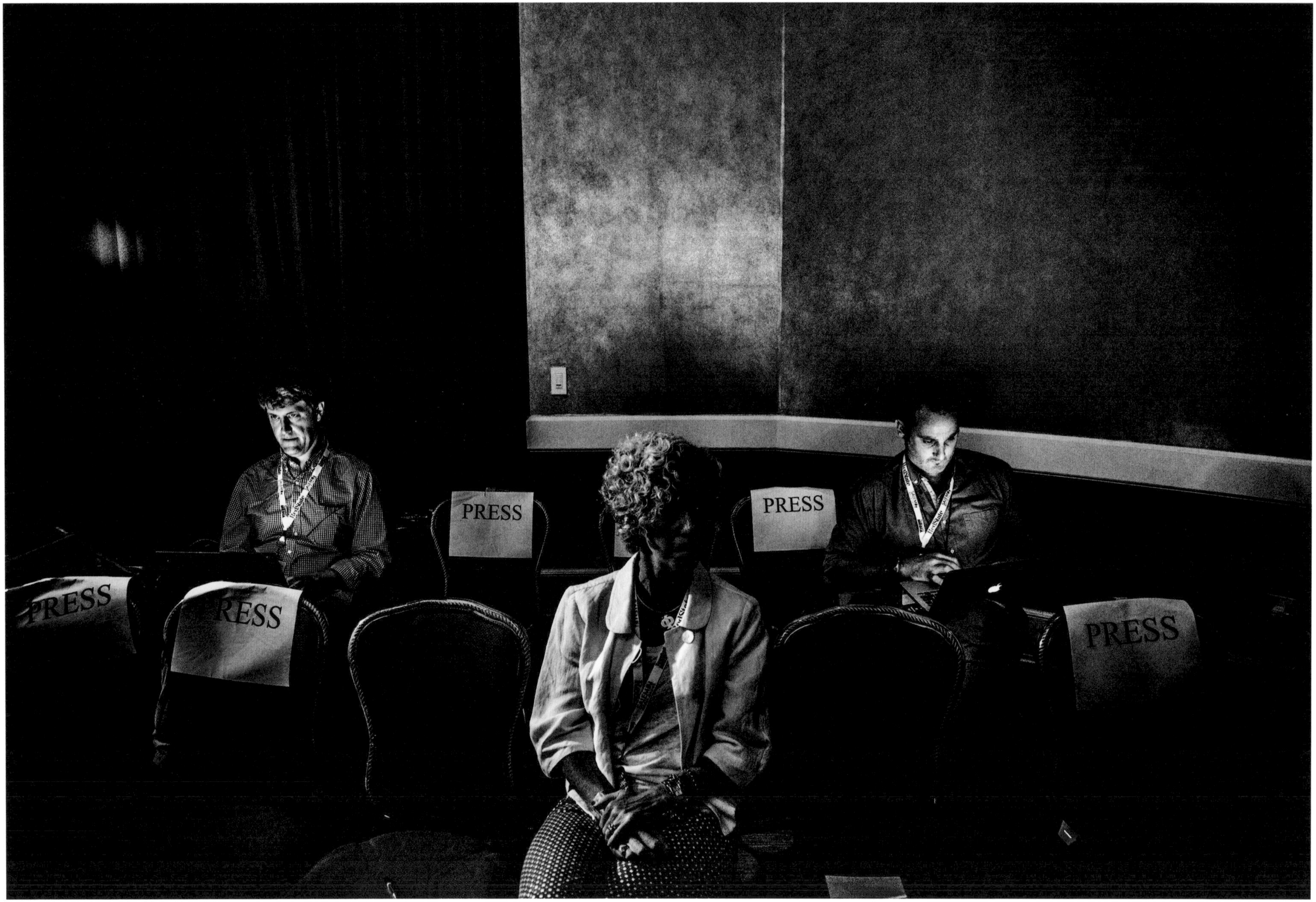
PRESS
PRESS
PRESS
PRESS
PRESS
PRESS

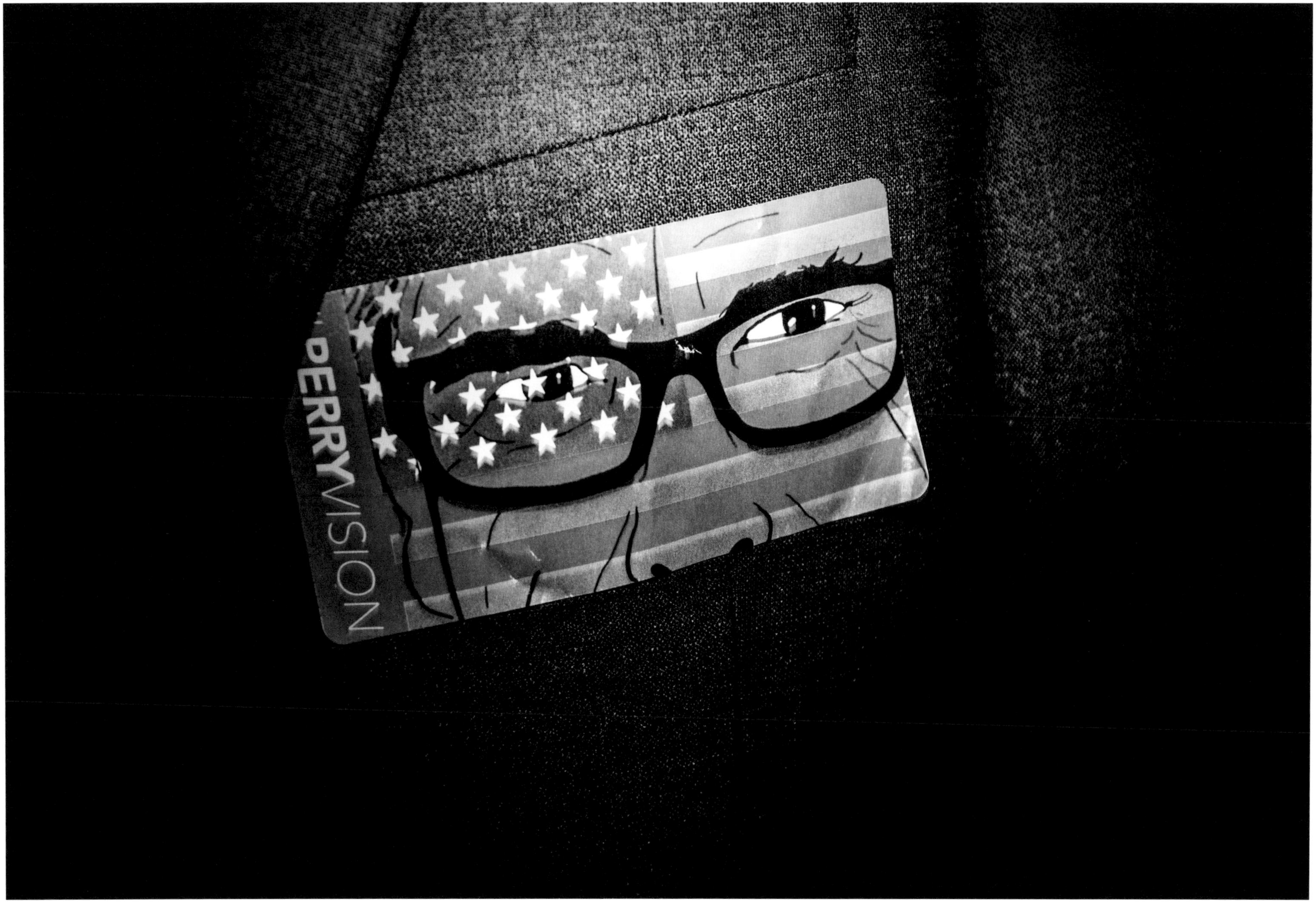
PERRYVISION

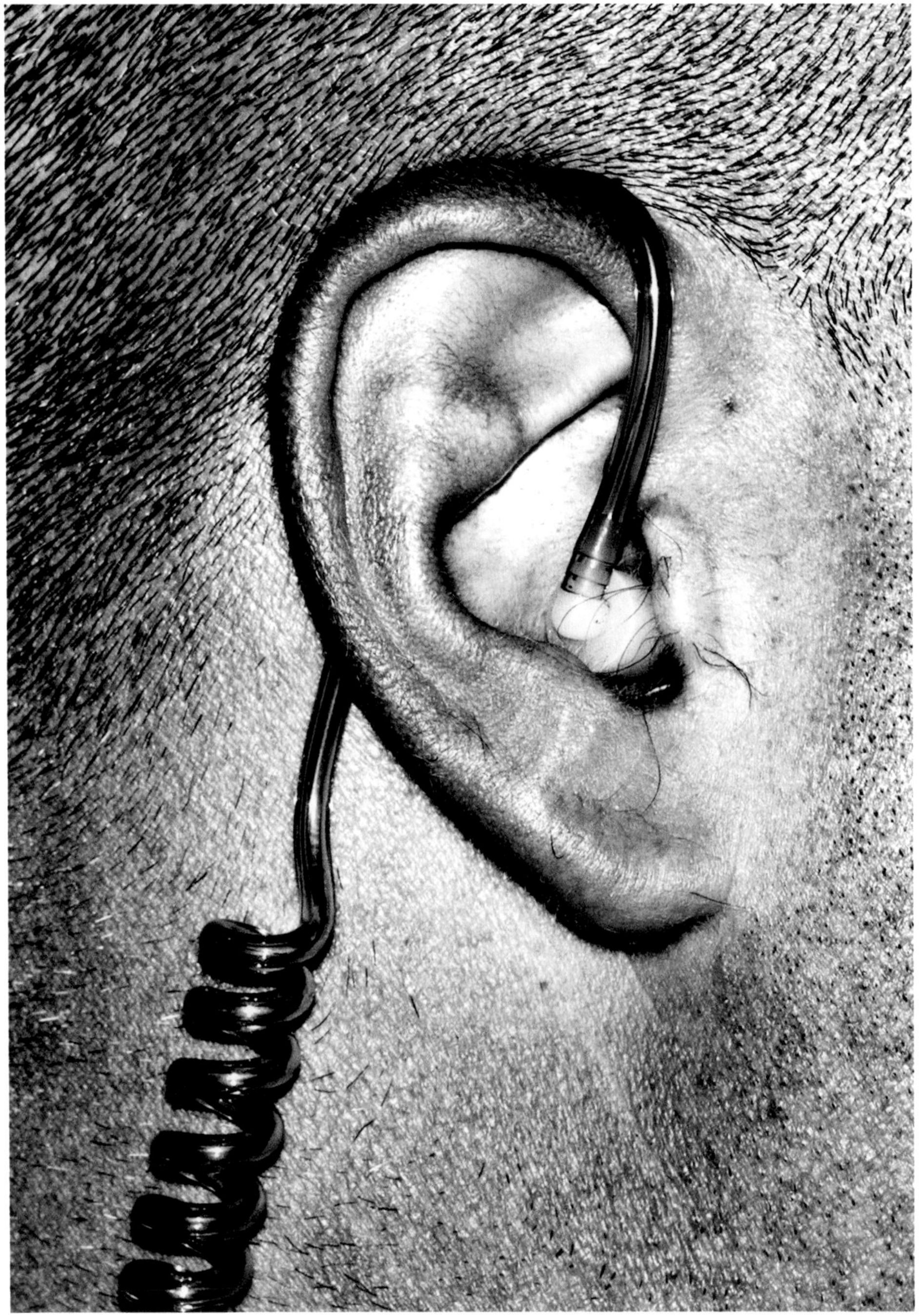

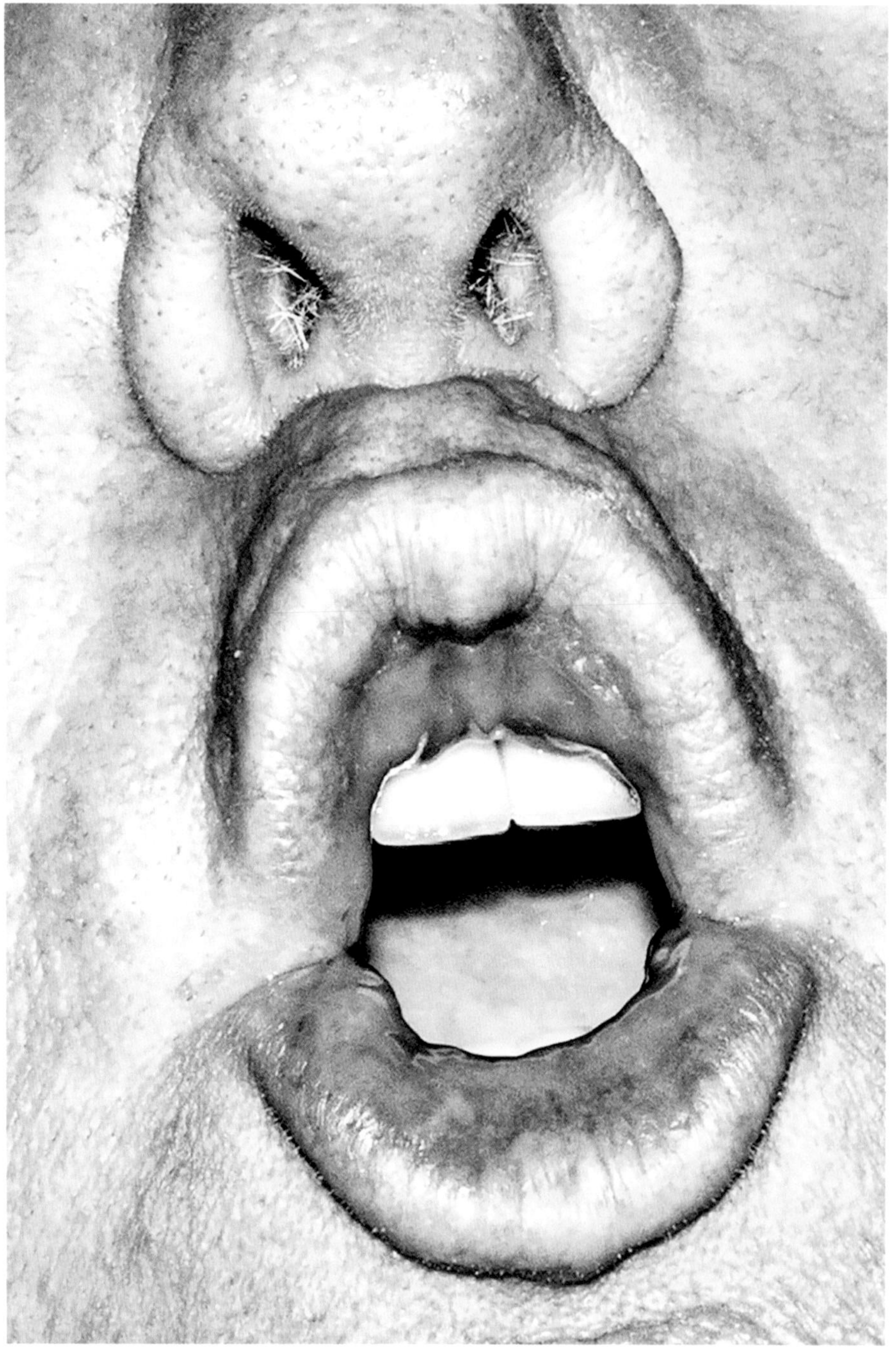

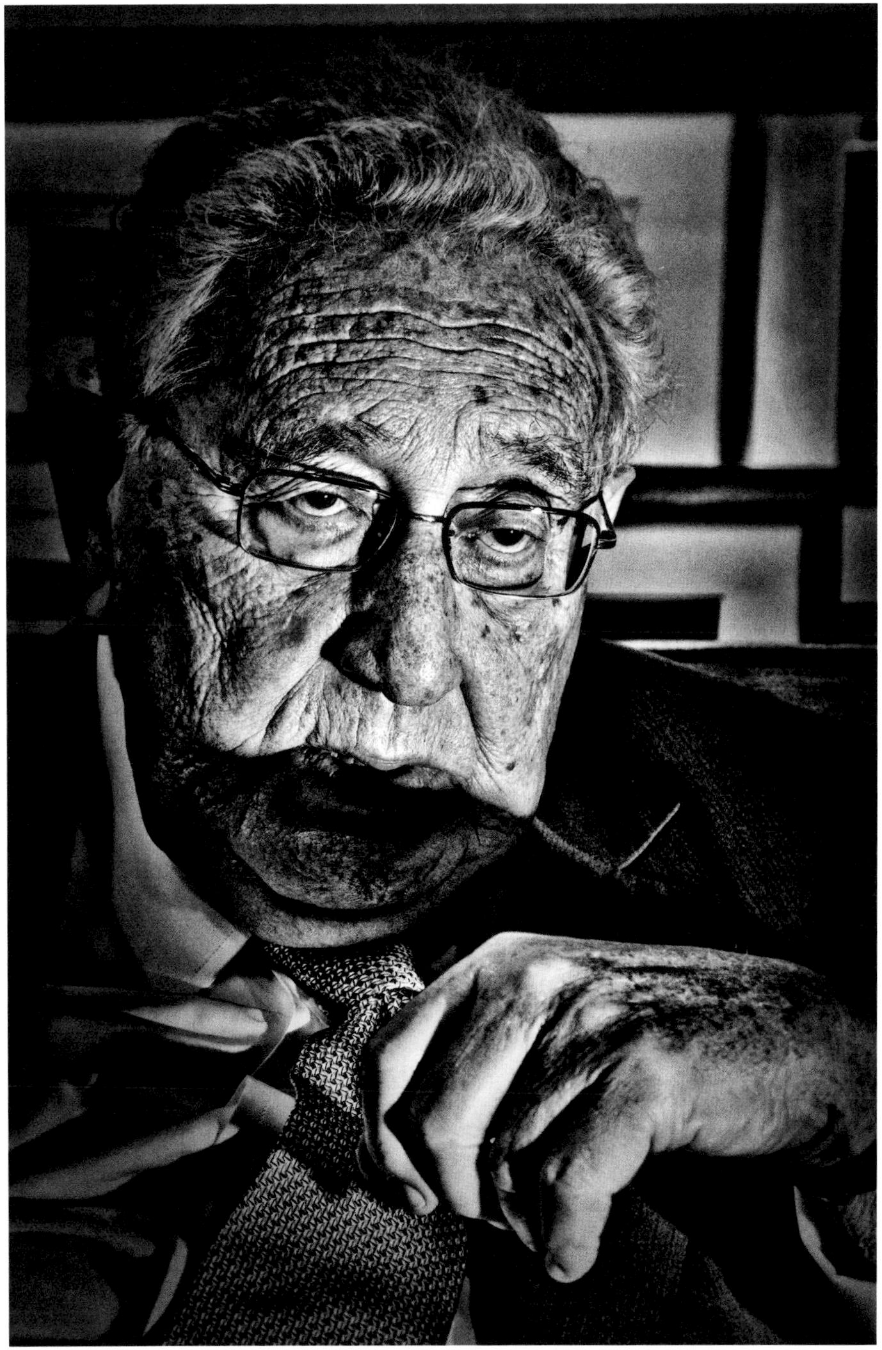

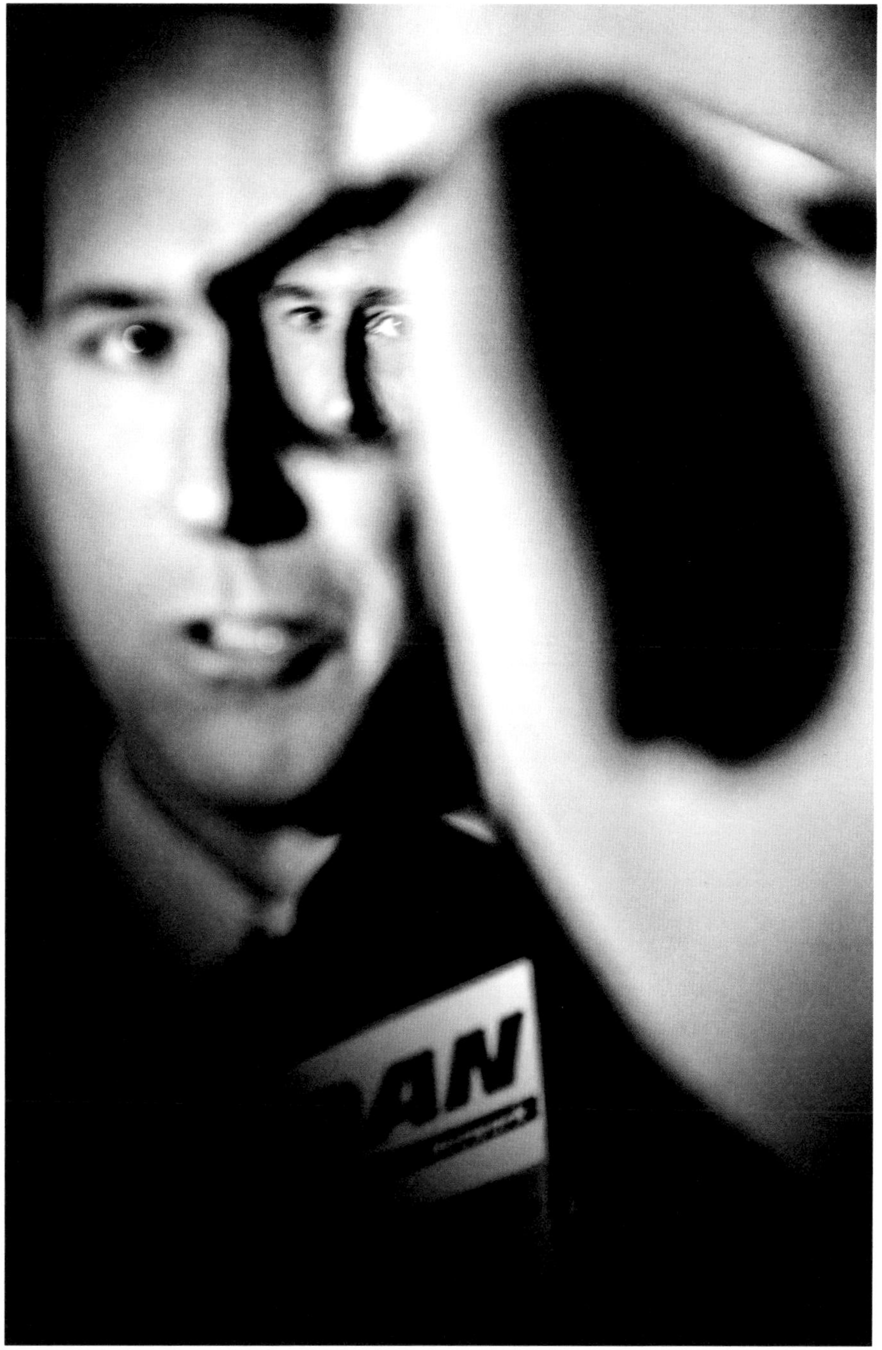

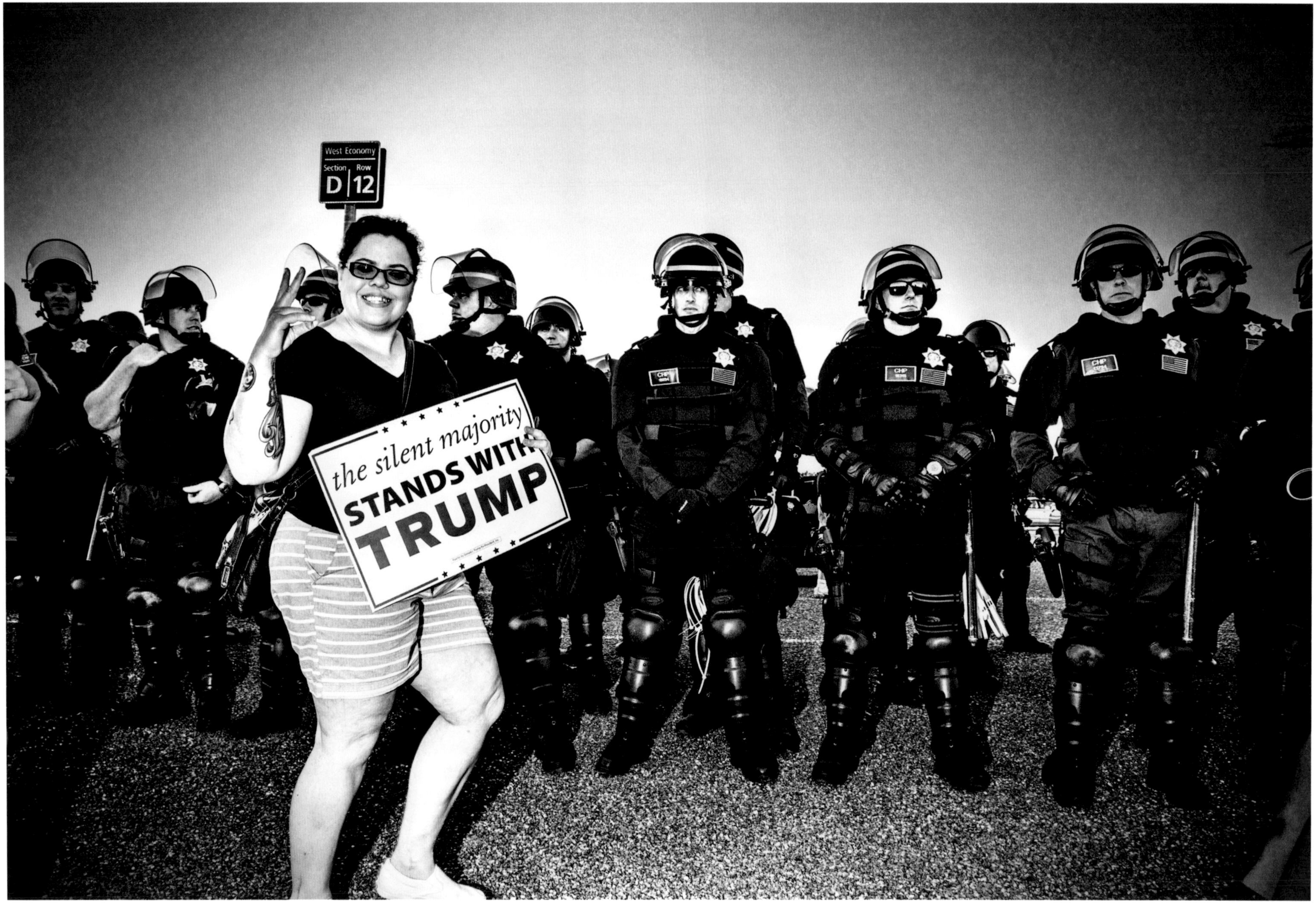
West Economy
Section Row
D 12
the silent majority
STANDS WITH
TRUMP

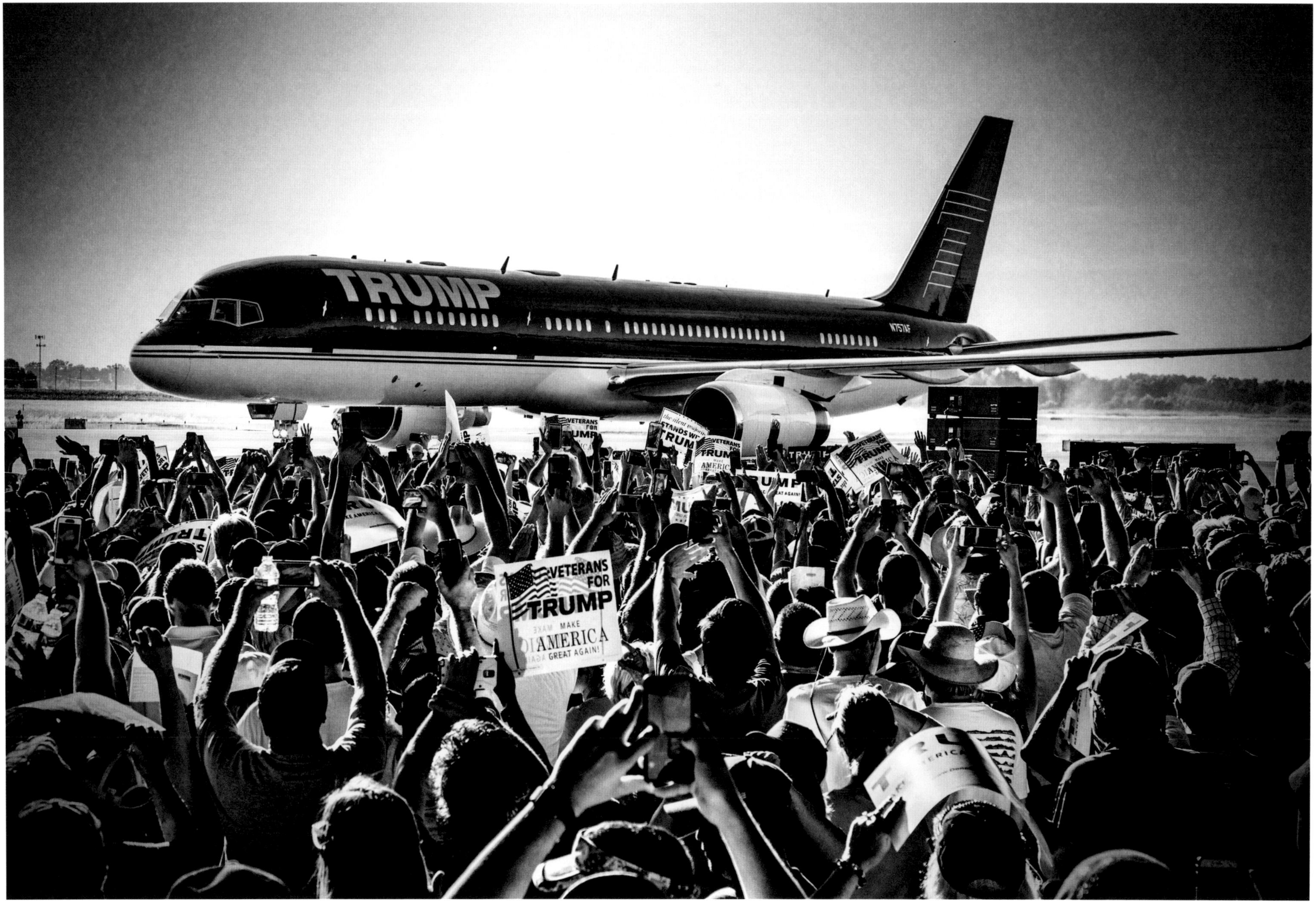
TRUMP
N757AF
VETERANS FOR TRUMP
MAKE AMERICA GREAT AGAIN!

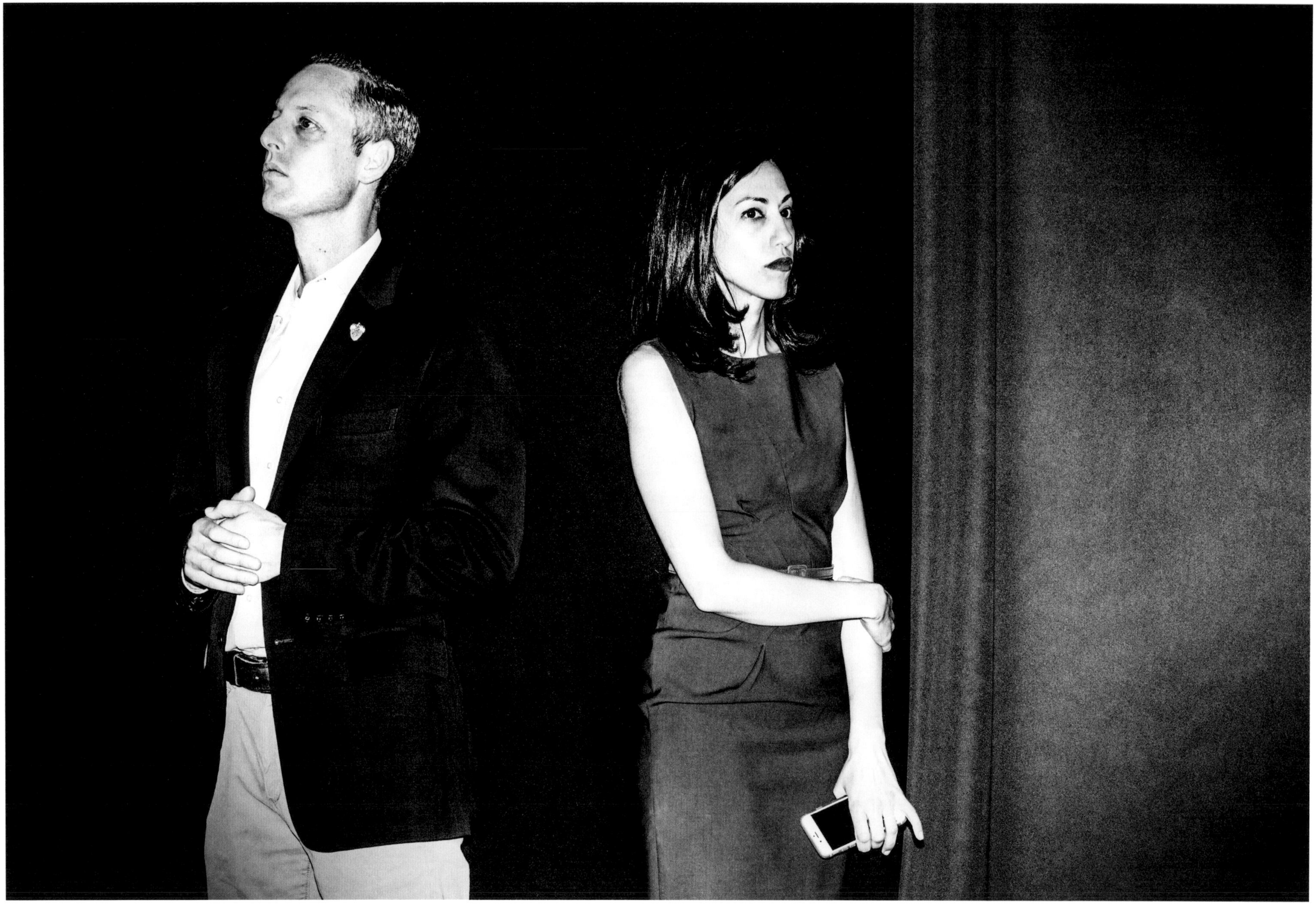

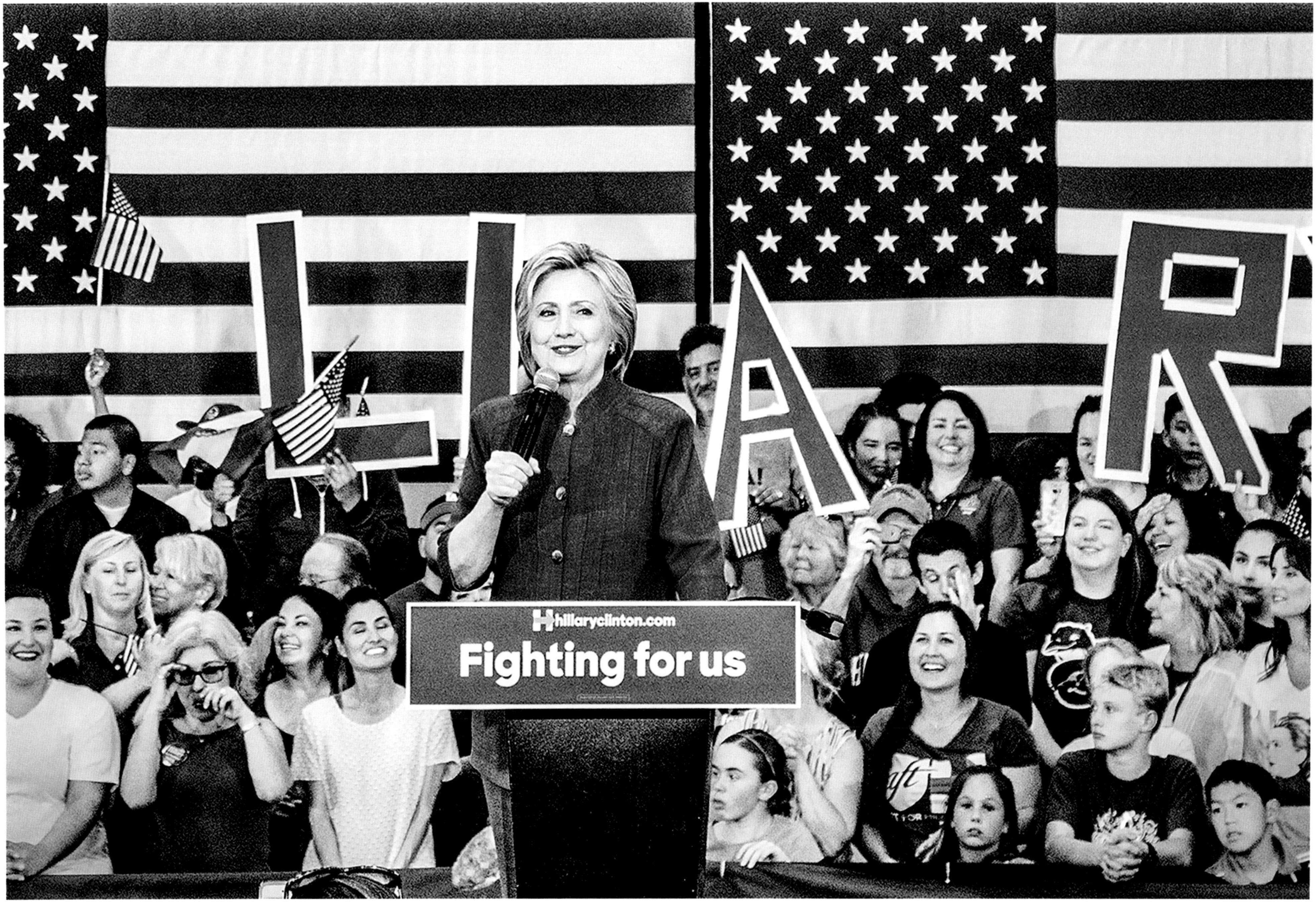
hillaryclinton.com
Fighting for us

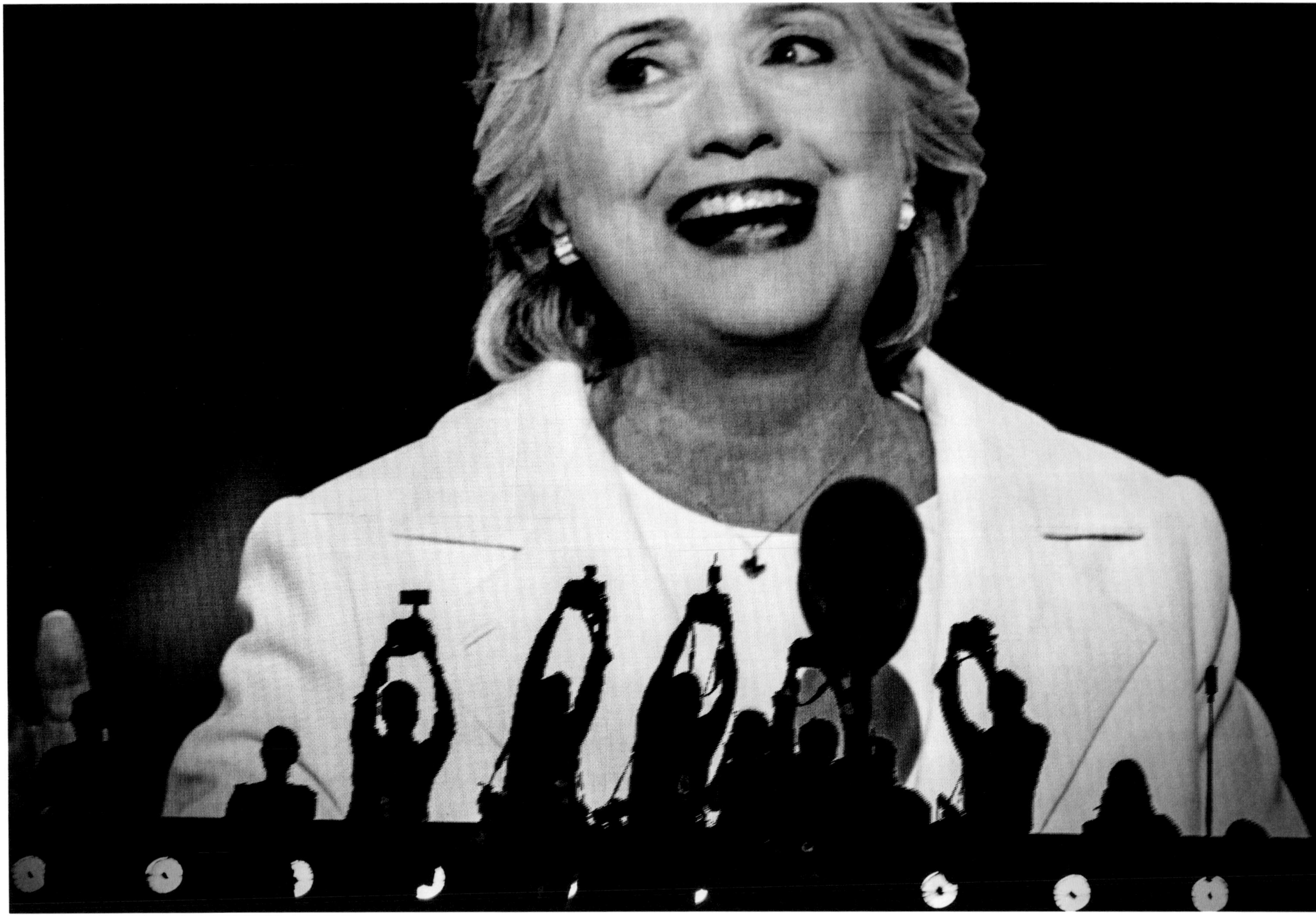

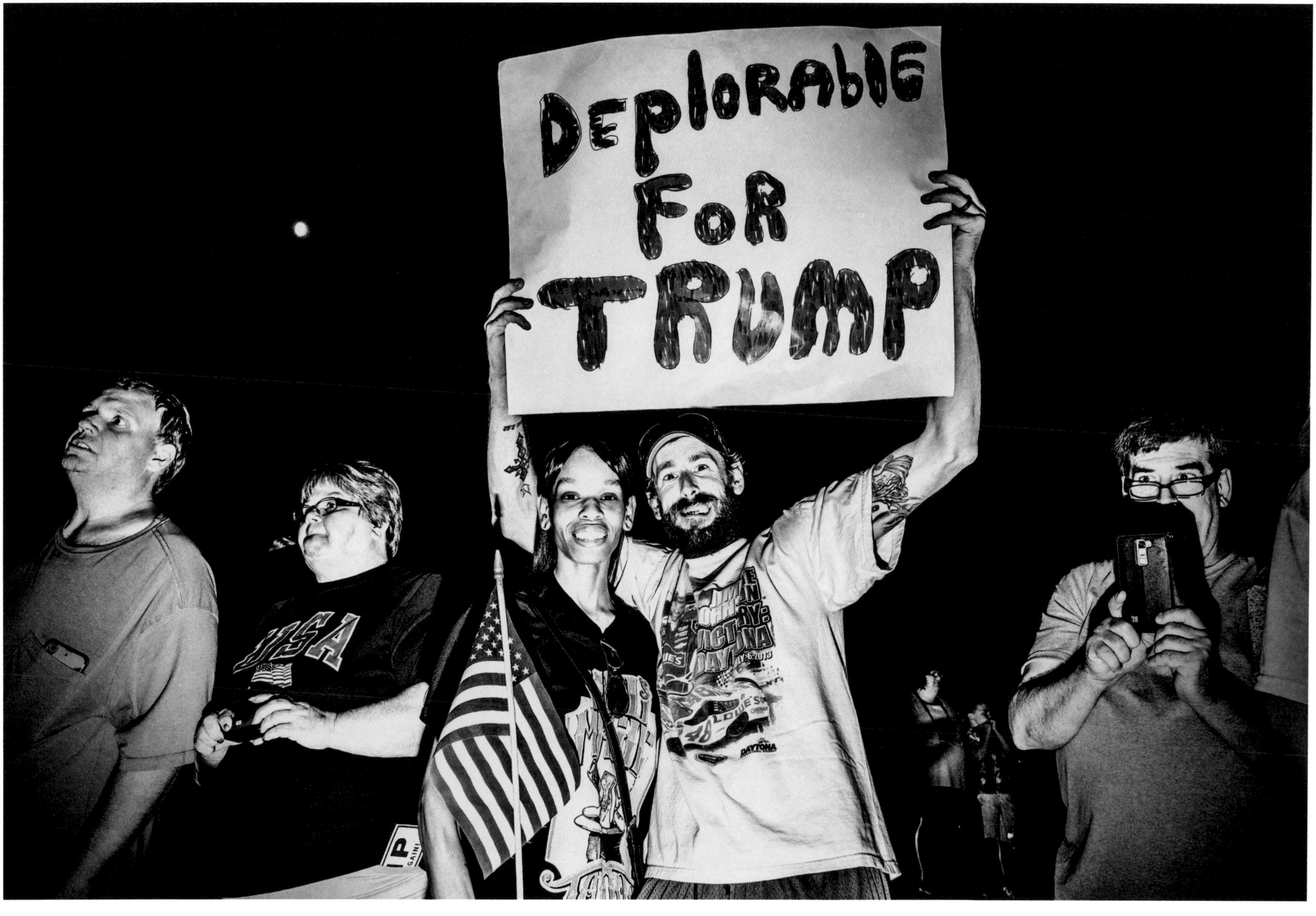
DEPLORABLE
FOR
TRUMP
USA

"You know, to just be grossly generalistic, you could put half of Trump's supporters into what i call the basket of deplorables. Right? The racist, sexist, homophobic, xenophobic, islamophobic—you name it.

And unfortunately there are people like that. And he has lifted them up... Now some of those folks, they are irredeemable, but thankfully they are not America." —**HILLARY CLINTON**

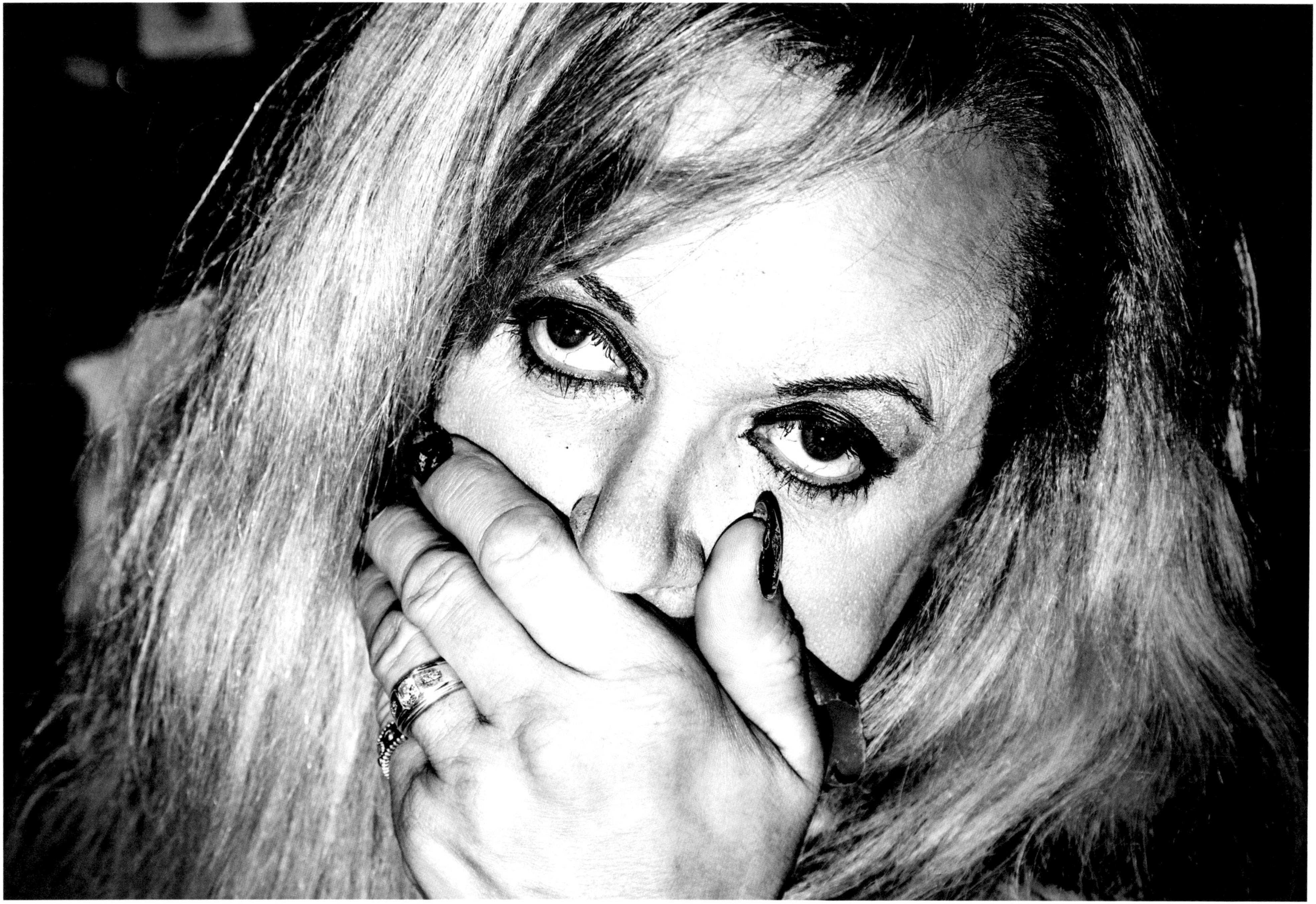

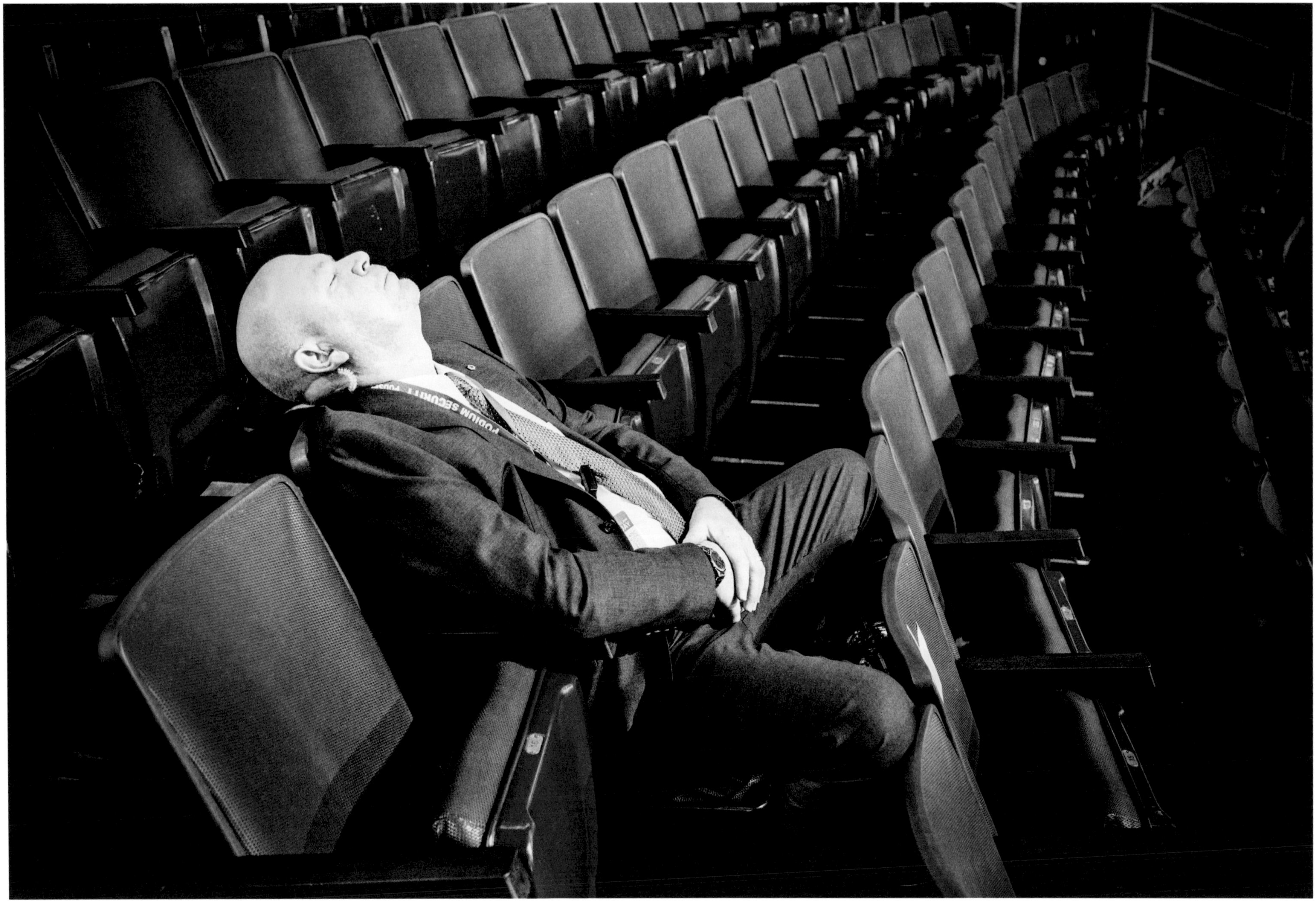
PODIUM SECURITY

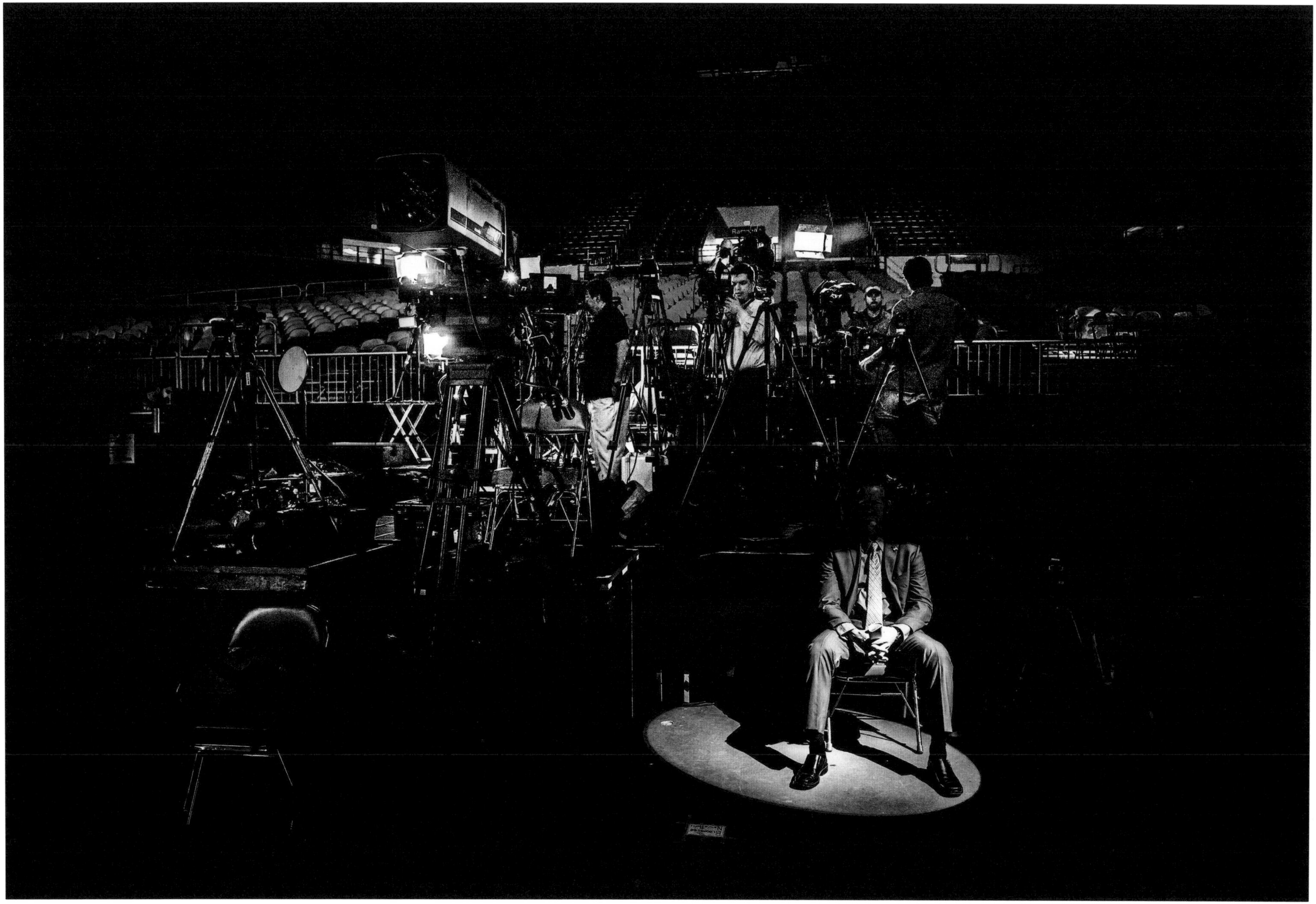

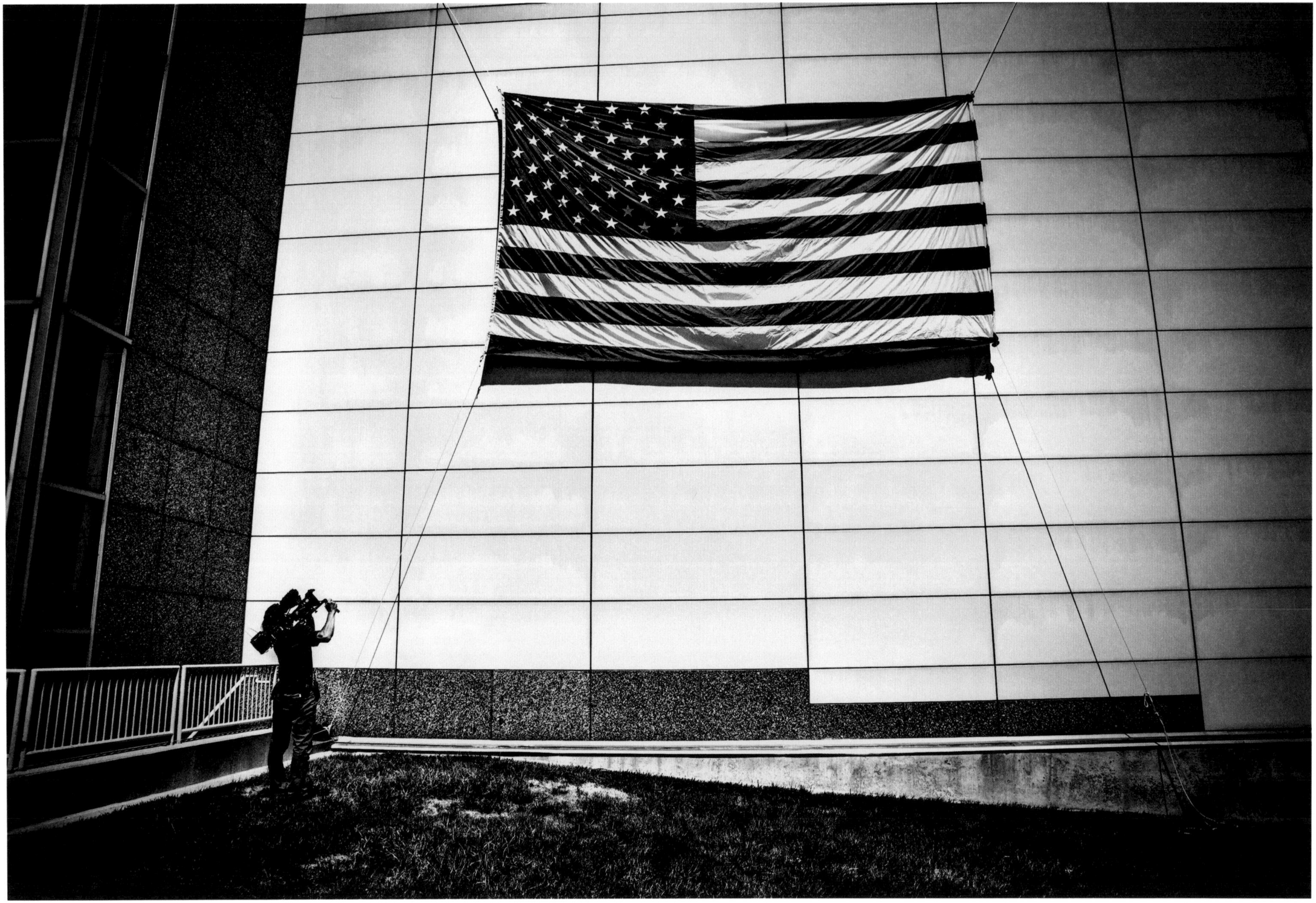

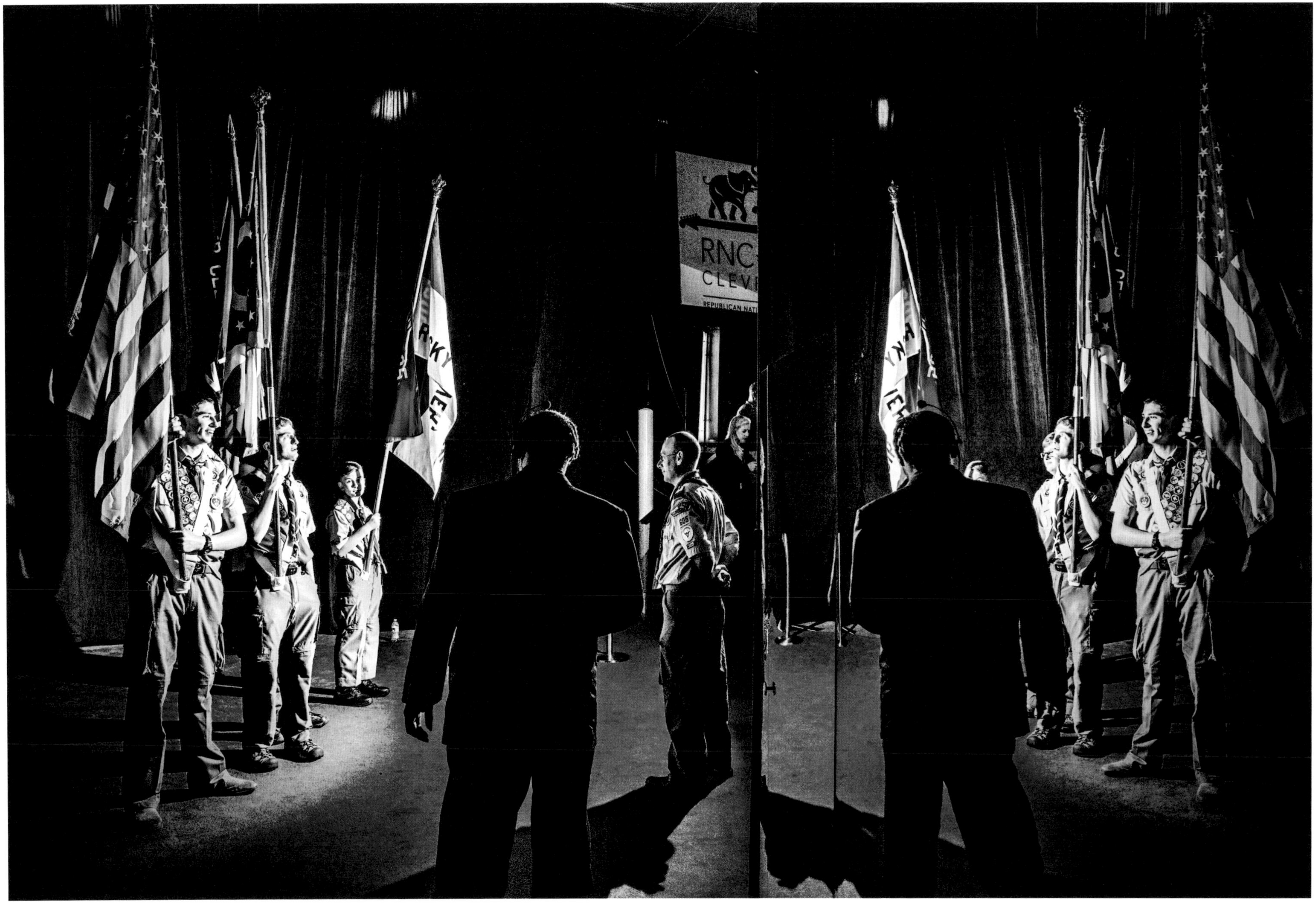
RNC

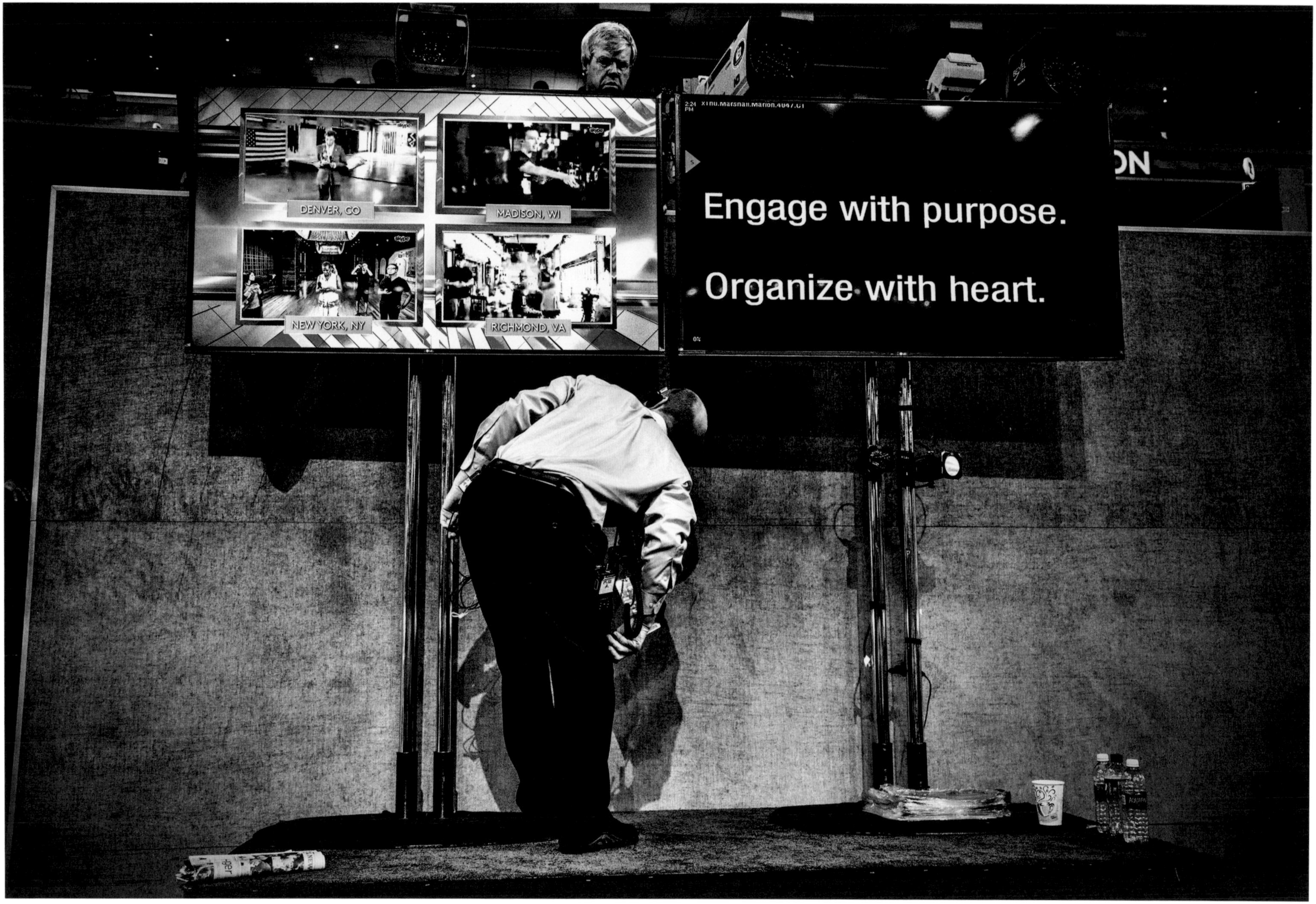
DENVER, CO
MADISON, WI
NEW YORK, NY
RICHMOND, VA
Engage with purpose.
Organize with heart.

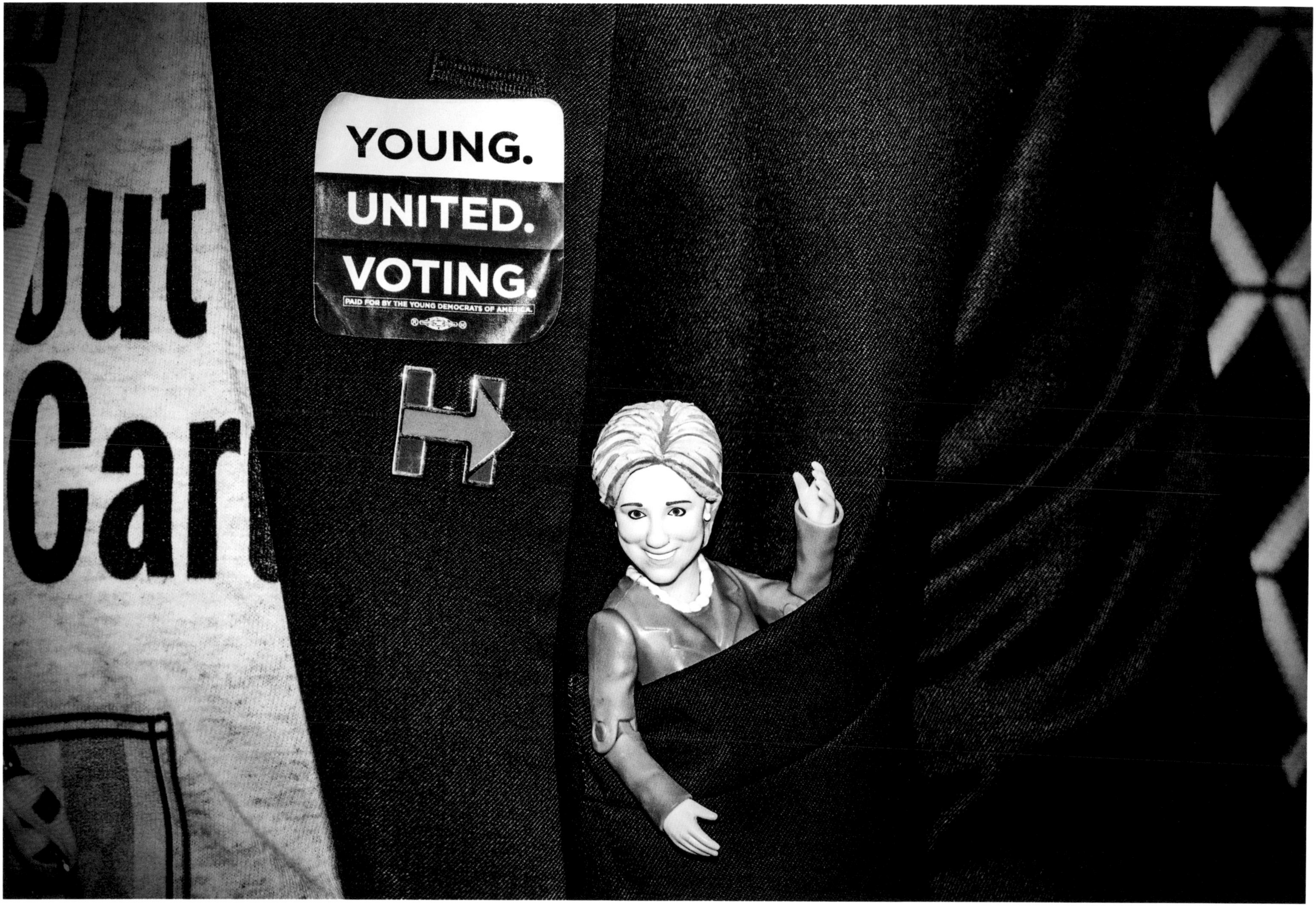
YOUNG.
UNITED.
VOTING.
PAID FOR BY THE YOUNG DEMOCRATS OF AMERICA.

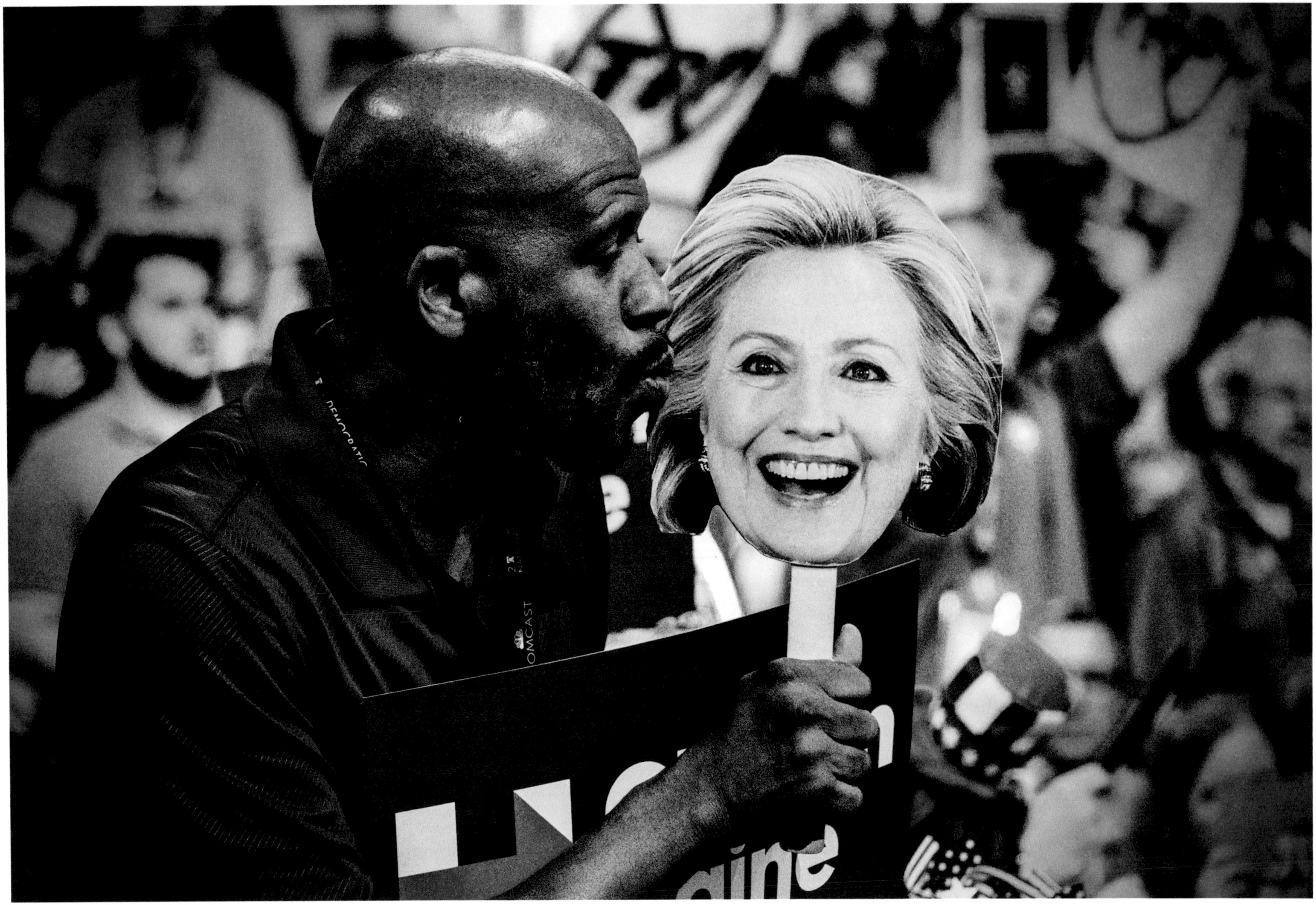
DEMOCRATIC

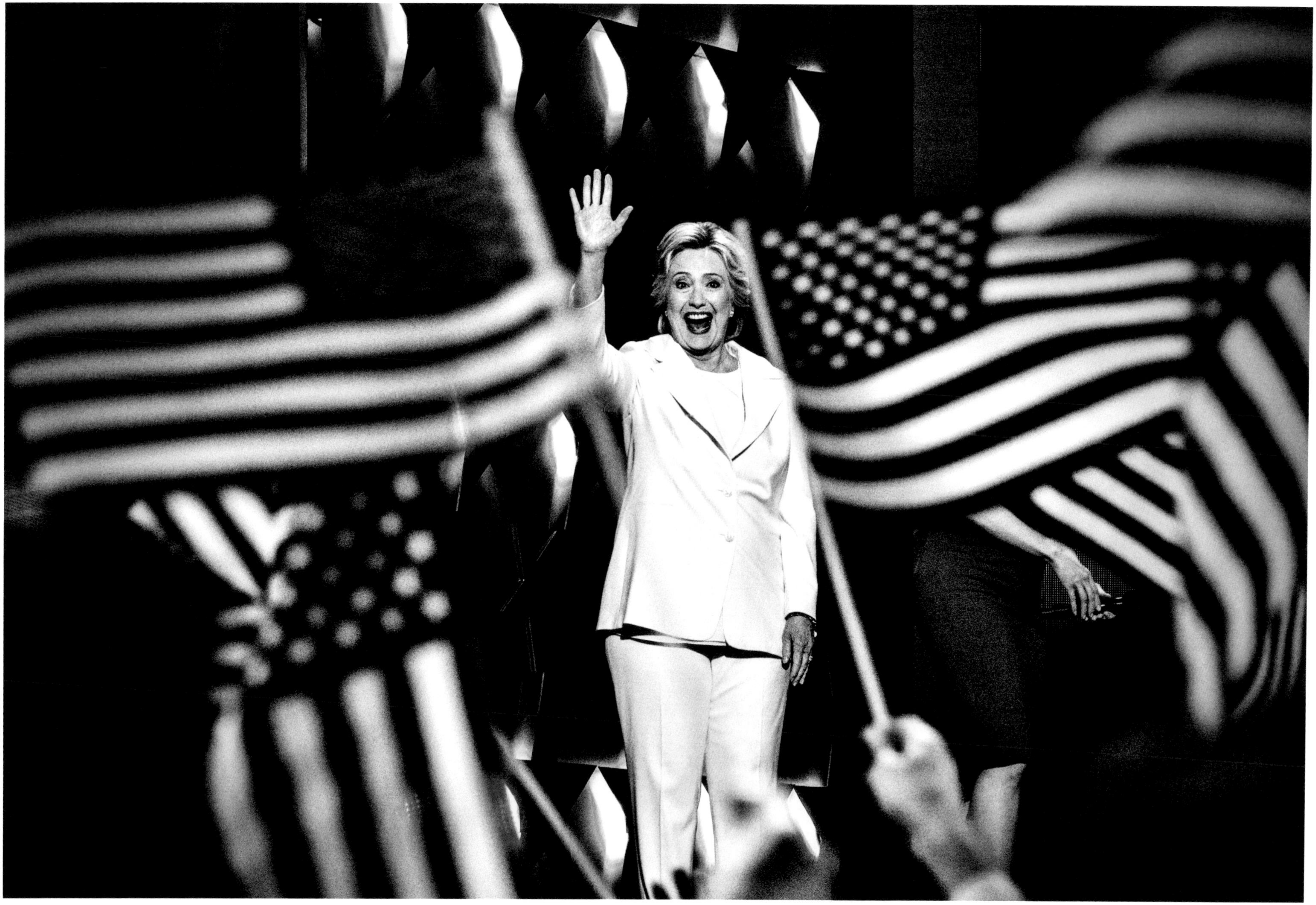

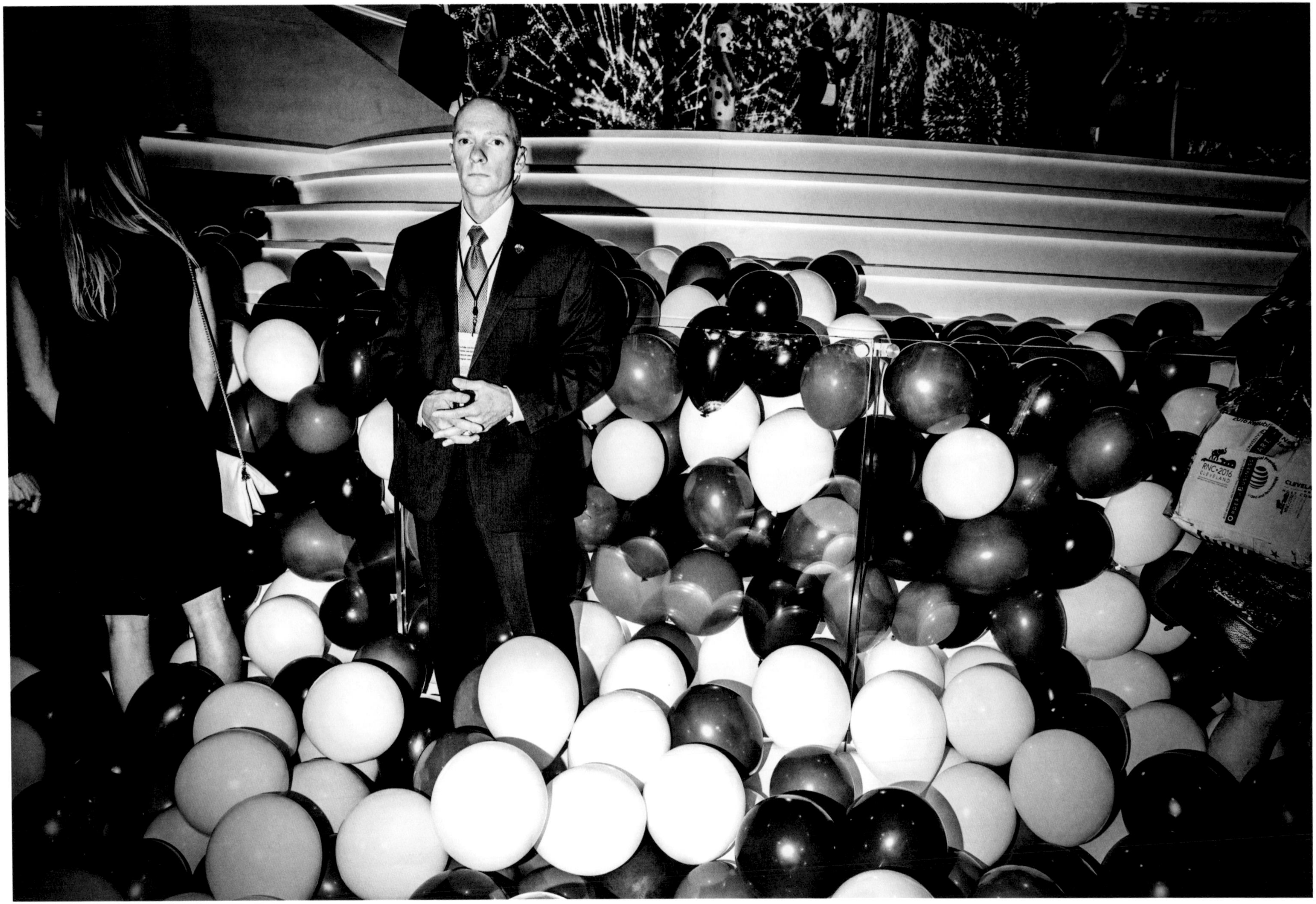
RNC•2016
CLEVELAND

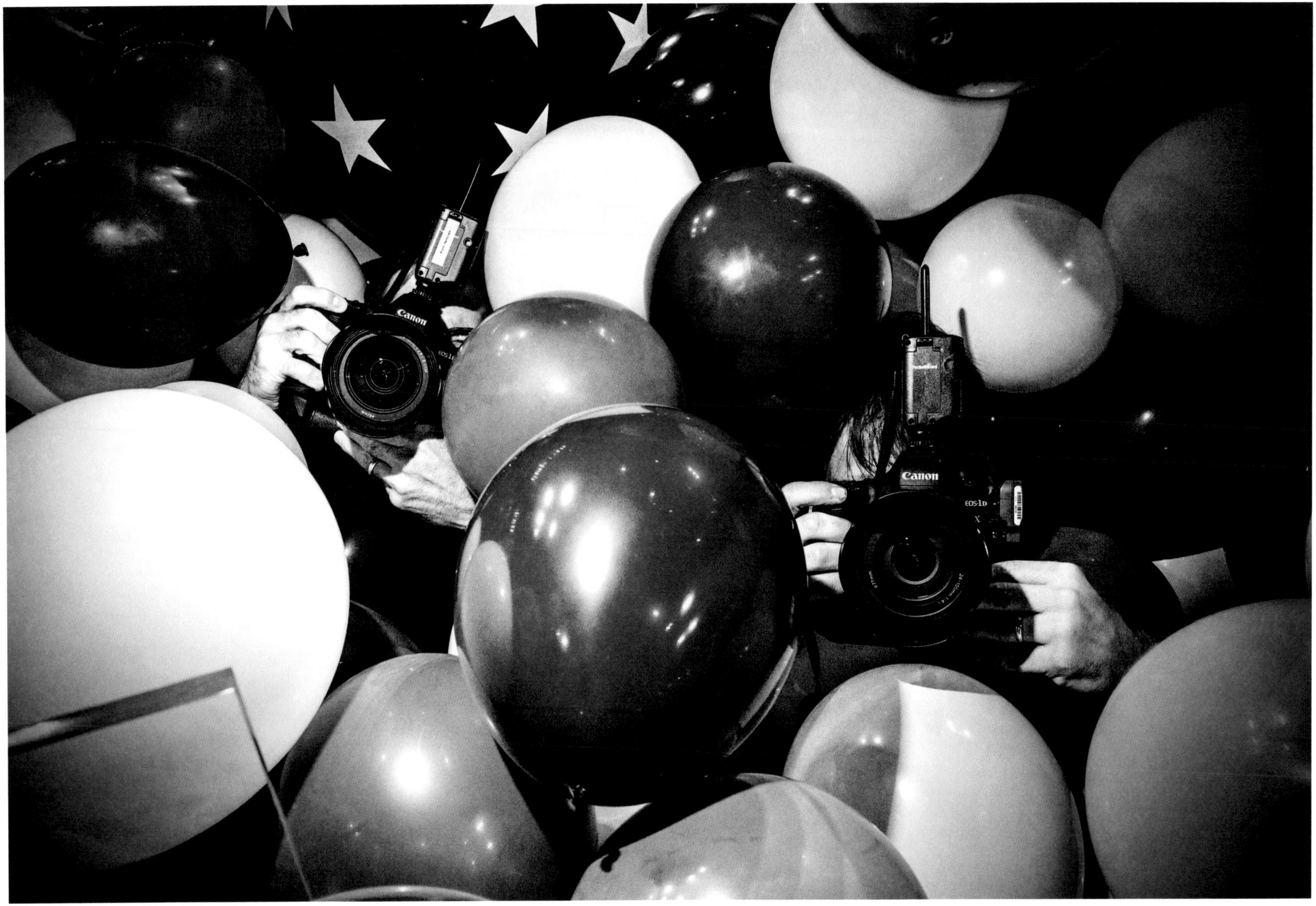
Canon
Canon
EOS-1D

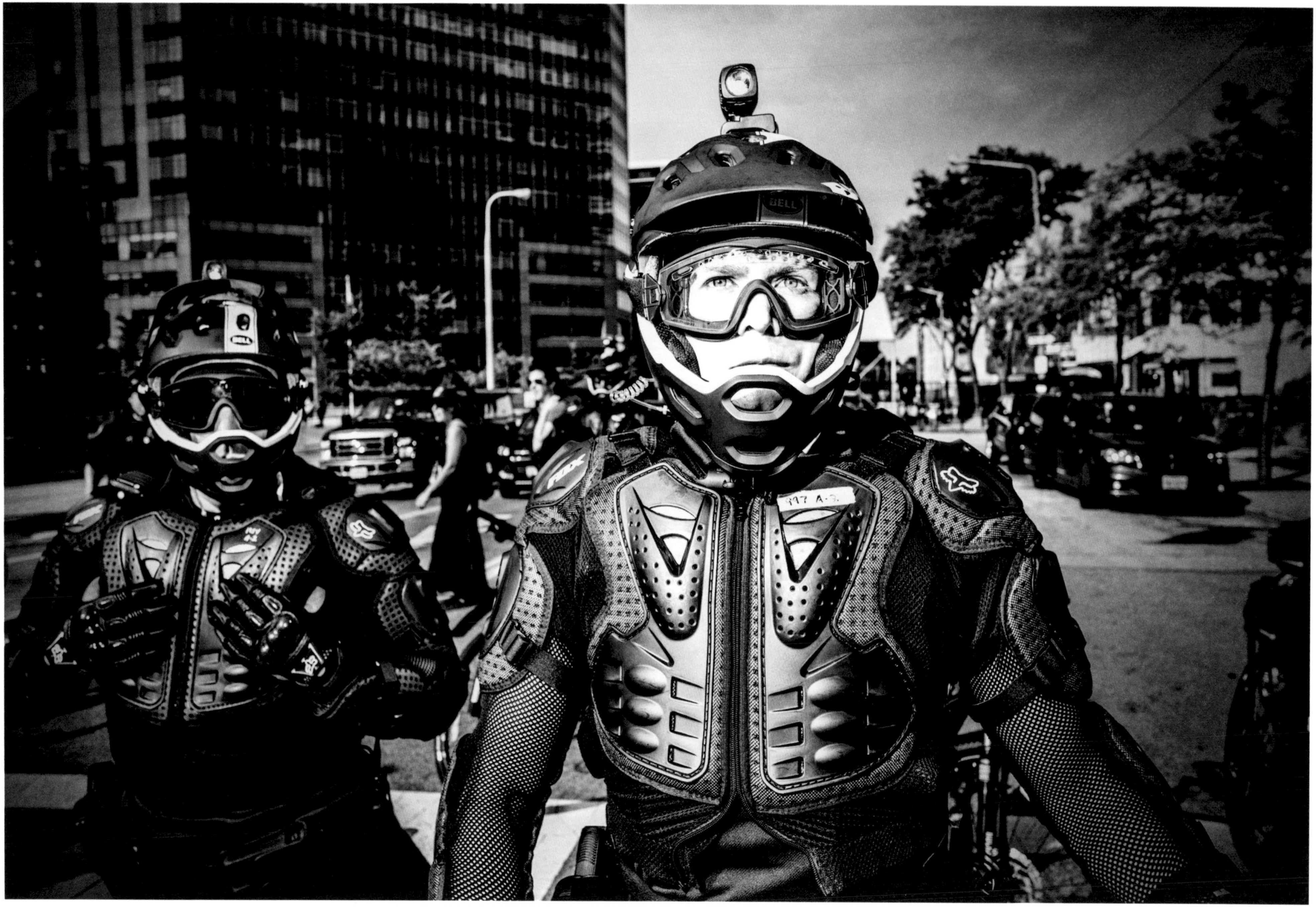
BELL

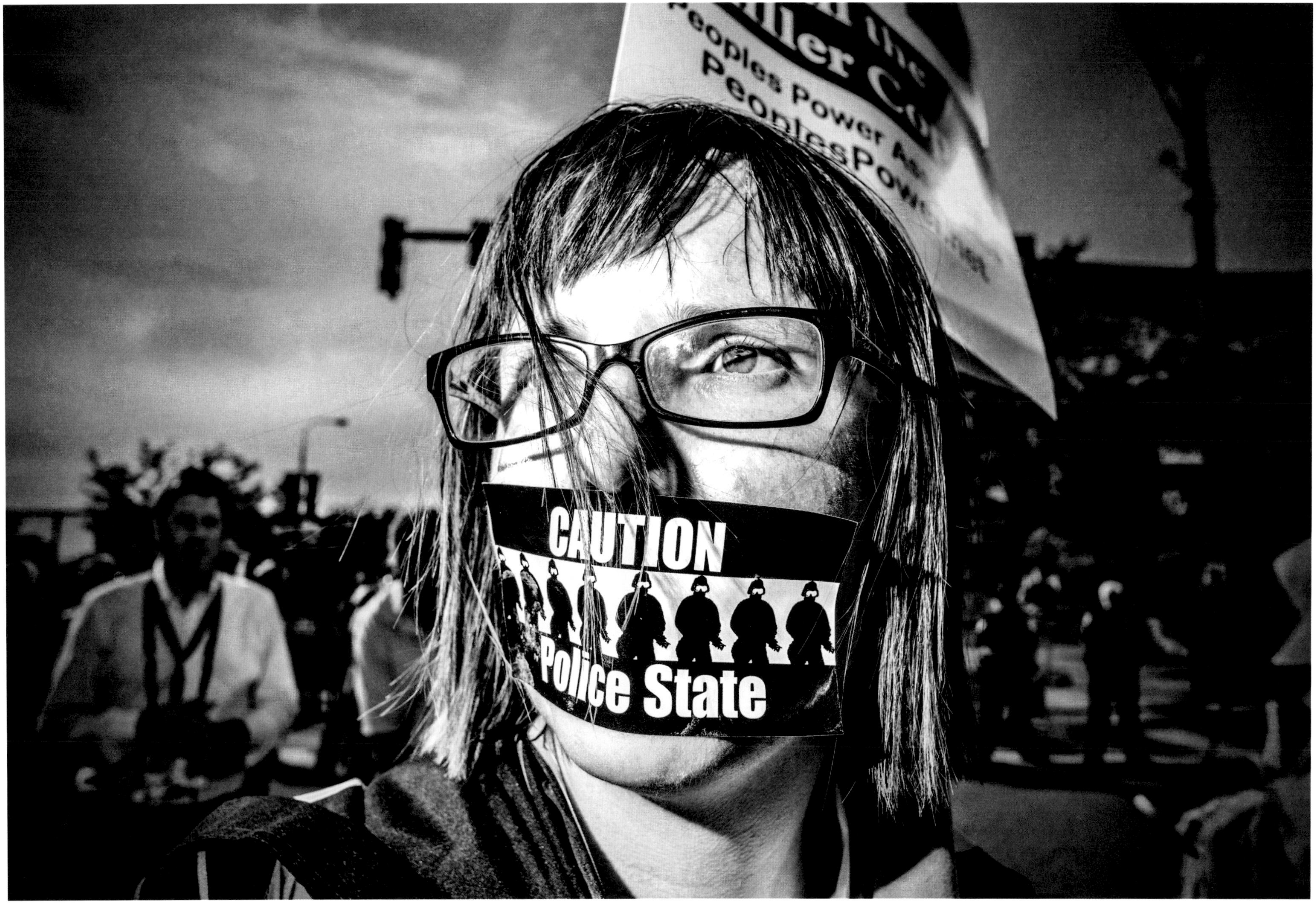
CAUTION
Police State

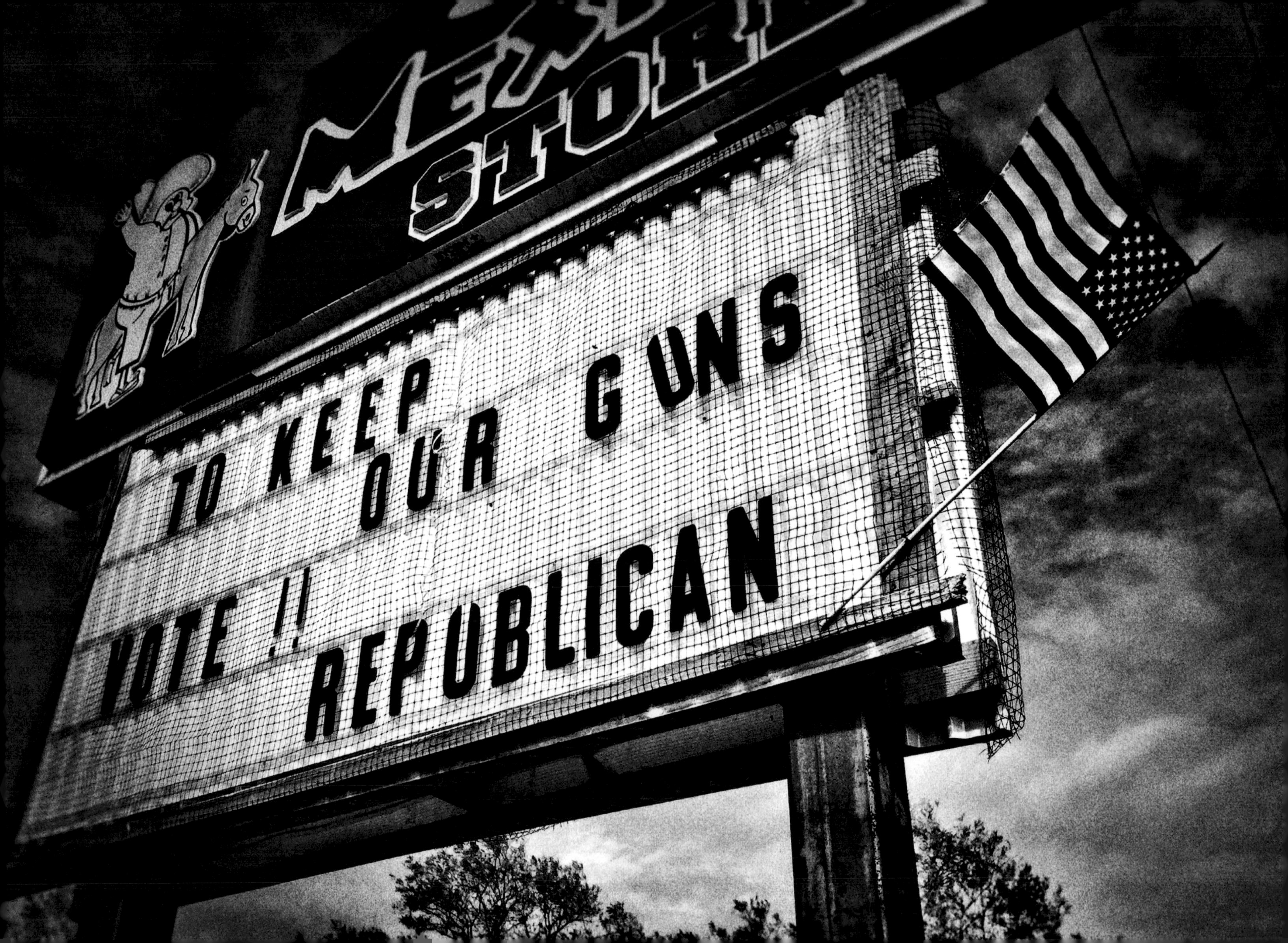
TO KEEP OUR GUNS
VOTE !! REPUBLICAN

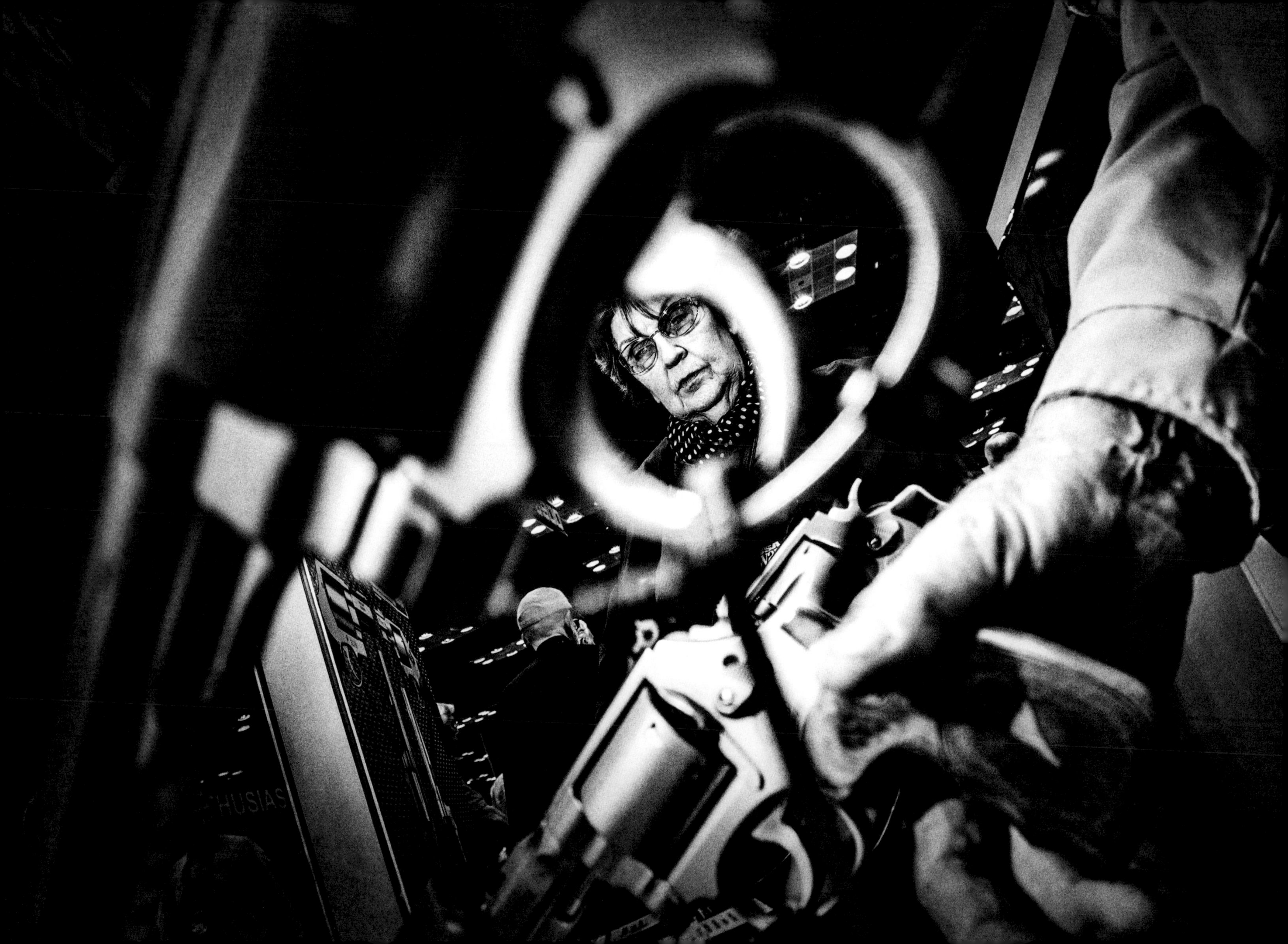

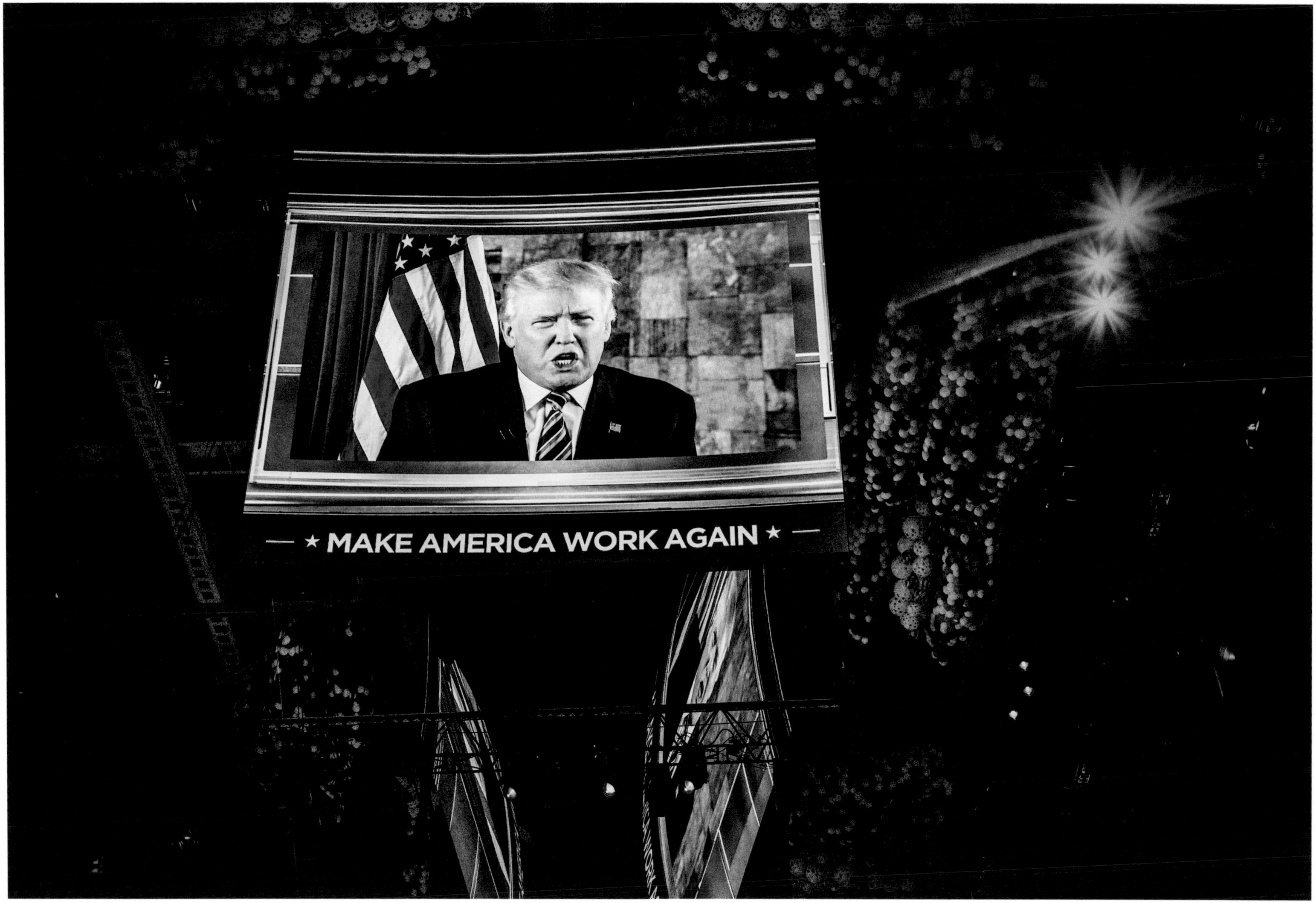
MAKE AMERICA WORK AGAIN

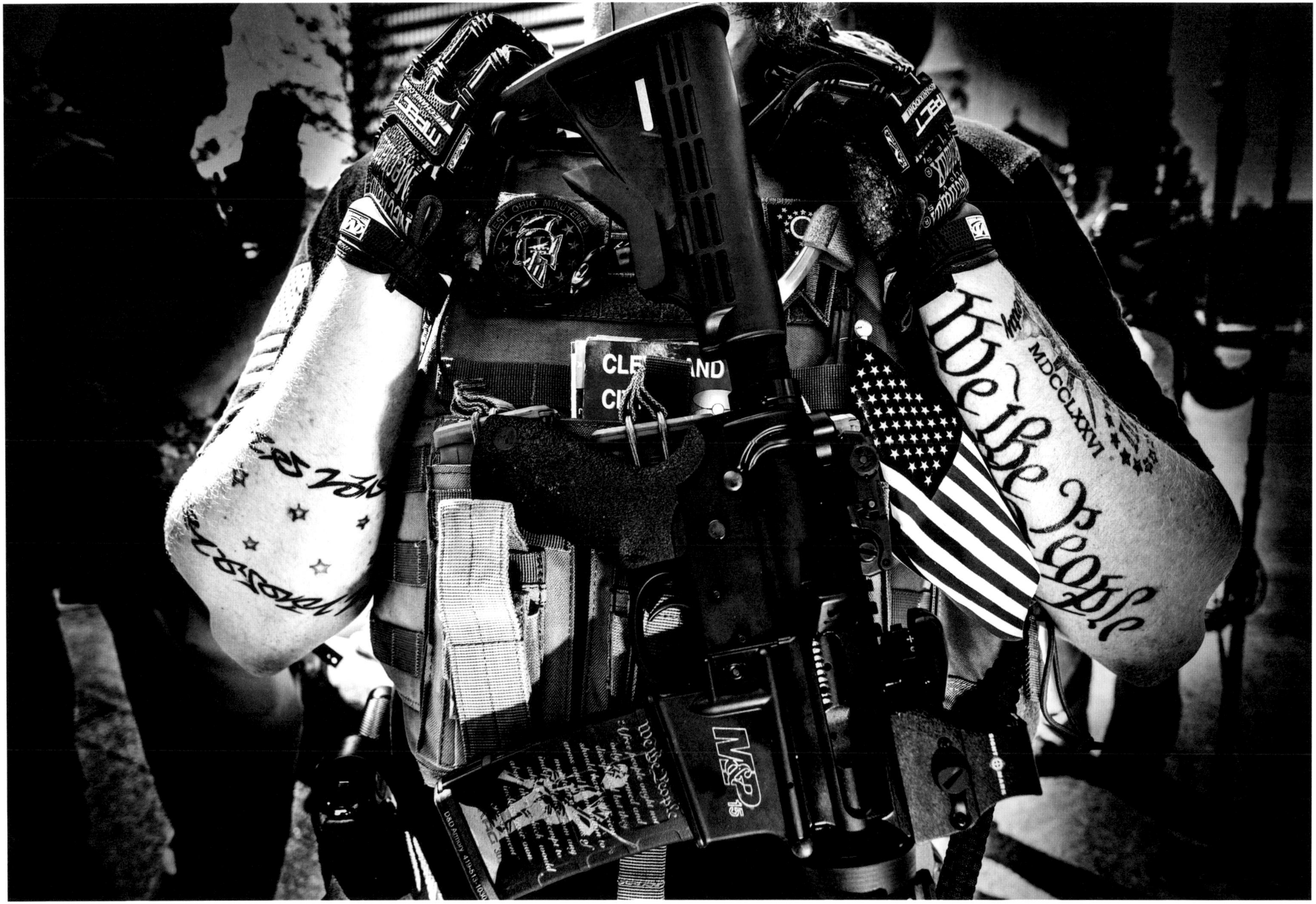
We the People
MDCCLXXVI
M&P 15

“Politics will eventually be replaced by imagery. The politician will be only too happy to abdicate in favor of his image, because the image will be much more powerful than he could ever be.” —**MARSHALL MCLUHAN**

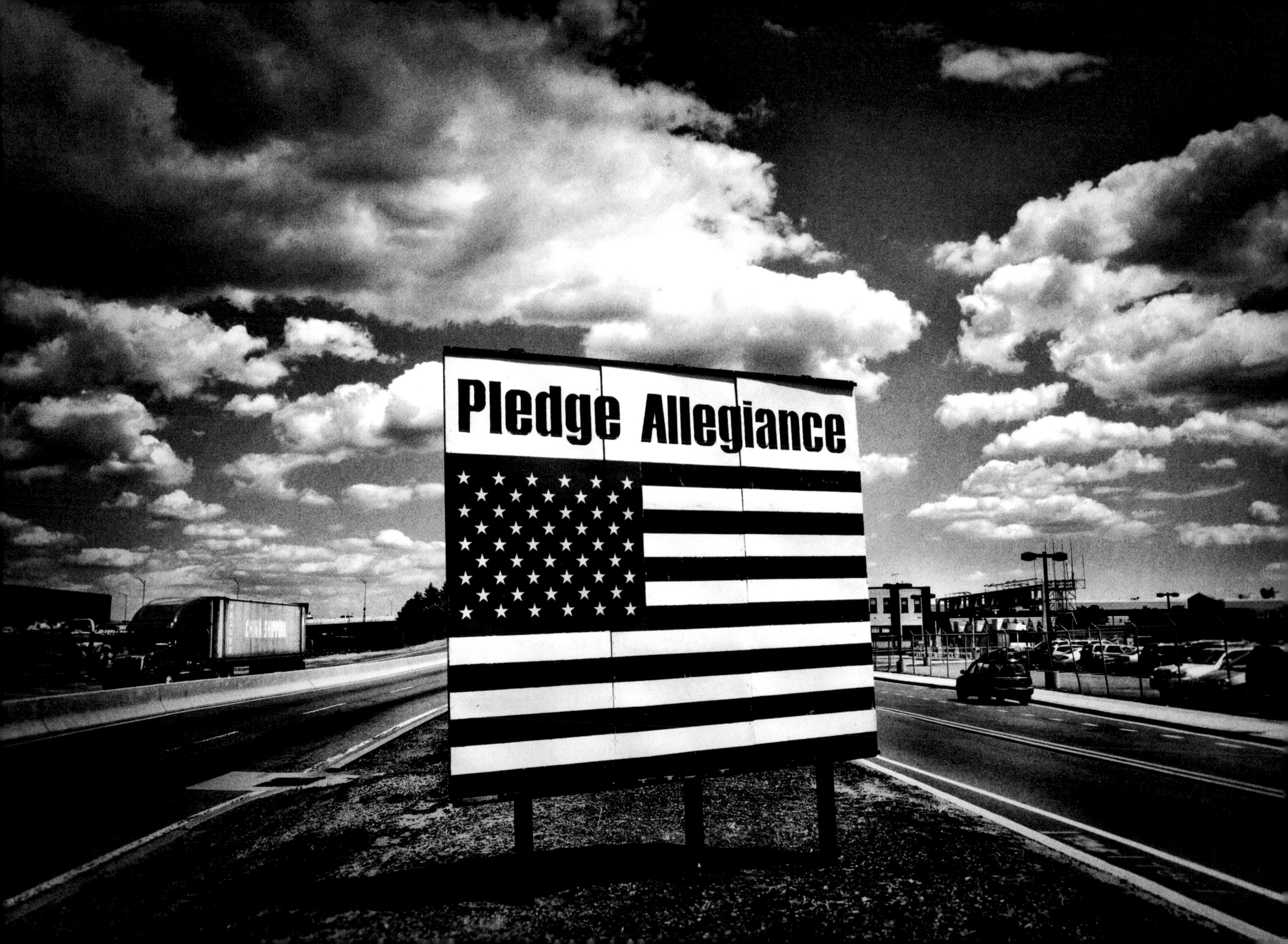
Pledge Allegiance

Donald J. Trump for President Press Office

To: Undisclosed recipients: ;
Your Media Credentials Have Been Denied

Hello,
If you are receiving this email, we are unable to credential you for the event in Terre Haute, IN on May 1st, 2016. Any name that does not appear on our list, will not be permitted to enter as credentialed media.
With the abundance of requests for media credentials, we have to take proactive measures with our credentialing process to ensure the success of each event.

During the 2016 Presidential Primary race, the Donald J. Trump Campaign fully recognizes and respects all media but due to various venue sizes, media space, and safety we must limit the number of credentialed media and give priority to our national and local outlets. We appreciate your understanding.

Best,

The Press Office

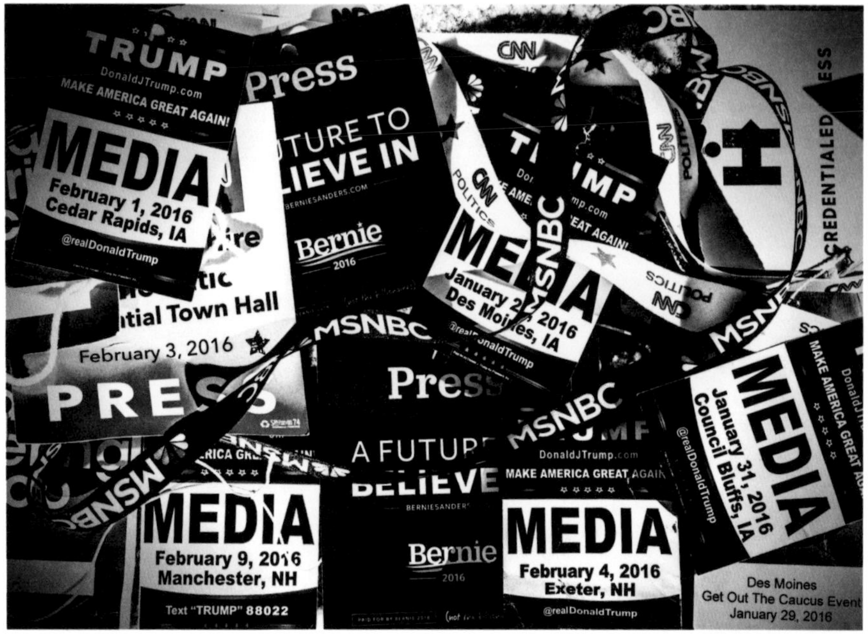

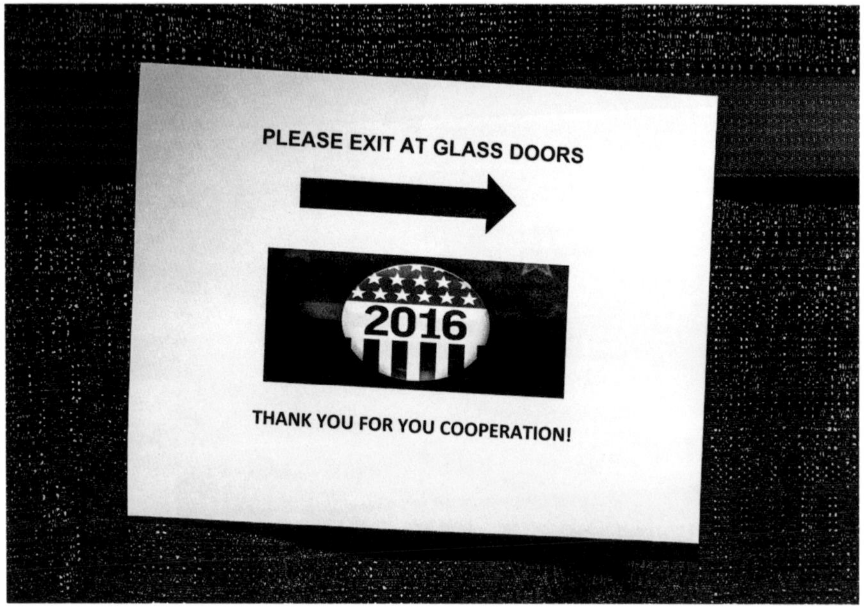

This book is for Axel and Rose.

I would like to thank several people who made this book possible.

Gerhard Steidl who has so graciously taken on this project and given it a home.

Amy Pereira has made this project possible with her vision and support.

MSNBC Photography has given me a free hand to make my pictures.

Redux Pictures and Marcel Saba have been instrumental in making all the pictures possible.

Joanna Milter who as a friend has always pushed me and help me make better pictures.

Paul Moakley who also has been a friend and supporter.

Kathy Ryan and Scott Thode who gave me great advice on the book.

Teru Kuwayama who from behind the scenes has supported this project from the beginning.

John Heilemann whose words have been a steady voice in this campaign, no matter which way the wind blows.

To my wife Greta Pratt who has always supported me and made me a better photographer.

And last I would like to thank all my fellow photographers who are shooting the campaign, who have always inspired me,

and have put up with my flash getting in their way.

First edition published in 2016

Book design: Mark Peterson, Bernard Fischer, Gerhard Steidl
Cover and typographic design by David Shields
Photo-editing: Amy Pereira
Separations by Steidl's digital darkroom
Production and printing: Steidl, Göttingen

Steidl
Düstere Str. 4 / 37073 Göttingen, Germany
Phone +49 551 49 60 60 / Fax +49 551 49 60 649
mail@steidl.de
steidl.de

ISBN 978-3-95829-183-6
Printed in Germany by Steidl

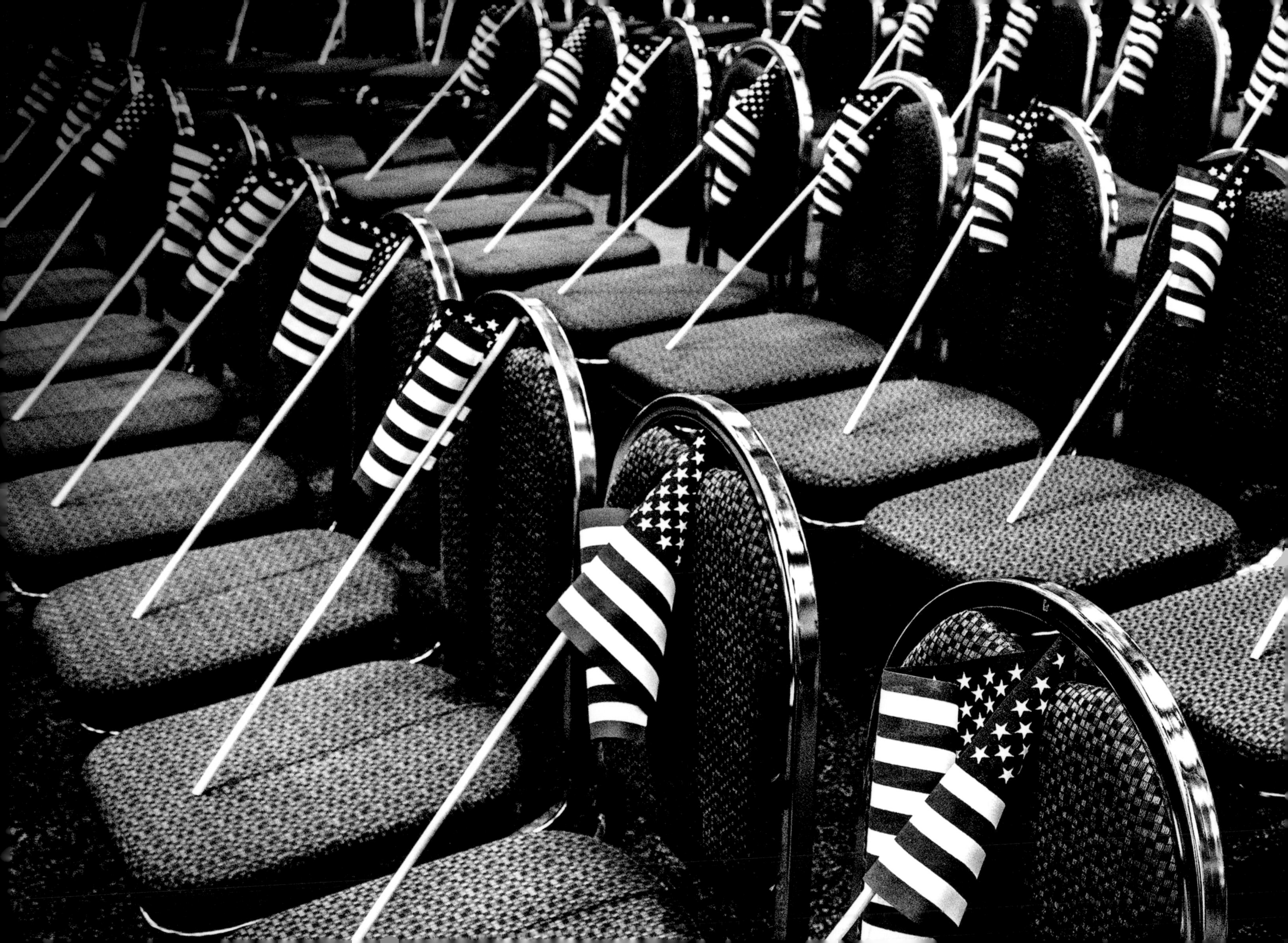